D0611346

PR
3637
.P6
A3

L-74013

Texas Woman's University
Library
Denton, Texas

BRO
DART   PRINTED IN U.S.A.   23-364-002

POPE'S ONCE AND FUTURE KINGS

·

POPE'S ONCE AND FUTURE KINGS

SATIRE AND POLITICS
IN THE EARLY CAREER

John M. Aden

THE UNIVERSITY OF TENNESSEE PRESS

KNOXVILLE

Publication of this book

was assisted by a grant from Vanderbilt University

COPYRIGHT © 1978

BY THE UNIVERSITY OF TENNESSEE PRESS.

ALL RIGHTS RESERVED.

MANUFACTURED IN THE UNITED STATES OF AMERICA.

FIRST EDITION.

.

Clothbound editions of University of Tennessee Press
books are printed on paper designed for an effective
life of at least 300 years, and binding materials are
chosen for strength and durability.

Library of Congress Cataloging in Publication Data

Aden, John M.
    Pope's once and future kings.
    Includes bibliographical references and index.
    1.   Pope, Alexander, 1688–1744—Political and social
views.   I.   Title.
PR3637.P6A3   821'.5   78–16618
ISBN 0–87049–252–7

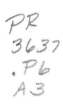

PR
3637
.P6
A3

TEXAS WOMAN'S UNIVERSITY LIBRARY

FOR

Gareth and Lorelei

BEST OF CHILDREN

1-74013

PREFACE

·

I HAVE HOPED in this study to suggest the unity of Alexander
Pope's career in satire and politics, aspects long acknowledged
in the later work but scanted, if even recognized, in the earlier.
If at times the result seems like two distinct inquiries, the impression is not amiss, for satire and politics do not always of
course go hand in hand. But in Pope they often do, and if there
is an emphasis here it is on their consolidation, with politics as
the prime mover.

For Pope and his age politics meant church if it meant anything: Protestantism versus Catholicism, Dissent versus the
Church of England. For this reason I have given introductory
attention to the penal history and predicament of English Catholicism into which Pope was born and under which he labored throughout his life. It was this handicap which, as much
as anything else, sealed him satirist, led him to Toryism, and
stirred in him sympathies deeply and instinctively Jacobitical.
As part of this same background I examine the question of
Pope's commitment to his religion and look into his early reading, study, and emulation of the great body of satire available
to him on this and related issues.

In the body of the book, except for a few well-worn examples, I examine Pope's work from the beginning to the neighborhood of 1728, after which the question of satire and politics
has never been in doubt. In doing so I have perforce dealt with
much that is no longer current in Pope studies, but this neces-

sity I hope will be found a benefit rather than a liability. The renascence of Pope studies in the last half-century has naturally concentrated itself upon the major works, but, while it has enriched us immeasurably in respect to those, it has by that very fact deprived us of much in Pope that is also significant and artistically noteworthy. I hope this book can help recover that lost Pope.

I call the book *Pope's Once and Future Kings* because I find in the title, obviously adapted, a perfect formula for expressing the axis around which Pope's career in satire and politics essentially ordered itself. Pope's work falls between, and gives answer to, the hopes and fears, the trust and distrust, of three royal houses: the Stuart, the Williamite, and the Hanoverian. It begins in the first minutes after noon of Stuart decline, falls quickly under the shadow of a militant Protestant regnancy, enjoys a brief if uncertain respite in the chequered sunshine of Anne, and falls again under a Hanoverian winter of discontent. Pope's kings (and a queen) constitute, in short, a synechdoche for the complex of issues—religious, political, and even literary —which defined the world he lived in and determined, in large measure, the direction of his literary career.

Acknowledgment of indebtedness must begin with the indispensable Mr. Sherburn, whose *Early Career of Alexander Pope* and whose edition of Pope's correspondence remain the starting point for all studies of this kind. It must include as well the Twickenham editors, Mr. Norman Ault (*Prose Works* and *New Light on Pope*), and Mr. James M. Osborn, whose new edition of Spence's *Anecdotes* is invaluable.

More personally, I would express my gratitude to Professor Aubrey Williams for encouragement, criticism, and valuable counsel in the early stages of this undertaking; to Professor R. W. Rogers for hospitality and entree to the Rare Book Room of the University of Illinois Library; to Mrs. Mary Ciebart, Assistant Rare Book Librarian there, for her gracious assistance; to Miss Mary Anne Kernan and Mrs. Howard Griest of the Joint University Libraries at Vanderbilt University, for favors both great and small; to Professor H. Lloyd Stow, then Chairman of Classical Studies at Vanderbilt, for his kindness and patience in seeing to it that I did no wrong he could prevent in coping with Homer's Greek; to Vanderbilt University for a leave of absence to complete the project; and to the Graduate Research Council of the University for a grant toward the cost of preparing the manuscript. For typing the manuscript, preparing the index, and taking a special interest in the accuracy of the proofing, I wish to thank Miss Elaine Goleski.

To the editors of *Philological Quarterly* and *Papers on Language and Literature*, I am indebted for permission to reprint as part of Chapter V revised texts of articles originally appearing in those journals.

I would not conclude these acknowledgments without expressing again my thanks to one who has now and ever shall have the greatest claim upon my gratitude and affection, my wife, Marie, who, not surprisingly perhaps, concurred heartily in my wish to dedicate this book to our children.

JOHN M. ADEN
Vanderbilt University

CONTENTS

·

xi

ABBREVIATIONS AND SHORT TITLES

.

Baxter	Stephen B. Baxter, *William III.* London: Longmans, 1966.
Corr.	*The Correspondence of Alexander Pope,* ed. George Sherburn. 5 vols. Oxford: Clarendon Press, 1956.
Early Career	George Sherburn, *The Early Career of Alexander Pope.* Oxford: Clarendon Press, 1934.
Guerinot	J. V. Guerinot, *Pamphlet Attacks on Alexander Pope, 1711–1744.* New York: New York Univ. Press, 1969.
Hooker	Edward Niles Hooker, ed., *The Critical Works of John Dennis.* 2 vols. Baltimore: Johns Hopkins Univ. Press, 1939.
Minor Poems	Alexander Pope, *Minor Poems,* ed. Norman Ault and John Butt, vol. VI, 1954, of *The Twickenham Edition of the Poems of Alexander Pope* (see work abbreviated TE following).
MLN	*Modern Language Notes.*
N&Q	*Notes & Queries.*
OBO	*The Iliad of Homer ... By Madam Dacier. Done from the French by Mr. OZELL* [along with William Broome and William Oldisworth]. 5 vols. London: for Bernard Lintott, MDCCXII.
PMLA	*Publications of the Modern Language*

	Association of America.
POAS	*Poems on Affairs of State,* gen. ed. George deF. Lord. 7 vols. New Haven: Yale Univ. Press, 1963–75. (Note: The state poems published originally were under various titles from 1689 to 1716. Mention of specific poems in the text often includes date first published.)
PQ	*Philological Quarterly.*
Prose Works or PW	*The Prose Works of Alexander Pope,* ed. Norman Ault. Oxford: Blackwell, 1936.
RES	*Review of English Studies.*
SEL	*Studies in English Literature.*
Spence	Joseph Spence, *Observations, Anecdotes, and Characters of Books and Men,* ed. James M. Osborn. 2 vols. Oxford: Clarendon Press, 1966. (Unless otherwise indicated, references are to entry numbers.)
Spingarn	J. E. Spingarn, ed., *Critical Essays of the Seventeenth Century.* 3 vols. Rpt. Bloomington: Indiana Univ. Press, 1957.
TE	Alexander Pope, *The Twickenham Edition of the Poems of Alexander Pope,* gen. ed. John Butt. 11 vols. London and New Haven: Methuen and Yale, 1939 ff.
Vieth	David M. Vieth, ed., *The Complete Poems of John Wilmot, Earl of Rochester.* New Haven: Yale Univ. Press, 1968.
Wakefield	*The Iliad of Homer Translated by Alexander Pope, Esq.,* A New Edition, by Gilbert Wakefield. London, 1806.

THE COLOURS
AND THE GROUND

I

CONVICT A PAPIST

.

IN 1923 GEORGE SHERBURN observed that "Most writers on the
literature of this period have no idea, apparently, of the furious
hatred of Catholics expressed in journals and pamphlets during the years here under consideration."[1] It is likely that many
still do not. It is likely too that many still do not appreciate the
enormity of the statutory plight of Catholics from the time of
Elizabeth I through the eighteenth century, or its effects upon
the personal and literary career of Alexander Pope. As late as
1737 he was still brooding about it:

> ... knottier Points we knew not half so well,
> Depriv'd us soon of our Paternal Cell;
> And certain Laws, by Suff'rers thought unjust,
> Deny'd all Posts of Profit or of Trust:
> Hopes after Hopes of pious Papists fail'd,
> While mighty WILLIAM's thundring Arm prevail'd.
> For Right Hereditary tax'd and fin'd,
> He [Pope's father] stuck to Poverty with Peace
> of Mind;
> And me, the Muses help'd to undergo it;
> Convict a Papist He, and I a Poet.[2]

Pope is decrying the penal laws against Roman Catholics, laws
reaching back as far as the first Act of Supremacy, 1534,
proclaiming Henry VIII head of the Church of England and
declaring it treasonable to maintain otherwise. The Protestant
movement legalized by this act gained headway under Edward
VI with the abolition of Latin services, the publication of the

3

Book of Common Prayer, and the formulation of the Articles of Religion. Still, though Thomas More and the Bishop of Rochester died in 1535 for refusing the Oath of Supremacy, a Catholic persecution as such did not emerge until after the counter-reformation under Mary, during whose reign (1553–1558) papal supremacy and the Roman rites were restored and Protestant dissenters ("heretics") ruthlessly put to the stake. The trauma this induced in the Protestant conscience for better than two centuries still quickens the pages of the *Book of Martyrs*.

Pope was legatee of everything that came thereafter in the way of reprisal against Catholics, and if we are to understand him, it is important that we know at least something of that grim history.[3]

i. ELIZABETH I

The statutory persecution of Catholics began with the reign of Elizabeth, which set the pattern and formed the basis of English Catholic policy for the next two hundred years. New acts of supremacy and uniformity repealed the Marian church legislation and restored power and jurisdiction over the Church to the Crown. Subjects were required to attend Sunday worship according to the English rite or pay a fine of 12p., a heavy penalty for most, being twice the daily wages of a laborer. Recusancy, created by this provision, carried additional provisos for excommunication and imprisonment. Additions to the Act of Supremacy increased the penalties for disobedience: on first offense *praemunire* (forfeiture of lands and goods), on second, execution. The Thirty-nine Articles, made statutory in 1571, explicitly renounced Romish doctrine in relation to purgatory, pardons, adoration of images and relics, invocation of saints, transubstantiation, and the number of sacraments.

After the excommunication of Elizabeth in 1570 it was made treasonable, among other things, for any subject to receive or propagate papal bulls or import Romish icons of any sort, and it was forbidden dissenters to leave the country to evade penalty or to be trained as missionaries. Still later it was made treasonable for a priest to proselytize or for a subject to be reconciled to Rome; and forbidden, on pain of indefinite imprisonment, to give aid or comfort to missionaries.[4] This legislation also increased the penalty for recusancy, imposing a fine of £20 a month for steady offenders, retaining the 12p. a Sunday, and levying heavy fines for saying or hearing Mass.[5]

Another act of 1581 made it criminal to traffic in seditious talk or rumor, at a cost of 200 marks and imprisonment for three months, or having the ears cut off in public. In 1585 an act against Jesuits, seminary priests, and "like disobedient persons," ordered all such to leave the kingdom within forty days or be judged guilty of treason. It was made a felony to aid or harbor them, and subjects were required to report the whereabouts of any Catholic priests. English students in continental seminaries were ordered to return and submit, and heavy penalties were imposed on any who sent their children abroad for Catholic training. Anyone giving assistance to foreign seminaries was subject to *praemunire*. Finally, even conformed recusants were forbidden within ten miles of the Queen without permission, on pain of death.

Subsequent legislation provided for stricter enforcement of existing laws, increased the penalties for recusancy, disallowed the conveyance of property for the purpose of evading penalty, made it a felony to harbor a recusant, allowed recusants to venture no more than five miles from their homes, and required anyone suspected of being a Catholic priest to stipulate whether he was "a jesuit, or a seminary or massing priest."

The repetition of laws suggests that, as throughout the history of the penal acts, enforcement was difficult and never wholly effective. There was simply not sufficient bureaucracy for the task, and there was, in addition, too much corruption and connivance among those available for it. But the dangers were ever present, and many did suffer, some grievously. It has been estimated that during the reign of Elizabeth 183 Catholics were put to death: 123 priests, 1 friar, and 59 laymen.[6]

ii. JAMES I

Any prospects of relief Catholics might have entertained upon the accession of James I were not long in being chilled. Perhaps as a result of the Bye Plot, though more likely out of ingrained prejudice, Parliament reenacted in 1604 all the Elizabethan penal laws against Jesuits, seminary priests, and recusants.[7] This setback was compounded the next year by the Gunpowder Plot, resulting in two of the most disabling acts since the Elizabethan high-water mark of the 1580s. The first, aimed primarily at occasional conformity, required "church papists" to take Communion according to the Anglican rite once a year or suffer escalating fines. Churchwardens were required to report absentees annually. The act also required an oath of allegiance to James as rightful sovereign, renouncing papal authority to depose, along with the doctrine that heretical kings could be lawfully murdered, all on pain of *praemunire*.

Even more severe was the second of these acts, one of the most sweeping in the whole penal record. By it Catholics could not come to court except at the King's command; come within ten miles of London unless in trade or menial occupation in the city, or without abode elsewhere;[8] practice any profession or hold any office; legally marry outside the established Church, or transfer land by any such marriage arrangement; possess Catholic books or devotional literature; keep arms or munitions; take degrees from the universities or pursue education abroad; be officers in the trainbands or the navy; import "relics"; or, if convicted Catholic women, act as executors or guardians or inherit chattels, being deprived at the same time of two-thirds of any other inheritance or jointure. All "recusants convict" were declared "excommunicate" and deprived of going to law except in cases involving landed property. Children of marriages not solemnized in the Church of England were ruled illegitimate, and parents of children not baptized in the Church of England were subject to a fine of £100. Finally, those convicted of clandestine burials (as papists were likely to be) were subject to a fine of £20.

In 1610 laws were added requiring the sacrament of Communion according to the Anglican rite, as well as the oaths of allegiance and supremacy for any seeking naturalization or restoration "in blood," and extending the application of the Oath of Allegiance to everyone over eighteen, on pain of *praemunire*. Proclamations for the enforcement of all the penal laws appeared with regularity thereafter, notably in 1621 and 1624. It is not surprising, given this record, that, as far as Catholic hopes were concerned, James turned out to be, in the words of one Katherine Gawen, "a King as good as no King."[9]

iii. CHARLES I

With the accession of Charles, Catholic hopes must have quickened again, as they did, pathetically, with every Stuart monarch, only to be dashed, either from not enough, from too much, or, as in the case of the first Charles, from falling somewhere between. In this instance Catholics suffered more from a tug of war between King, Parliament, and Council than from any renewal of the penal frenzy under Elizabeth and James. Charles vacillated between personal and connubial inclinations toward Catholicism on the one hand and Parliamentary alarms on the other. He tried suspension of the penal laws, Parliament countered with investigations and arrests; he renewed the penalties, the Council ordered the disarming of recusants. Charles and government alike profited from the mulct of Catholic recusants. Parliament passed an act in 1628 "To restrain the Passing or Sending of Any to be Popishly Bred Beyond the Seas," and subsidy acts regularly provided that Catholics should pay double.[10] By 1640–41, as events moved toward their climax, Jesuits, priests, and seminarians were banished by royal proclamation. The Grand Remonstrance of the latter year placed the blame for distress in the realm on "Jesuitical Papists," high Anglicans, and councillors serving foreign interests.

It is hardly surprising that Catholics were predominantly royalist during the Civil War, but the cost was great. They were the object of intense mob hatred and violence on its eve, and suffered singular depredation at the hands of Parliamentary forces during the rebellion, notoriously at Basing House in 1645, "one of the few real atrocities of the Civil War."[11] In 1643 Parliament passed ordinances for the sequestration of suspected papists' estates, with an oath abjuring papal authority, transubstantiation, purgatory, and the like. After the war Catholic "delinquents," those who fought for the King, were made subject to loss of four-fifths of their lands and simple "Papists" two-thirds, though many managed to salvage by compounding or by fictitious sales.[12]

iv. The Commonwealth

During the Commonwealth the laws of Elizabeth and James remained on the books, except for the oaths of allegiance, obedience, and supremacy, which, along with church attendance laws, were repealed. But Mass was still forbidden, and it was still treasonable for a Roman Catholic priest to be in England, let alone to act as a priest. Jesuits and priests alike were excluded from the Act of General Pardon. Restrictions on Catholic travel were reenacted; papists earning less than 20 marks a year or possessing goods and chattel less than £100 in value were required to abjure the realm; disarming acts were renewed; and further sequestration ordinances were enacted.

Elizabethan and Jacobite laws were again reenacted under the Protectorate, with violations punishable as treason. A new test for papists was enacted in 1657, "the worst," as Forbes puts it, "that a junto of theologians and lawyers could devise."[13] Under Richard, Parliament (now restored) passed acts for the disarming and "dismounting" of Catholics, making it treasonable for them to live within twenty miles of London or to remain in England without giving security for good behavior.

In February of 1660 a Council of State was created and charged with enforcement of laws against "Jesuits, priests, and popish recusants." March saw still another act for disarming and for enforcement of the penal laws. Apparently the Interregnum was not so tolerant of Catholics as some, then and since, have alleged.

v. THE RESTORATION, CHARLES II

Perhaps the only real difference brought about by the Restoration was that the Catholics now shared persecution and reprisal with the Protestant nonconformists. Though Protestant dissent did effect a certain diffusion of the onus of penal harassment, it did not significantly alter the status of Catholics, especially as old fears and animosities were kindled anew by various circumstances surrounding the personal life and public conduct of Charles II and the Duke of York, and as these came to a head in the Popish Plot, the Exclusion movement, and the birth of parties.[14]

Under Charles the Test Act of 1678, passed in the wake of depositions alleging a popish plot, was the only new anti-Catholic legislation to reach the statute books, but it was seriously disabling. It excluded Catholics from both houses of Parliament by requiring an oath quite impossible for a conscientious Catholic to take. With the exception of the Duke of York, who was exempted, no Roman Catholic sat in Parliament again until 1829.[15]

Charles, who was not ill-disposed toward Catholicism, had already issued (1672) a Declaration of Indulgence ostensibly for the relief of nonconformists but also permitting private worship, in their homes, to Roman Catholics. This he was forced to rescind the next year, at which time Parliament passed its first Test Act, forcing the Duke of York to resign the Admiralty and in so doing to make public what had been suspected all along, his conversion to Catholicism. This, and his marriage in November to the Catholic Mary of Modena, brought the old popish fears and animosities once again to the fore.

Recognizing the realities of politics, Charles issued proclamations banishing priests and ordering enforcement of the penal laws. Recusancy presentations and convictions soared, reaching in 1673 the highest figure for any year of the reign. Bonfires and "pope-burnings" were carried out 5 November on a scale unprecedented for thirty years. Early the following year came still another order for enforcement of the penal laws and a bill to incorporate in the Test Act a declaration of impiety for resistance to constituted authority and an oath not to alter the established government in church and state. Fear continued to mount, and to be played upon, until it finally burst into national panic with the Popish Plot. Even though the Plot was pure fabrication, and proved so at the time, there was little consolation for Catholics in the exposé.

The real thorn in the side of all this of course was the Duke of York. He had never been popular, even before the Plot and the Exclusion movement, and he pursued his Catholic conviction and intent with fatal obduracy. He proved, as a consequence, not more alarming to the Protestants than disquieting and disconcerting to the Catholics, to whose rescue he brought only ruinous zeal and arrogance. It was with him not a case of too little, but too much.

vi. James II

James lost no time agitating the Catholic cause, with the result that he was forced first to prorogue and then dissolve his only Parliament and undertake the dangerous venture of rule by prerogative. In 1687 he issued the Declaration of Indulgence suspending all penal laws, dispensing with the oaths and the test, and proclaiming the free exercise of religion to all. In May of the following year he ordered the reading of the declaration aloud in churches throughout the kingdom. When Sancroft and six other Anglican bishops resisted, they were arrested and sent to the Tower. This was the last straw. Sympathy flooded to the side of the bishops, and, when on 30 June they were acquitted, the country went wild with celebration. James had finally forced a choice.

It was a choice made easier by an event scarcely three weeks earlier, the birth to the royal family of a son and Catholic heir. The night of the acquittal of the bishops, a committee gathered at the house of the Duke of Shrewsbury and drafted an invitation to William of Orange to intervene. By mid-December 1688 it was all over. James had fled to France and William was in London. So was Alexander Pope, by seven months.

vii. WILLIAM III AND MARY

The monarch who displaced James was his nephew and son-in-law, grandson of James's own father, Charles I. He had been raised in the Dutch Reformed faith and was already the foremost Protestant leader in Europe. He had, moreover, been deep in the English scene for some time. In 1677 he had married his cousin, Princess Mary, eldest daughter of James. He had also been involved in the Exclusion movement, and James would later attribute the beginning of William's conspiracy for the English throne to his failure to intervene in James's behalf during that crisis. James's suspicions were not unfounded: in 1680 William went so far as to send a representative to Parliament to see to it that he rather than Monmouth would benefit if any change were made in the succession.[16]

Though William made peace with his newly enthroned father-in-law, he continued his contacts with Protestant leaders in England. By the summer of 1687, following the Declaration of Indulgence, members of the English nobility were visiting him and he was being steadily importuned to intervene.[17] When he did it was, in effect, to seat himself on the throne.

William's reign proved a strong if not, for all its fancied promise, a popular one. The honeymoon was brief, even for the leadership that had brought about the match. William proved as jealous of prerogative as his Stuart kinsmen, though he was more politic in its exercise. He too filled the administration with his own, the Dutch; he too turned English foreign policy to his own special interests—the protection of the Netherlands from the Catholic threat of Louis XIV—and he too played off one English faction against the other in an effort to remain as independent as possible of Parliamentary government. He was, even for his promoters, more Dutch than Stuart, more European than English; and his government proved painfully oppressive in taxation.

As for his Catholic policy, William never showed any inclination to persecution, though Pope and his fellow religionists would have been little disposed to believe it, assuming they were even in a position to know it. William, it is true, had intervened as the champion of Protestantism, but he came, as Lecky reminds us, from a country where toleration was already well established and without any disposition of his own to behave otherwise.[18] Upon his arrival he had declared for freedom of conscience for all willing to live peaceably, and he did what he could in the beginning to discourage penal excess. But Parliament, always the real enemy of Catholicism, could not have been reformed even if William had tried harder, and he did not choose to resist any of the penal measures enacted during his reign.

That particular history began with the Act of Toleration, 1689, which abolished none of the penal statutes affecting Catholics or dissenters, but exempted Protestants from enforcement under certain conditions easy enough to subscribe to. On the other hand, the act explicitly declared that nothing in it was to be construed as affording relief for Roman Catholics. The Bill of Rights, in the same year, prescribed new oaths of allegiance and supremacy, oaths which affected Anglicans as well as Catholics, and so gave rise to nonjuring. As for Catholics, the bill specified that no Roman Catholic or anyone marrying same could ever succeed to the throne and that all future sovereigns must subscribe to those articles in the second Test

Act of Charles II relating to transubstantiation, invocation of saints, and the Roman Mass.

Not only were the old Catholic laws left in force, but new ones were added, including two right off against conspiracy and insurrection. By one Catholics were excluded from London and Westminster; by the other no Catholic was to possess arms or a horse worth more than five pounds.[19] A new Oath of Allegiance included specific disavowals of Romish interference. Still another statute limited the power of a Catholic to bring an action in law, or to claim part of a husband's estate, and withdrew the right of presentation to benefices. In 1692 Catholics refusing the oaths were made subject to double taxation; in 1695 a further act closed to them the various professions of the law.[20]

In 1700 "An Act for the further preventing the growth of Popery" subjected any bishop, priest, Jesuit, or Catholic teacher to perpetual imprisonment, offering a reward of £100 to anyone securing conviction of any apprehended in the performance of a priestly function. By the same act no parent could send a child abroad for the purpose of Catholic education, on pain of a fine of £100, payable to the informant! Any person who did not within six months of attaining eighteen subscribe to the oaths and the declaration against transubstantiation became disqualified to inherit or purchase land, and any inheritance such a person would otherwise have been eligible for was ordered passed to the nearest Protestant heir. This last provision must have figured in Pope's father's conveyance, in 1700, of the Binfield property (purchased in 1698) to his nephews-in-law, Samuel and Charles Mawhood. In the last year of William an Abjuration Oath required office holders and members of Parliament to abjure the Pretender.

viii. ANNE

For many the accession of Anne must have seemed the restoration of the Stuart line undefiled, and with it the hope of continuing that line, by fair means or foul. For Catholics it must have seemed, in spite of experience, still another promise of liberation from bondage. Though they were to be denied again, the reign of Anne, especially as it stood out against that of William and held out the possibility of forestalling Hanover, was for Catholics (and other Englishmen as well) one of mixed hopes and fears, and, in respect to the penal laws, nothing worse than they had grown hardened to.

Meanwhile the changeover began in the familiar way. The Act of Settlement (1701), prompted in large part by the death in 1700 of the Duke of Gloucester, Anne's only surviving heir, provided that if William and Anne should die without issue, the succession would pass to the Electress Sophia, granddaughter of James I, or to her heirs, and that in no event should a papist, or anyone married to a papist, succeed to the throne. Anne's first Parliament passed acts adopting the loyalty oath of William's reign, substituting Anne's name in the Abjuration Oath, and making it high treason to interfere with the Protestant succession.

The issue of succession would continue to agitate the nation throughout the lifetime of Pope. From 1702 on it became the more unsettled as Anne's reign progressed without heir and the prospect of Hanover became more and more eminent. Meanwhile the Pretender himself was not idle, and in 1707 the Regency Act made additional provision against the possibility of an attempt by the Pretender should the Queen die suddenly.[21] The suspense over the union with Scotland further agitated the Jacobitical issue, and in 1708 James Edward undertook an invasion of Scotland, though it never even got him ashore. Its failure proved a setback to Catholic interest, breaking the spell of Anne's remorse and prompting her to declare against her half-brother as a popish pretender.

This, in the wake of Harley's dismissal from the ministry on suspicion of Jacobitical intrigue, drew the Whig faction closer to the Hanoverian cause. Though the Tories triumphed in 1710, bringing Harley and St. John to the fore, their negotiations for peace laid them open once more to suspicion of betrayal and thus vulnerable to reprisal later on. The suspicions regarding them, if exaggerated, were not without foundation. Toward the end, Harley sent the Pretender a draft declaration for renouncing the Catholic Church, and Bolingbroke discussed the Prince's response at a meeting with members of Parliament. Anne fell ill in December of 1713 and never fully recovered. Hanoverian partisans in both houses proclaimed the succession in danger and complained of French and Jacobitical biases in the Treaty of Utrecht. The uneasy partnership of Oxford and Bolingbroke came to open breach as the former sought accommodation with the Whigs and the latter consolidation of Tory strength. Bolingbroke eventually sought Oxford's dismissal, but was put off until late July, when Anne finally relieved the Lord Treasurer, giving the reins of government to Shrewsbury, instead of Bolingbroke. Anne died 1 August 1714, and the Tories were broken.

Meanwhile, the anti-Catholic agitation had been kept alive at all levels and in all parts of the realm. Pope could have read in *The Flying Post* 17/20 February 1705 a report from Edinburgh of the seizure and order for burning of popish vestments, trinkets, crucifixes, and the like.[22] Narcissus Luttrell records 25 January 1705 the Queen's approval of an Irish act for "preventing the further growth of popery in that Kingdom." On 4 April 1706 the Council, through the archbishop and bishops, circularized the clergy to the effect that her Majesty, being apprized of "the very great Boldness and Presumption of the Romish priests and Papists in this Kingdom," directed them thereby to take a census of papists in every parish along with their "Qualities, Estates and Places of Abode" and to report their findings to her.[23] This was followed shortly by a royal proclamation for enforcing the laws against any attempting "to Pervert her Majesties Subjects to the Popish religion," citing the laws of 23 Eliz. "to Retain the Queen's Majesties Subjects in their due Obedience," and of 3 Jas. I "for the Discovering and Repression of Popish Recusants." In March 1710 a proclamation for the apprehension of certain Sacheverell rioters included clauses commanding all papists sixteen years and over to repair, as legislated, to their domiciles and not to move therefrom beyond five miles distant, and all papists, saving householders and those in trades, to remove within the week from London and Westminster. A like proclamation for papists to remove from the cities was issued the following March. The *Protestant Post Boy* for 17/20 November 1711 reported government interference, out of concern for riot, in the customary "pope-burning" of 17 November that year. Toward the last days of Anne (17/20 July 1714) *The Flying Post* reported a bill of indictment against one Hanmer, popish priest in Chelmsford, for saying Mass "according to the custom of the Romish Church."

It is indicative of the divided loyalties of the kingdom that, apart from additions to the crushing penal code in Ireland, the reign of Anne did not add appreciably to the laws against Catholics, nor, on the other side, do anything to remove those already in effect.

ix. HANOVER

Pope affected to be indifferent to the health of Anne and the prospect of Hanover. "I never inquire if the Queen be well or not," he wrote to Jervas 28 July 1714, pretending to be more concerned about the progress of the Homer.[24] But in a letter to Caryll after the death of the Queen, though for a moment he tries again to appear insouciant, he cannot suppress his concern. The passage is so revealing that it warrants quotation at length:

> . . . I could not but take a trip to London [from Binfield] on the death of the Queen, moved by the common curiosity of mankind, who leave their business to be looking upon other men's. I thank God that as for myself, I am below all the accidents of state-changes by my circumstances, and above them by my philosophy. Good will to all, are the points I have most at heart; and I am sure those are not to be broken for the sake of any governors or government. I am willing to hope the best and that I more wish than my own or any particular man's advancement, that this turn may

put an end entirely to the divisions of Whig and Tory, that those parties may love each other as well as I love them both, or at least hurt each other as little as I would either; and that our own people [the Catholics] may live as quietly as we shall certainly let theirs, that is to say, that want of power itself in us may not be a surer prevention of harm, than want of will in them. I am sure, if all Whigs and all Tories had the spirit of one Roman Catholic that I know [Caryll], it would be well for all Roman Catholics; and if all Roman Catholics had ever had that spirit, it had been well for all others; and we had never been charged with so wicked a spirit as that of persecution. It is indeed very unjust to judge of us in this nation by what other members of our communion have done abroad. Our Church Triumphant there is very different from our Church Militant here (if I may call that a Church Militant which is every way disarmed). The greatest fear I have under the circumstances of a poor papist is the loss of my poor horse; yet if they take it away, I may say with the resignation of Job, tho' not in his very words, *Deus dedit, Diabolus abstulit,* I thank God I can walk. If I had a house and they took it away, I could go into lodgings; if I had money and they took it away, I could write for my bread . . . if my own works would not do, I could turn writing master at last and set copies to children. . . . Whatever befalls me, I only desire to keep my own integrity and your love. The rest I leave to Heaven.[25]

This is a remarkable testament, not only to the reality of the problem, but to the burdens of conscience, tact, adjustment, and cunning it placed upon Pope and doubtless others of his faith: the instinct for advertising the innocence of his motives and behavior and the necessity of wording with utmost scruple sentiments both dear and dangerous; the whistling in the dark and protestations of insignificance and philosophic indifference while at the same time making a show of fortitude; the less than ingenuous disavowal of property and means; but most of all the almost defiant casting aside of fear in the audacious rewording of Job, where *diabolus* leaps forth like a glove in the face of Hanover.[26]

Pope had reason to be concerned. Homer was as much his refuge and distraction as it was his preoccupation, but he would find means even there to enlarge, under cover of translation, upon the political crisis. Meanwhile the changeover was breathing hard upon the backs of many, including his own friends. Swift, in despair, had retired to Letcombe. Bolingbroke had watched helplessly as power slipped from his grasp into that of Shrewsbury, and on the day of the Queen's death had gathered with Ormonde, Bathurst, Wyndham, and Atterbury at Harcourt's to consider what, if anything, might be done to redeem the situation. Atterbury was for desperate measures. They should proclaim James III, put an army under Ormonde, and enlist the aid of France. He would himself read the Proclamation in lawn sleeves at the Royal Exchange. Bolingbroke said they would get their throats cut, for "England would as soon have a Turk as a Roman Catholic for king." Later that same day all but Atterbury signed the document proclaiming George, and marched in the procession for its reading.

The king who reached Greenwich from Hanover on 18 September 1714 was fifty-five years old, without a shred of English or any knowledge of or real interest in the country he had reluctantly come over to rule. Whether he was in effect the captive of his Whig promoters, or whether he molded that clay to suit his own will may be moot, but his reign brought about an overthrow of power that lasted the better part of Pope's lifetime. Within a month of his arrival the remainder of the old Tory ministry had been purged and replaced by Hanoverian Whigs and fellow travelers.

The new Parliament, overwhelmingly Whig, immediately initiated impeachment proceedings against Bolingbroke, Oxford, Ormonde, and Strafford. Bolingbroke (and later Ormonde) fled to France, whereupon both were declared traitors and their estates and rights placed under attainder. Oxford went to the Tower, where he remained for two years before being acquitted in 1717.

Meanwhile there was the Fifteen, a badly mismanaged rising in behalf of "James III," followed by other abortive plots in 1716, 1719, and 1722. In the last of these Atterbury was implicated, tried, found guilty, and exiled. Pope was a witness for his defense. This was the end, until the Forty-five, of serious Jacobite effort, though, as Basil Williams points out, Walpole continued to find the Jacobitical bogey useful at election times and continued the policy of guilt by association between Jacobites and Tories.[27]

The Jacobitical activity, designed to promote the Catholic cause, only succeeded in worsening it. The anti-Catholic laws not only went unmitigated in the early Hanoverian period, but as a consequence of the risings and plottings were compounded. The resulting complication of the Catholic disability is impressively summarized by Lecky:

> By a law which was enacted in the first year of George I. all persons in any civil or military office, all members of colleges, teachers, preachers, and lawyers of every grade were compelled to take the Oath of Supremacy, which was distinctly anti-Catholic, as well as the Oath of Allegiance and the declaration against the Stuarts. By the same law any two justices of the peace might at any time tender to any Catholic the Oaths of Allegiance and Supremacy if they regarded him as disaffected. They might do this without any previous complaint or any evidence of his disaffection, and if he refused to take them he was liable to all the penalties of recusancy, which reduced him to a condition of absolute servitude. A Popish recusant was debarred from appearing at court, or even coming within ten miles of London, from holding any office or employment, from keeping arms in his house, from traveling more than five miles from home, unless by licence, under pain of forfeiting all his goods, and from bringing any action at law, or suit in equity. A married woman recusant forfeited two-thirds of her jointure or dower, was disabled from being executor or administratrix to her husband, or obtaining any part of his goods, and was liable to imprisonment unless her husband redeemed her by a ruinous fine. All Popish recusants within three months of conviction, might be called upon by four justices of the peace to renounce their errors or to abandon the kingdom; and if they did not depart, or if they returned without the King's licence, they were liable to the penalty of death. By this Act the position of the Catholics became one of perpetual insecurity. It furnished a ready handle to private malevolence, and often restrained the Catholics from exercising even their legal rights. Catholics who succeeded in keeping their lands were compelled to register their estates, and all future conveyances and wills relating to them.

They were subjected by an annual law to a double land-tax, and in 1722 [/23] a special tax was levied upon their property.[28]

We have already remarked Pope's involvement in some of these disabilities, and the politics in which they were caught up, but other particulars of that story, along with Pope's attitude toward his religion, are better reserved for another chapter.

II

THE POETS STATE

·

FOR THE CATHOLIC who would live and let live in Pope's time politics must have seemed desperate indeed—little better than a state of war. Pope's own resentment of the "Violence of Party" was early and not, we may be sure, an affectation of political wit.[1] That the violence was real and that Catholicism was at the heart of it cannot but have been painfully evident to him from the start.

His father, a convert to Catholicism, was a linen merchant in London from at least 1678, the eve of the Plot and the turbulence of its aftermath, both immediate and lasting. How we do not know, but the family apparently weathered the earlier upheaval successfully enough, for the first known record of its discomfiture dates from the year of the Revolution, when, the risks evidently proving too great, Mr. Pope retired from business. How long the family remained on Lombard Street, where the poet was born in that year, is not certain, but sometime before 1698 it moved out of the city to Hammersmith, some six miles from St. Paul's, close enough to the ten-mile limit to afford a greater sense of security. By that date, probably as a result of the petition of Commons the year before for stricter enforcement of the penal laws, Pope's father purchased some fourteen acres at Binfield in Windsor Forest, whither the family removed about 1700. Either in anticipation of or in response to the legislation of that year disqualifying Catholics from purchasing land, Mr. Pope conveyed the property to his wife's

21

Anglican nephews, Samuel and Richard Mawhood, to be kept in trust for his son.[2]

In Binfield not only were the Popes out of reach of London's more imminent threats but in something of a Catholic neighborhood. The manor of Binfield was owned by a Catholic, John Dancastle. Just a few miles away was Whiteknights, home of Anthony Englefield, Catholic, and grandfather of the Blount sisters of Mapledurham, itself nearby. At Bagshot lived the poet's half-sister, Mrs. Rackett, from whose husband Mr. Pope had bought the Binfield property. Other friends and relatives were in Pangbourne and Reading. Professor Sherburn cites a religious census for Berkshire in 1676 showing 24 Catholics in Binfield, 16 in Cookham, 16 in Inglefield, and 28 in Upton. The population was probably much the same when the Popes came to the Forest.

They remained at Binfield until, probably to escape the added land taxes and inquiry into their title, though also perhaps to accommodate the poet's access to London, they moved in 1716 to Chiswick, where they rented a house near the estate of the Earl of Burlington. After the death of his father in 1717 Pope moved the next year to the slightly farther remove of Twickenham, a change which, if not specifically attributable to Catholic causes, must have included that consideration.[3] Pope remained in Twickenham for the rest of his life, though there were times, as when the Court was meeting in Richmond, when he found it advisable to be away from home. We know too that toward the end of his life he could not safely go to London for medical attention he sorely needed.

What sort of Catholic was the poet whose place of residence was so often dictated or influenced by his religious affiliation, and whose whole political existence was affected by it? That Pope's parents, and many of his friends, were more strict in Catholic observance than the poet himself should not be taken to mean that his Catholicism was nominal only. Even if it had been, of course, that fact would not have lessened his political liability; but the point is that the handicap was not just the misfortune of a profession meaningless in the first place. Pope was an earnest, as well as steadfast Catholic. As a nonjuror, indeed, and in other ways as well, he was a defiant Catholic. At the same time, to be sure, a certain impatience of religious rigor, coupled with an early welcome into the worldliness of London, elicited in him a readiness for adventure, even misadventure, in the intellectual life of a less than conscientious society, as a result of which he more than once brought disquiet to his Catholic acquaintance and no doubt to his parents as well, though we have no record of that. But in spite of these ventures in the world of wit, and a lifelong disposition to broadmindedness in religious matters, no one who has studied Pope closely can doubt the sincerity and fidelity of his Catholicism. At home, as Francis Thornton rightly infers, he was certainly accustomed to regular prayer; he knew his catechism, was required to read the Bible and *The Following of Christ*, attended Mass at the homes of the Dancastles, Blounts, and Englefields, and was schooled in the lives of the saints. Though he never permitted this training and observance to tyrannize either his conscience or his conduct, Pope was, as Thornton says, an altogether "traditional Catholic."[4]

His education, aside from family precept and practice, was almost exclusively Catholic in supervision, starting at home with a priest named Bannister (alias Taverner), whom he followed to a school at Twyford in 1696, only to be withdrawn after a whipping for writing a satire on his master.[5] He was then sent for a time to the school of another priest, Thomas Deane, in Marylebone, near Hyde Park Corner. After the move to Binfield he resumed study at home under the Reverend William Mannock, of the Rackett household. If we are to believe Mannock, Pope's only venture in non-Catholic education may have been tutoring in French and Italian in London "when he was about fifteen," though this too could have been under Catholic tuition. Mannock does not say. If the story is true, the London outing may have been the beginning of Pope's induction into a world with less than devotion on its mind. Mannock says the family "looked upon it [the outing] as a wildish sort of resolution." The family was probably righter than it suspected; still nothing really disabling came of it.[6]

However Pope flirted, or affected to flirt, with the fashion of freethinking and however much he seriously detested certain aspects of Roman dogmatics and practice, he never toyed with atheism or with another faith, though he was, with respect to the latter, more than once invited to do so by his Anglican friends. One of these was Swift, who sometime in 1713 wrote him, no doubt partly in jest, partly in earnest, offering him twenty guineas to convert. Pope answered in kind, but one can read between the lines not only his resolve but its implications for him. He compares the offer to the thirty pieces of silver, and suggests that at that rate he might better have put his faith than his Homer out to subscription. If Swift will undertake to raise a like amount among the government, he might consider the offer, but only under certain conditions: that he would renounce the Pope only when he could be assured of indulgences from the Queen, that he would undertake Communion in both kinds as soon as ever the ministry would provide him "wherewithal to eat and to drink," that he would invoke sinners instead of saints whenever he could be convinced that the former were as willing to serve him as the latter, and finally that he be allowed to retain at least one Catholic practice with the perquisites necessary thereto, that is, prayers for the dead—like old Dryden, a papist and a poet; Walsh, a Socinian and a Whig; Tory L'Estrange; and a pair he intended (God willing) to outlive, Jervas and Swift himself.[7]

This of course is wit play between friends on a subject important to them both. A more serious exchange on the subject took place between Pope and Atterbury after the death of the poet's father in 1717. Pope's response can be appreciated only in contrast with the nature of the proposal. "When you have paid the Debt of Tenderness you owe to the Memory of a Father," writes Atterbury, "I doubt not, but you will turn your Thoughts towards improving that Accident to your Own ease and Happiness. You have it now in your Power to pursue that

Method of Thinking and Living which you like best. Give me leave, if I am not too early in my Applications . . . to assure you, that there is no man living, who . . . would be more pleas'd to contribute any ways to your Satisfaction, or Service."[8]

The Bishop had plainly misjudged his friend and his friend's preferences. Pope declined the somewhat less than flattering overture first (but not only) on his mother's account. What he says further of the offer tells us much about Pope's conscience and its political cost:

> Whether the change would be to my spiritual advantage, God only knows: this I know, that I mean as well in the religion I now profess, as I can possibly ever do in another. Can a man who thinks so, justify a change, even if he thought both equally good? To such an one, the part of *Joyning* with any one body of Christians might perhaps be easy, but I think it would not be so to *Renounce* the other.
>
> .   .   .   .
>
> . . . In my politicks, I think no further than how to preserve the peace of my life, in any government under which I live; nor in my religion, than to preserve the peace of my conscience in any Church with which I communicate. I hope all churches and all governments are so far of God, as they are rightly understood, and rightly administred: and where they are, or may be wrong, I leave it to God alone to mend or reform them . . . . I am not a Papist, for I renounce the temporal invasions of the Papal power, and detest their arrogated authority over Princes, and States. I am a Catholick, in the strictest sense of the word. If I was born under an absolute Prince, I would be a quiet subject; but I thank God I was not. I have a due sense of the excellence of the British constitution. In a word, the things I have always wished to see are not a Roman Catholick, or a French Catholick, or a Spanish Catholick, but a true Catholick: and not a King of Whigs, or a King of Tories, but a King of England. Which God in his mercy grant his present Majesty may be, and all future Majesties![9]

There is more here, to be sure, than the expression of faith and fidelity, impressive as that is. This is also what may be called an "inspector's letter," one written on the supposition of its likelihood of being opened and read by government agents or informers. But even under that rubric it is impressive. Pope not only drops the necessary reassurances of political submission and renounces the temporal authority of Rome, but lectures his potential censors on good government and just kingship. He also makes it clear, for whatever audience—princely or ministerial, Anglican or Roman, civic or religious of any sort—that he believes in separation of church and state in matters of conscience.

Later in his career Pope received a letter from Henry Brooke, the poet and dramatist, expressing disbelief at having heard, more than once, that Pope "had too much wit to be a man of religion, and too refined a taste to be that trifling thing called a Christian," to which Pope replied:

> I do not deserve the tenth part of what you say of me as a writer; but as a man I will not, nay, I ought not, in gratitude to him to whom I owe whatever I am, and whatever I can confess, to his glory, I will not say I deny that you think no better of me than I deserve; I sincerely worship God, believe in his revelations, resign to his dispensations, love all his creatures, am in charity with all denominations of Christians, however violently they treat each other, and detest none so much as that profligate race who would loosen the bands of morality, either under the pretence of religion or free-thinking. I hate no man as a man, but I hate vice in any man; I hate no sect, but I hate uncharitableness in any sect; this much I say, merely in compliance with your desire, that I should say something of myself.[10]

One should not overlook, either, Pope's response to Louis Racine's attack in *La Religion* (1742) upon the *Essay on Man.* "Upon the whole," says Pope, "I have the pleasure to answer you in the manner you most desire, a Sincere Avowal that my Opinions are intirely different from those of Spinoza; or even of Leibnitz; but on the contrary conformable to those of Mons: Pascal & Mons. Fenelon: the latter of whom I would most readily imitate, in submitting all my Opinions to the Decision of the Church."[11]

But Pope was far more troubled by complaints about his fidelity than by any hopes or fears of his infidelity. "I find by dear experience," he wrote to Caryll in 1714, "we live in an age, where it is criminal to be moderate .... It is certainly to be lamented, that if any man does but endeavour to distinguish himself, or gratify others by his studies, he is immediately treated as a common enemy . . . and assaulted as generally, as if his whole design were to prejudice the State, and ruin the public."[12] Pope was thinking immediately, it would appear, of the Homer and the partisan push and pull around that, not of the change of scepters, though that too was much on his mind. A week later Anne was dead, and the clouds that had low'rd upon his house from that prospect crowded out all other considerations.

By the end of August, uneasy over the reactivation of the penal laws, he was writing to Blount: "May I venture to say, who am a *Papist* . . . to you who are a *Papist*, that nothing is more astonishing to me, than that people so greatly warm'd with a sense of Liberty, should be capable of harbouring such weak Superstition, and that so much bravery and so much folly, can inhabit the same breasts?"[13]

With the turn of the year came greater uneasiness, and sadness as well, in the face of political reprisals against Oxford and Bolingbroke. In late June, Jervas wrote him of the Whig notice of his salute to Bolingbroke in the Preface to Homer, suggesting that he might wish to "make room for Walpole" in his next.[14] Pope wrote the Blount sisters in July of Oxford's imprisonment and Ormonde's flight, and mustered (perhaps as much for the inspectors as for the sisters) a sally upon the Pretender's coming, with the flurry of battle and fashion which that would bring to the ladies. But he concluded as he began, on a sober note: "So much for the present, & as for the future, I neither know what will become of myself, or of the nation."[15]

Nor was he merely posturing when, more than a year later, he wrote to Lady Mary, homesick from her travels, that it was not for him "to talk of it with tears in my eyes; I can never think that Place my Country, where I can't call a foot of paternal Earth my owne." Nor when, fancying himself in flight to Turkey in search of liberty, he said, "for who would not rather live a free man among a nation of Slaves, than a Slave among a nation of free men?"[16]

His friendship with Atterbury was also to bring him grief and embarrassment. Atterbury was implicated in the Jacobite plot of 1722, went to the Tower in August, and, notwithstanding insufficient evidence for capital indictment, was finally deprived and exiled in May of 1723, largely through Walpole's doggedness. At Atterbury's request, Pope had been called before Lords as a character witness, perhaps on the assumption that a Catholic disavowal of complicity would somehow carry weight, though for Pope such a qualification made it anything but easy for him to meet the summons. Under fire already for his edition of the works of Buckingham (suspect of Jacobitical content), Pope himself was accused in *Pasquin* (20 February 1723) of complicity in the plot and later of perjuring himself in his testimony for Atterbury.[17] Even Lord Harcourt, Pope's friend, to whom he had spoken in Atterbury's behalf, advised him to lie low and keep quiet.[18] The fact that Atterbury wrote him secretly on the tenth of April expressing the hope that his ill fortune would never catch up with Pope or Arbuthnot suggests the extent to which Pope was vulnerable, if not actually implicated, in the whole affair. But the strongest proof of his vulnerability is a letter he wrote to Harcourt on the opening day of the trial. Harcourt had already advised him, but Pope expressed a desire to confer again with his lordship. Meanwhile he ventures and questions as follows:

> I resolve to take any opportunity of declaring (even upon Oath) how different I am from what a reputed Papist is. I could almost wish, I were askd if I am not a Papist? Would it be proper, in such case, to reply, That I dont perfectly know the Import of the word, & would not answer any thing that might for ought I know, be prejudicial to me, during the Bill [a tax measure] against such, which is depending. But that *if to be a Papist be to profess & hold many such Tenets of faith as are ascribd to Papists, I am not a Papist. And if to be a Papist, be to hold any that are averse to, or destructive of, the present Government, King, or Constitution; I am no Papist.* I very much wish I had your Lordships opinion a little more at large, since probably I may not be calld upon this day or to morrow.[19]

But for all his alarm and fear, obviously warranted, Pope remained as loyal to Atterbury as he had to the faith which Atterbury had sought to lure him from and which he had now brought to the extremity of forcing Pope to the study of legal double talk. Pope visited Atterbury in the Tower before the trial, testified for him at the trial, and corresponded with him after he was banished, even though to do so was illegal. The bill "depending," to which Pope referred in the letter to Harcourt, was one for additional punitive tax on Catholics. It was introduced in Commons 26 April, passed there on 17 May (after the trial), in Lords on the twenty-second, and was affirmed law by royal approval on the twenty-seventh. On the day it passed Commons, Pope wrote Caryll bespeaking repayment of a £200 loan so that he might invest in annuities to help absorb the shock.[20]

Earlier the Popes had been under the necessity of registering their change of residence from Binfield to Chiswick, as a result of the act for mulcting Catholics passed in the wake of the uprising in 1715. Pope wrote to Thomas Dancastle, brother of John Dancastle of Binfield Manor, asking if he could arrange to have the commissioners of inquiry and registry come to Chiswick so as to spare his parents, especially his mother, the "trouble and fatigue of going to London" for the registration. From the same letter it is evident that Pope was finally to give up his poor horse.[21] The Fifteen had also led to a requirement that Catholics and nonjurors take revised oaths of allegiance by 23 January 1716 or suffer the usual penalties. Pope refused and undoubtedly, as Thornton says, "prepared for the worst."[22]

Pope's Catholic liabilities were not merely governmental of course, though they always threatened to come back to that. They included a sedulous and relentless campaign on the part of Grubstreet to blacken his character and question his loyalty. This vendetta must have proved among the most painful and disquieting of all his experiences as a Catholic. It began with Dennis's *Reflections Critical and Historical, Upon a Late Rhapsody, Call'd An Essay Upon Criticism* (1711), an outburst and libel that might better have been styled "critical and hysterical." Dennis was a rabid anti-papist and Francophobe. He was also, like Addison, "too fond to rule alone," and Pope had made free with his reputation that way in the *Essay on Criticism:*

> ... *Appius* reddens at each word you speak,
> And *stares, Tremendous!* with a *threatning Eye,*
> Like some *fierce Tyrant* in *Old Tapestry!*

Dennis, to be sure, had as much right to tit-for-tat as Pope, but apart from some admittedly useful criticisms of the poem qua poem, which Pope acknowledged by adopting, the *Reflections* far exceeded the provocation in malice and virulence. In addition to a brutal and unwarranted attack upon Pope's person ("a hunchback'd Toad"), along with no little caviling at the poem, Dennis went out of his way to advertise Pope a papist and Jacobite. Citing Pope's line, "As *Kings* dispense with *Laws* themselves have made" (v. 162), Dennis extracts the last full measure of sinister intent:

> In the beginning of the 12th Page, we find what that is which so happily reconcil'd him to it [the reign of James II, as against those of Charles II and William III], and that was the Dispensing Pow'r, which was set on foot in order to introduce and to establish Popery, and to make it the National Religion. Now I humbly conceive that he who Libels our Confederates [the Dutch], must be by Politicks a *Jacobite;* and he who Libels all the Protestant Kings that we have had in this Island these threescore Years, and who justifies the Dispensing Pow'r so long after we are free'd from it, a Pow'r which as was hinted above was set on foot on purpose to introduce Popery: He who justifies this when he lyes under the Tye of no Necessity, nor ev'n Conveniency to approve of it, must, I humbly conceive, derive his Religion from St. *Omer's,* as he seems to have done his Humanity and his Criticism; and is, I suppose, politickly setting up for Poet-Laureat against the coming over of the Pretender, which by his Insolence he seems to believe approaching.[23]

What must have made this all the more painful for Pope is the fact that there is, for all the overreading, just enough truth in the accusation to be politically awkward. Pope does take occasion in the *Essay* to allude favorably to the Stuarts (Dennis overstates his exceptions to Charles II) and unfavorably to

William and the Dutch; and, though Dennis fetched the Jacobitical inference from the grossest distance and carried it to
the grossest exaggeration, the truth is that Pope probably was
Jacobitical in sentiment, if only wistfully so. But that he ever
seriously entertained the idea of translating that sentiment
into disloyal or rebellious conduct is something that only now
the evidence would discredit. Enough then to have the charge
made; trial was summary. But Pope-baiting was too easy, popular, and potentially self-serving to be foregone on grounds no
better than fair play or hard evidence. Pope continued to be
branded Jacobite and popish henchman in such libels as *A Farther Hue and Cry after Dr. Sw[if]t* and *The High German
Doctor* of 1714; the *Homerides* and *Grumbler* of 1715; and
the *Flying Post, Weekly Packet,* and *Homerides* of 1716, to
name only the most conspicuous.

Oldmixon, in the "Petition" appended to *The Catholick
Poet* (1716), accused Pope of turning Homer for the benefit of
the Pretender: "he makes *Homer* say, *that the Priest can pardon Sins,* which is downright Popery. Upon which your Pe-
titioner, could not forbear crying out, z-nds, *This Popish Dog
has ruin'd me, he has translated HOMER for the Use of the
PRETENDER.*"[24] Dennis returned to the attack in the same
year, with *A True Character of Mr. Pope,* impugning Pope's
protestations of and efforts at political impartiality:

> he is . . . a Whig and a Tory, a virulent *Papist* and yet forsooth, a
> Pillar of the Church of *England,* a writer at one and the same
> time, of GUARDIANS and of EXAMINERS, an assertor of Liberty and
> of the Dispensing Power of Kings . . . a Jesuitical Professor of
> Truth, a base and foul Pretender to Candour . . . however, he may
> cry up HOMER for being every where a *Graecian-Trumpeter* in the
> Original, I can see no *Trumpeter* in the *Translator,* but the King
> of *Spain's.*[25]

In *Remarks upon Mr. Pope's Translation of Homer* (1717),
Dennis continues the attack with still greater pointedness:

> I regard him as an Enemy, not so much to me, as to my KING, to
> my COUNTRY, to my RELIGION, and . . . LIBERTY . . .

that Protestants . . . Lovers of Liberty, and . . . Country, should encourage him . . . to suborn Old HOMER to propagate his ridiculous Arbitrary and Popish Doctrines . . . is . . . a Prodigy.[26]

Cibber joined the hue and cry in 1718 with asides on Pope's Catholicism and Jacobitism in the *Non-Juror*. In 1724 Curll brought out *Madame Dacier's Remarks upon Mr. Pope's Account of Homer*, "Made English," in which the French translator took mischievous notice of Pope's political talents, something that proved especially awkward for him at this juncture in his affairs.[27] In 1728 (the outer limit of this study) Pope was noticed for his papistry in *The Twickenham Hotch-Potch, Gulliveriana*, and *Codrus;* for his Jacobitism in the miscellany *A Complete Collection;* for both in *Characters of the Times*, and for his disloyalty in *An Essay on the Dunciad*.

For all their spite and unfairness, Pope's critics were not wholly wide of the mark where his politics lay. Their principal disservice was that they hit him as much as they missed (or misrepresented) him. Pope's Catholicism was not an insignificant factor in his public career, though it did not include the papism so often alleged, for Pope rejected papal authority in the state, as we have seen. His critics were less wide of the mark on the score of Jacobitism, even if they did overstate it. Pope probably was, as we have said, loosely Jacobitical in sentiment, but he was not an agitator or conspirator. What he really wanted was not a James, but an Anne, though he would have settled for any government not hostile to Catholics.

Where the critics came closest was in alleging political import to his literary work, and therein lies an irony, for Pope was manifestly engaged in political writing and obviously wanted to be so understood, at least this side of the law. His critics, as far as reading went, did precisely what he had hoped; that is, they perceived his drift. Where they went wrong was in not agreeing with him, in overreading him and publishing his intent as criminal.

That Pope suffered no worse than he did from the penal laws and their critical informers is due to no quarter granted him on either part, but to his talents, which the Whigs coveted; to his friendships among important persons of both parties; and to his genius at political satire—satire that could, if worse came to worst, always be disavowed or placed at another's doorstep. That he suffered as much as he did goes far to explain his resort to satire and politics in the first place.

III

FULL EARLY PUT TO SCHOOL

·

POPE WAS NOT DEPENDENT upon personal or domestic experience
alone in forming his attitudes toward political tribulation. He
was schooled as well, especially in the dislike of royal offenders, by a teeming satiric press, a press which also served in one
degree or other as singing master to his muse. His apprenticeship in both respects, apart from the Drydenian, is less well
known than it should be and deserves more attention than can
be given here.[1] The schooling in question is that of *Poems on
Affairs of State*.[2] It will be useful to consider what that schooling tells us of Pope and politics on the one hand, and of Pope
and the art of satire on the other.

i. TARQUIN AND TULLIUS

" 'What is Truth?' said jesting Pilate; and would not stay for
an answer." Had he asked it of the people, his indifference
would have been less censurable, for he would have found it
difficult indeed to sort where human perception is concerned—
little else, often, than opinion or belief, with as uncertain relation to what is called fact as the latter bears to truth. Something
of this dilemma must be borne in mind as we assess Pope's attitude toward William III. It is in relation to the common barriers
to truth, not to perversity and certainly not to a "corrupt love
of the lie itself," that we must judge his understanding in this,

as in other matters of political import. All of which is not to say that he was wrong in any or every particular, only that he was not always right. William, as it proves, was not in fact so bad as he was made out to be, but neither was he so good. This, however, must be acknowledged as something we are in a better position to know than his contemporaries. True or not, at any rate, we are compelled, for the purposes of literary history, to see William as his age saw him, for better and for worse. Where Pope is concerned, and many of his persuasion, that means seeing him for the worse.

In the state poems William was attacked for his face and figure, his "usurpation," familial ingratitude and betrayal; his Whiggish backing and appointments, his preoccupation, at the expense of the English, with affairs of Europe, particularly the Provinces; for the costliness of his government and the resulting burden of taxation; for his Dutch extraction, attitudes, favorites and favoritism; for corrupting English religion and trampling upon Rome; for his alleged homosexuality and many lesser faults and crimes—little of which is likely to have escaped the notice of Pope, even in his boyhood, and thus to have authorized, where it did not foster, his own resentment and distrust.

One of the most scurrilous caricatures of William appears in *The Coronation Ballad* (1689) by Ralph Gray, a reputed papist, who includes Mary in the family portrait. To the usual sneer at physique, Gray adds the sexual innuendo, breach of promise to the English nation, and, along with Mary, filial impiety. A few stanzas will illustrate its vein:

> Some people were glad at the monster's invasion,
> Had the knave but stood to his Declaration.
> But now 'tis too plain; he hath cheated the nation.
> A dainty [fine King indeed.]
>   · · · · · ·

> An unnatural beast to his father and uncle;
> A churl to his wife without e'er a pintle;
> But excuse me in this for I hate to dissemble.
> A dainty, &c.
>   · · · · · ·

35

Huzza to the King and his delicate mate!
She was a most lovely princess of late,
But now a contemptible object of state.
A dainty fine Queen indeed.

. . . . . .

Then may the confusion they hither have brought us
Always attend them until it hath brought us
To bring back great James as loyalty taught us.
Our gracious good King again.[3]

Of greater merit, owing in part to its Drydenian extraction,
is Arthur Mainwaring's *Tarquin and Tullia* (composed 1689,
published [augmented?] 1704). Mainwaring, like Dryden,
takes the way of allegory, catching up the usurpation theme in
terms of a violent and impious chapter in Roman legend. In the
transposition James becomes Tullius and William Tarquin,
while Tullia is now Mary, now Anne, now both. The story
lends itself perfectly to Mainwaring's argument:

In times when Princes cancelled nature's law
And declarations (which themselves did draw),
When children used their parents to dethrone
And gnawed their way like vipers to a crown,
Tarquin, a savage, proud, ambitious prince,
Prompt to expel yet thoughtless of defence,
The envied scepter did from Tullius snatch,
The Roman King, and father by the match.

. . . . . .

Vain promises the people's minds allure;
Slight were their ills, but desperate the cure.

. . . . . .

'Twas now high time for Tullius to retreat
When even his daughter [Anne] hastened his defeat.
When faith and duty vanished, and no more
The name of father, nor of King, he bore:

. . . . . .

This King removed, th'assembled states thought fit
That Tarquin in the vacant throne should sit,

. . . . . .

36

But Tarquin, guided by destructive fate,
Wasted the country, and embroiled the state,
Transported to their foes the Roman pelf,
And by their ruin hoped to save himself.

    . . . . . .

Men who renounced their God for dearer trade
Were then the guardians of religion made;
Rebels were sainted, foreigners did reign,

    . . . . . .

The trade was sunk, the fleet and army spent,
Devouring taxes swallowed lesser rent,
(Taxes imposed by no authority:
Each lewd collection was a robbery).
Bold self-creating men did statutes draw,
Skilled to establish villainy by law,
Fanatic drivers, whose unjust careers
Produced new ills exceeding former fears.[4]

Mainwaring avoids the abuse of William's person, even softens
the indictment of Mary ("sobbing" and "maudlin in her cups,"
v. 112), but he touches very nearly every other complaint, and
gives no quarter where tyranny is concerned:

    ... brutal Tarquin never did relent,
    Too hard to melt, too wicked to repent,
    Cruel in deeds, more merciless in will,
    And blest with natural delight in ill.
                  (vv. 113–16)

At the same time he is studious in the praise of James:

    A King whose right his foes could ne'er dispute.
    So mild, that mercy was his attribute.

    . . . . . .

    His active soul did ne'er from labours cease,
    Valiant in war, and sedulous in peace,
    Studious with traffic to enrich the land,
    Strong to protect, and skillful to command,
    Liberal and splendid, not without excess,
    Loth to revenge, and willing to caress.
    In sum, how godlike must his nature be,
    Whose only fault was too much piety.
                  (vv. 83–96)

As in the case of William, there is both truth and error in this characterization, but many a loyal Englishman, papist or not, believed it as an article of unassailable truth. Pope was not, I think, one of those, but the idea behind the characterization, abstracted from the man, would have been deeply compelling for him.

A shorter, but no less caustic attack on William and his English confederates, *Suum Cuique*, also attributed to Mainwaring, appeared in a broadside edition without date, but probably belonging to 1689 or 1690.[5] In it Mainwaring, if he is the author, executes quick satiric portraits of Gilbert Burnet (who "betrayed a master and a prince"); John Tillotson ("grave Socinian"); William Lloyd, Bishop of St. Asaph (the "treason of old age"); Henry Compton, Bishop of London (the "scum and outcast of a loyal race"); and, finally, of William himself, this time in the physical and deviant aspect.[6]

Mainwaring is one of those who read Pope's *Pastorals* in manuscript. By that time his defection from the Jacobite cause to that of William would not have troubled Pope overmuch, though it may account in part for his later judgment of Mainwaring's work as of "very little merit." Later still Pope would speak of "That very hot copy of verses against King William and Queen Mary ('Tarquin and Tullia') . . . writ by the famous Mr. Mainwaring, though he was so great a Whig afterwards."[7]

Pope may or may not have known *On the Late Metamorphosis* (1690), a brief satiric commentary on an emblematic engraving of the conquering Cromwell altered to show the head of William. The burden of the satiric comparison is the violation of the constitution, with glances sober and facetious at the popish plight:

> . . . See Rome trampled down,
> See his victorious sword thrust through the crown,
> See his triumphant foot on papists' necks.
> See *Salus Populi Suprema Lex*.
> See Magna Charta. Can all this agree
> With any man but Oliver and *he?*
> Then talk no more of taxes and excise;

Such little thoughts true Protestants despise:
What though they come at times when money's scanty,
Whilst our religion's safe, it's all not tanti.
Let no free quarter grieve you or disturb you,
Nor think that Dutch or Dane came here to curb you.
What though they spoil your goods and pox your wives
So long as all our throats 'scape Popish knives?[8]

It is even less certain that Pope would have seen *A Litany for the Reducing of Ireland* (c. 1690), which sums up much of the Jacobite sentiment of the times:

From a Parliament that can make it no sin
For a son to dethrone both father and King;
From tearing up popery to bring atheism in;
For ever, good Lord, deliver us.[9]

But whether either piece came to Pope's attention, he could scarcely have been unacquainted with the analogies, charges, and petitions expressed in them.[10]

He almost certainly would have seen, on the other hand, *A Panegyric*, written by Jack Howe (?) and published in POAS 1703, the opening lines of which ring changes especially likely to have engaged him: filial ingratitude (Mary), disloyalty (Marlborough), subversion of the law, economic oppression, and the like.[11] Pope may have read too, and with feeling, the burning epitaph *On Sir John Fenwick* (POAS 1703). Fenwick was executed without due process in January 1697 for complicity in the Jacobite plot of the preceding year. The epitaph is in the high vein of Jacobitical outrage:

Here lie the relics of a martyred knight,
Whose loyalty, unspotted as the light,
Sealed with his blood his injured Sovereign's right.

The state his head did from his body sever
Because, when living, 'twas his chief endeavor
To set the nation and its head together.

He boldly fell, girt round with weeping soldiers,
Imploring Heaven (for the good of the beholders)
So to cut Holland's head from England's shoulders.[12]

Pope's "downright Shippen" (*Sat.* II. i. 52) may have been

the author of the *Advice to a Painter*, written in 1697 and published in POAS 1703, a cutting indictment of political corruption under William, with a strength of verse and image that Pope would have responded to. The poet directs the painter "With War and Slav'ry the vast Canvas [to] fill," not only with the scene abroad but that at home, "When *Fenwick* yielded to the cruel Stroke." To which end, says the poet,

> First draw the Hero seated on the Throne,
> Spite of all Laws, himself observing none;
> Let *English* Rights all gasping round him lie,
> And native Freedom thrown neglected by.

The painter is instructed to draw the minions of the conqueror —Tennison of Canterbury, Lord Chancellor Somers, the Dutch ganymedes Bentinck and Keppel, the Earl of Sunderland ("Trusted [by James], yet always forfeiting his Trust"), the "brib'd Senate," "florid warlike *Cutts*," and others—all sketched with fine dispatch by the poet himself, who concludes.

> Some few untainted Patriots still remain,
> Who native Zeal and Probity retain;
> These sullen draw, disgrac'd and discontent,
> Mourning the Ruin which they can't prevent.
> But Painter hold—Reserve the vacant Room
> For Knaves in Embrio, and Rogues to come;
> Who undiscover'd, yet will us betray,
> And sell their Country in a closer way.[13]

The death of James, late 1701, and of William, early 1702, brought forth a spate of elegies, mock and serious, on both sides, some of which at least Pope must have seen. He certainly saw, sooner or later, an anti-Williamite piece published in POAS 1703 which, in his own 1705 copy, he attributed to Bevil Higgons. Whoever the author, he defines the grounds for mourning the lost leader in terms Pope could scarcely have failed to find congenial:

> Mourn on, you foolish fashionable things,
> But mourn your own Condition, not the King's;
> Mourn for the mighty Summs by him mis-spent,
> Those prodigally given, those idly lent;
>
> . . . .

Mourn for ten Years of War and dismal Weather,
For Taxes, strung like Necklaces together,

. . . . . .

Tho now you mourn, 't had lessen'd much your Wo
Had *Sorrel* stumbled thirteen Years ago.[14]

Pope would not, on the other hand, have been impressed with
the sentiment, whatever he thought of the style, of Walsh's
The Golden Age Restored (POAS 1703), a Whiggish retort on
the Tory hopes of Anne, though he is apt to have found its
provocation, *The Golden Age* (1703), palatable Toryism:

Now Banish'd Justice takes its Rightful Place,
And *Saturn's* Days return with *Stuart's* Race.[15]

Some of the lines of this piece anticipate Pope's own celebration of the golden age in *Windsor Forest:*

Fearless of loss, and confident of Gain,
The Merchant shall in Safety Plough the Main;
The lab'ring Hind shall cleave the Country Soil,
And Plenty rise and Court the Farmer's Toil.
As every Subject sees his Wrongs Redress'd,
Views Faction quell'd, and Anarchy Suppress'd,
And Prince and People Mutually Bless'd.[16]

Among the pieces published in the collection owned by
Pope, *Faction Displayed* (1704), attributed by him to Shippen,
may have made a lasting impression on him. It not only etches
more deeply the brand of usurpation but canvasses political
evils and ideals which Pope touched upon both early and late in
his own career.

Faction, a restless and repining Fiend,
Curdles their Blood, and gnaws upon their Mind;
Off-spring of *Chaos,* Enemy to *Form,*
By whose destructive Arts the World is torn.

. . . . . .

'Tis She, that wou'd, for ev'ry slight Offence,
Depose a True Hereditary Prince;
That would *Usurpers* for their Treason Crown,
Till Time and Vengeance drag them headlong down,
And *Exil'd Monarchs* Reassert their rightful Throne.

. . . . . .

41

O *England* how revolving is thy State!
How few thy Blessings! how severe thy Fate!

. . . .

Where is the Noble *Roman* Spirit fled,
Which once inspir'd thy antient Patriots dead?
Who were above all private Ends, and joy'd,
When bravely for the publick Weal they dy'd.[17]

We have remarked Pope's detestation of faction, and we know how he came to espouse the philosophy of the Patriot King and ministry of the later Bolingbroke. That he in fact anticipated the formal promulgation of that doctrine may be attributable in part to Shippen's expression of it here.[18] Shippen may also have figured in such embellishments of the Statius, composed during this same period, as "O *Thebes!* for thee what Fates remain," and the like.[19]

Faction Display'd also contains (vv. 24–43) an account of the English constitution, a *mixt* government, and not one in which monarchs are but the "Tools of State." The English system avoids extremes, admitting neither "Tyranny" nor "Commonwealth," but ordaining a "Successive Monarchy . . . / With all the Lawful Sanctions of a Crown." Pope understood these principles long before he gave them expression in the *Essay on Man.*[20]

The state poems undoubtedly contributed much to the development of Pope's views, not only of William, but of politics and politicians in general. Some of their lessons he took to his bosom only, and withheld from his pen; others he gave vent to, either directly or indirectly. He never resorted to the abuse of William's person so conspicuous in these poems, perhaps because of his own misfortune that way, but perhaps as well because he found such argument incompatible with his concept of satire. Nor does he invoke the sexual slander or innuendo— not, we may assume, out of any moral scruple, but because he deemed that charge the least of consequence. But he does touch upon just about every other item in the bill of complaint. He clearly accepted the view of William as Catholic persecutor; as an intruder upon the constitutional succession; as a foreigner, invader, and overlord; as a Socinian heretic and corrupter of religion and morals; as pickpocket of the English (and especially Catholic) purse; as the abridger of English liberties; and, in all likelihood, as presider over the consolidation of faction in English politics.

As for James, the picture is less certain, no doubt in part because of the sensitivity of the subject, especially for one in Pope's position. Though he said almost nothing of record about that unhappy monarch, what he did say reveals no very great regard for him. He told Spence, in 1735, that the reign of James I "was absolutely the worst . . . we ever had—except perhaps that of James the Second."[21] Even so, it is difficult to escape the impression that Pope entertained resentments as much in behalf of that pitiful figure as in detestation of William. He was accused of being a Jacobite, and it is by no means certain that the accusations, irresponsible as they are, were without foundation. Insofar as the label implies Stuart loyalty, there can be no question of its justification. Pope obviously thought of the reign of Anne as a Stuart restoration, and he clearly dreaded and resented the prospect of Hanoverian succession, against which he protested as much as he dared.

Meanwhile, in absorbing, sorting, and forming these particular viewpoints, he was also framing, both independently and with the stimulus of certain poems on affairs of state, other more general and philosophical views of politics and the political order. These included disapproval of faction as a way of political life, commitment to the patriotic ideal, the constitutional principle of monarchical succession, the doctrine of political tolerance, especially in matters of conscience, and the concept of the mixed state or balance of powers. We may now consider how, in part at least, he learned to voice these and other views.

ii. LIBELS AND SATIRES

Pope found more in the poems on affairs of state than talk of Catholics and kings. He also found examples of the satiric craft, from Dryden and the mob of gentlemen who wrote with ease to the journeymen of libel and lampoon. We need not reopen the case with respect to Dryden and Garth, but it will be worthwhile to consider his schooling at other hands.

Pope was much into the Court Wits, and, one suspects, quite early. He was especially drawn to Rochester, in whom he found, at that one's best, a style answerable to his own bent. We can track him everywhere in Rochester's snow:

But women, beggar-like, still haunt the door
Where they've receiv'd a charity before.[22]

What though the excrement of my dull brain
Flows in a harsh, insipid strain.

Yet most men show or find great want of wit,
Writing themselves or judging what is writ.

But men will censure, yet 'tis ten to one
When'er they censure they'll be in the wrong.[23]

. . . hasty Shadwell and slow Wycherley.

Proceed from want of judgment or of wit.

I lothe the rabble: 'tis enough for me
If Sedley, Shadwell, Sheppard, Wycherley,
Godolphin, Butler, Buckhurst, Buckingham,
And some few more, whom I omit to name,
Approve my sense. I count their censure fame.[24]

. . . 'tis such a baffl'd fop
That ev'ry schoolboy whips him like a top,
And, with his arm and head, his brain's so weak
That his starv'd fancy is compell'd to rake
Among the excrements of others' wit,
To make a stinking meal of what they s———.
So swine for nasty meat to dunghill run,
And toss their gruntling snouts up when they've done,

So have I seen, at Smithfield's wondrous fair. . . .[25]

Though Pope found it wise and no doubt attractive (especially in the early period) to follow more openly in the higher style of Dryden, Rochester is ultimately more nearly his model in tone and idiom that perhaps any other English satirist. Stripped of its coarser elements, Rochester's satiric voice is somewhere near the dead center of the Popeian at its most direct: spare, downright, and aggressive. Pope had a wider range than Rochester and a more elaborate rhetorical and dramatic texture, but Rochester seems as much as any other to have afforded him that unceremonious middle register around which he could play the high and low while executing those flourishes of wit, irony, and allusion which set him off from any other satirist in the language.

Carr Scroope, though but a satellite in this galaxy, added a knack of adversarial rhetoric which Pope might well have found instructive. We find evidence of that likelihood in his *In Defence of Satire* (1677), modeled loosely on Horace's *Sat.* I. iv:

a.   These and a thousand fools unmention'd here
    Hate poets all because they poets fear.
    "Take Heed!" they cry, "Yonder mad dog will bite.
    He cares not whom he falls on in his fit.
    Come but in's way, and straight a new lampoon
    Shall spread your mangl'd fame about the town."

b.   E'er that black malice in my rhymes you find
    That wrongs a worthy man or hurts his friend.
    But then perhaps you'll say, "Why do you write?
    What you call harmless mirth the world calls spite.
    Why should your fingers itch to have a lash
    At Simius the buffoon, or Cully bash?
    What is't to you if Alidore's fine whore
    F———— with some fop while he's shut out of door?
    Consider, pray, that dang'rous weapon, wit,
    Frightens a million where a few you hit.[26]

This is a mode Pope would not turn to until later in his career, but it would have impressed him from the outset.

Another piece mined both early and late is Buckingham's

Essay upon Satire, published originally in 1689, but again in POAS 1697 and in the *New Collection* owned by Pope. Buckingham is Pope's friend, John Sheffield, acknowledged among the modern critics of note in *An Essay on Criticism* and edited by Pope in the difficult period of Jacobitical unrest already alluded to. Pope's debt to him extends beyond the *Essay upon Satire,* but it alone afforded instruction and example aplenty for putting himself to school. Buckingham (then Mulgrave) commends conscience and subtlety in satire, argues the greater virtue and art in finding "nicer faults" than "grossest follies," and then launches into a series of satiric characters which he himself is forced to admit violate his own principles. Meanwhile he laid down lines, among many poor ones, that echo in Pope's own verse:

> Poets alone found that delightful way
> Mysterious morals gently to convey.

> As men aim rightest when they shoot in jest.

> But who can rail so long as he can keep.

> T'a teeming widow but a barren wife.

> Where one poor thought's sometimes left all alone
> For a whole page of dulness to atone.[27]

Oldham, whom Pope must have found distressing as well as fascinating, may have furnished the closest model for the "Dregs and *Squeezings* of the Brain" of the *Essay on Criticism,* but there is little else in Oldham's style or technique that Pope could have found attractive, at least not in the *Satires upon the Jesuits.*[28] There Oldham was not only too shrill but too much of a Catholic alarmist to have commended himself to Pope.[29] On the other hand, Pope would have been drawn, and for more reasons than one, to *Naboth's Vineyard* (1679), a protest against the hue and cry after popery and a forerunner of *Absalom and Achitophel.* This poem was written by John, Lord Caryll, Jacobite uncle of Pope's friend, John Caryll of Ladyholt. From it, among other things, Pope is likely to have remembered especially Naboth's (= the Catholic's) complaint of being envied his "spot of land" and the echo of Milton in "Whilst thus he pour'd his venom in her ear."[30]

The contemporaries of Pope's own coming out also contributed to his schooling. Frank Ellis, editor of the sixth volume of POAS, speculates that Pope may have found Defoe's *Pacificator* (1700) a breeding ground for the *Dunciad*.[31] While that particular association seems uncertain, there are others to suggest that Pope did consult the *Pacificator*, along with Blackmore's *A Satyr against Wit*, published in the same year, that he learned from both something about the crisis in the republic of letters and took away hints and impressions later to become part of the ambiance and argument, not only perhaps of the *Dunciad*, but almost certainly of the *Essay on Criticism* and the *Essay on Man*.[32] The war on wit, broken out anew with Jeremy Collier, was heated by this time, and Pope unquestionably followed it closely, both in and out of the state poems, including Sedley's *Upon the Author of the Satyr Against Wit* (1702) and Tom Brown's *A Lent-Entertainment*, of the same date and target.[33] Of the various attacks on Blackmore, however, Pope is more apt to have been impressed with Dryden's contribution in the Prologue to *The Pilgrim* (1700), from which at least two verbal echoes are discernible in Pope's later work: "Dead-born Doggrel" and the observation that Blackmore "Traduc'd Two Kings, their kindness to requite / One made the Doctor, and one dubb'd the Knight."[34]

Of all the candidates for influence in Pope's apprenticeship, Defoe is perhaps the most surprising, but certainly one of the most likely. Pope's statements about him, later on, suggest not only that he was well read in Defoe but that he was sensitive to his strengths as well as his weaknesses. In the *Peri Bathous* he dubs Defoe the "Poetical Son of *Withers*," though it may be as much for their satiric tribulations as for anything else; and, if "D. F." really stands for Defoe, as seems likely, Pope includes him among the ostriches in poetry, "whose Heaviness rarely permits them to raise themselves from the Ground; [whose] Wings are of no use to lift them up, and [whose] Motion is between *flying* and *walking*; but then they *run* very fast."[35] In the variorum *Dunciad* Defoe is made the descendant of the puritan Prynne, also punished for satire. Pope calls the one "restless Daniel" and identifies the pair as "writers of Verses, as well as of Politicks," citing as an example Defoe's *De Jure Divino* (1706).[36] But in 1742 Pope told Spence that "Defoe wrote a vast many things, and none bad, though none excellent. There's something good in all he has writ."[37] There is reason to believe that Pope thought so from the beginning and that he found Defoe instructive, especially in satiric verse.

Pope is certain to have read, if with mixed emotions, Defoe's *True-Born Englishman* (1700), which, for all its Williamite platform and prolixity, abounds in stout lines and couplets. The latter Pope would have appreciated. "The Grand Contention's plainly to be seen, / To get some men put out, and some put in," though doubtless a commonplace by the time Pope got to it, approaches the briskness of his own "I think your Friends are out, and would be in" (*Epilogue*, ii, 123). Closer still is Defoe's "Their strong Aversion to Behaviour's such, / They always talk too little, or too much." (vv. 461–62) to Pope's "Avoid *Extreams;* and shun the Fault of such, / Who still are pleas'd *too little,* or *too much*" (*Essay on Criticism*, vv. 384–85).

The True-Born Englishman also has some satiric portraiture of note (cf. *Colon*, vv. 521 ff.), but there is more and better of that in *Reformation of Manners*, published in the same year. One example will do:

> *Clayton* superbly wise and grave of Life,
> Cou'd every one reform, except his Wife:
> Passive in Vice, he Pimps to his own Fate,
> To shew himself a Loyal Magistrate.
> 'Tis doubtful who debauch'd the City more,
> The Maker of the Masque, or of the Whore.
>
> . . . .
>
> With decent Zeal, to Church he'll gravely come,
> To praise that God which he denies at home.
>
> . . . .
>
> And yet he *Covets* without Rule or End,
> Will sell his Wife, his Master, or his Friend.

> To boundless Avarice a constant Slave,
> Unsatisfy'd as Death, and greedy as the Grave.[38]

Here is not only a shrewd eye to character, but a verse not unlike the more intricate style of Pope's. Defoe's lines are crisp,
balanced, antithetic, hemistichal, varied in the pause, strong in
rhyme, effectively alliterated, sylleptic in at least one instance
and triplicate of structure in another. Pope could have found
much of this sort of thing throughout Defoe.

In satiric theme, vigorously enforced, Pope would have been
impressed with the scourge of the venal (vv. 299–322), the
missionary barbarous (vv. 333–58), and the atheistic (vv.
367–96) in the same poem. The following, on satire and satirists, is reminiscent in tone and theme of the *Epilogue to the
Satires:*

> Thou may'st Lampoon, and no Man will resent;
> Lampoon but Heaven, and not the parliament:
> Our Trusties and our Welbelov'ds forbear;
> Thou'rt free to banter Heaven, and all that's there;
> The boldest Flights thou'rt welcome to bestow
> O'th' Gods above, but not the God's below.[39]

Part II of the *Reformation* affords more of the candid couplet, tersely marked off, that Pope employed so frequently:

> The Scandal of the Law, his own Lampoon,
> Is Lawyer, Merchant, Bully, and Buffoon.
> (vv. 449–50)

> Thro' all Degrees of Vice the Father run,
> But sees himself out-sin'd by either Son.

> In Matrimony finds a learned flaw,
> A Wife in Honour, and a Wife in Law.[40]

Pope is also likely to have remembered Defoe's impatience with
priestcraft and metaphysics (vv. 853 ff.) and the following version of "all things *needfull* to be *known*" religiously:

> Religion's no divided Mystick Name;
> For true Religion always is the same,
> Naked and plain her Sacred Truths appear,
> From pious Frauds, and dark Ænigma's clear:

The meanest Sence may all the Parts discern,
What Nature teaches all Mankind may learn:
And what's reveal'd, is no untrodden Path,
'Tis known by Rule, and understood by Faith.[41]

It may have been Defoe's account of Dr. Pelling, who, in the hyp, "Fancy'd himself with Child" (v. 967), that gave Pope the idea for his allusion to the doctor in *The Rape of the Lock*: "Men prove with Child, as pow'rful Fancy works" (IV, 53). The *Reformation* affords grist for the fop mill too and may, finally, have lent something to the moral stance of the *Essay on Criticism*.[42]

More Reformation. A Satyr upon Himself, published in 1703 after Defoe had been arrested for *The Shortest Way with Dissenters*, is a satiric apologia. From it Pope could have learned a great deal about the problems of the satirist, and some few things acceptable to his own theory and practice of satire, though he did not, obviously, accept Defoe's proscription of satire on royalty, his disallowance of personal names, or his counsel to shun irony and ambiguity. The last advice was prompted, as we know, by the stem that scores the hand: Defoe had been bit. Pope would, on the other hand, have been impressed with Defoe's occasional deftness in couplet caricature:

> K———'s a Dissenter and severe of Life,
> Instructs his Household, and *Corrects his Wife*.
> (vv. 248–49. POAS, VI, 560)

> Whores are his Daily Consorts and Delight.
> Is Lewd all Day, but very Chaste at Night.
> (vv. 787–88, p. 580)

Among other Defovian pieces of this vintage that Pope undoubtedly read is *The Dyet of Poland* (1705), another example of political allusion by way of allegory. *The Dyet* may have provided (vv. 12–25 ff., 1183 ff.) hints toward the method of the Atticus portrait as well as partisan authority for the view of William as a "Thundring Arm" (vv. 92–101, 158); it certainly afforded God's plenty of satiric vignette:

In Law upright, and prudent in the State,
In Council deep, in Execution great.

Strong in Opinion, in his Judgment Weak.

A thinking, plodding, *wise*, substantial *Fool.*

False to Himself, his Monarch, and his Friends,
But to the lowest Step of Pride descends.

Zeal on his *Tongue,* and *Fury* in his *Face.*

A Scolding Clamouring Member, Vain and Loud,
Noisy in Words, and *not a little Proud.*

Ambition now his antient Thoughts Employs,
And all the little Grace he had Destroys.

In Council *Hasty,* in Performance *Slow.*[43]

There is much in this style that suggests close study by Pope. In fact the whole question of Pope's debt at this door merits closer attention than it has received. Though Pope and Defoe were on opposite sides of the Williamite-Hanoverian fence, though one was a Puritan and the other a Catholic, one essentially a journalist, the other a poet, there were still grounds to accommodate respect on Pope's part, in spite of his published condescension. Defoe was an interminable writer and unconscionably prolix in verse, but when he hit his vein he was vigorous and far from unimpressive. He was to be sure a kind of political opportunist, at least from the standpoint of livelihood; but he had done a tour of duty under Harley and, like Pope, he despised faction. "I have always thought the only true fundamental maxim of politics that will ever make this nation happy is this, That the Government ought to be of no party at all," he wrote in the *Review.*[44] It may be too that Pope felt something in common between his Catholic and Defoe's dissenting tribulations, and that he responded to Defoe's aggressive spirit, in this as in other matters. For all their differences, in any case, there were grounds for respect open to Pope, and he not only admired Defoe more than he let on, but learned from him more than has been recognized.

As for the state poems in general, they almost surely exerted a profound influence on the shape of Pope's career. They brought copious ratification of grievance and the means of redressing it to a young poet smarting under the one and gifted toward the other. They as much as anything else must have confirmed him in the political calling of satire.[45]

SATIRE
WILL HAVE
ROOM

✠

IV

THE BEGINNINGS: TO 1710

·

THE EARLIEST LITERARY RECORD we have of Pope is that of a satirist. At the age of eight, while in school at Twyford, he wrote a satire on his master, for which he was punished and on that account withdrawn.[1] Of this precocious venture we know only that it was prompted by "some faults he had discovered" in his master, probably, to judge from his later comments on education, of the sort memorialized in *The Dunciad*:

> We ply the Memory, we load the brain,
> Bind rebel Wit, and double chain on chain,
> Confine the thought, to exercise the breath;
> And keep them in the pale of Words till death.
> (IV, 157–60)

Beyond the suspect testimony that it was "a Libel of at least one hundred Verses," we know nothing of the form of Pope's youthful sally.[2] It cannot have been an impressive performance, else there would have been further trace of it in the anecdotes or in Pope's later poetry, where he was wont to introduce whatever of merit he could salvage from his discarded apprentice-work. The most we can say is that the report shows Pope to have entered early upon his vocation as satirist, and that his inaugural theme was most likely dullness. If, on top of that, his *Successio* dates as claimed from 1702 and if, as his editors have speculated, it was aimed at Elkanah Settle's effusion on the prospect of Hanoverian succession, it is evident that Pope was not long adding politics to his agenda.

Neither biography nor criticism has been particularly alert to these tokens of Pope's initiation into poetry. It is commonly assumed that in the early period his energies were directed essentially to fledging himself in the practice of translation and imitation, or, with slight exception, to exploring fancy's maze. The fault with such an assumption is not that it is untrue, but that it is only partially true. That Pope was putting himself to school to a variety of masters, and exercising his own talents and fancy, is obvious enough, but what is generally overlooked is that satire and politics play an early and abiding part in that activity. With Pope, it is important to recognize, a translation is rarely just a translation, or an ode just an ode. It is likely to be a satire as well, or at least satiric, and frequently political in motive. As Geoffrey Tillotson said, in connection with *The Temple of Fame*, Pope as well as Dryden could have written

But Satire will have Room, where e're I write.[3]

The earliest surviving product of his muse seems to confirm the point. Written, according to Pope, when he "was not twelve years old," the *Ode on Solitude* is more apparently than an exercise in rural hymnody after the fashion of Horace and Cowley. Its textual history suggests that it is a reflection as well of personal experience, the family's removal from London to the sanctuary of Binfield. Some such confluence of form and pressure, of satire and song, is probably characteristic of all retirement literature. It is certainly true of the retirement poetry of Pope's later period, as Maynard Mack has demonstrated.[4] But Pope begins, I suspect, as he will end, for the fellowship of retirement and satire seems evident from the start. The *Ode* as now printed begins:

> Happy the man, whose wish and care
> A few paternal acres bound,
> Content to breathe his native air,
>   In his own ground.

Revision has all but obliterated the trace of personal interest in these lines, but in the earliest version, an autograph dating anywhere from 1700 to 1709, a satiric coefficient is discernible:

"Happy the Man, who free from Care, / The Business and the Noise of Towns." If this is conventional, it may be so only in respect to business and noise. The *care*, I would suggest, is Pope's, and appositional not to business or noise, but to the anxiety of a Catholic in the thick of an anti-Catholic state. Horace, who is the ultimate model, speaks only of *business: Beatus ille qui procul negotiis.*[5] The disclosure is even more pointed in the first printed version of Pope's ode (1717): "How happy he, who free from care, / The rage of courts, and noise of towns." This, we must remember, is how the lines read for almost twenty years of Pope's lifetime. Whether allusive or not, the lines were eventually improved in style and decorum, but as earlier conceived they suggest that the *Ode* was prompted in part at least by political malaise.[6]

In 1701, whatever else he may have done, Pope experimented further with the lyric, producing some nine imitations of Waller and Cowley; but by 1702 he was back to satire, imitating Dorset and Rochester. *To the Author of a Poem, intitled Successio,* alleged to be an imitation of the former, resumes the attack on dullness, to which is now added politics.[7] Though the poem as we have it (1712) cannot be assumed to be identical with the poem as first written, there is no compelling reason to suppose it greatly different. It is brief enough to quote in full:

> Begone ye Criticks, and restrain your Spite,
> *Codrus* writes on, and will for ever write;
> The heaviest Muse the swiftest Course has gone,
> As Clocks run fastest when most Lead is on,
> What tho' no Bees around your Cradle flew,
> Nor on your Lips distill'd their golden Dew?
> Yet have we oft discover'd in their stead,
> A Swarm of Drones, that buzz'd about your Head.
> When you, like *Orpheus,* strike the warbling Lyre,
> Attentive Blocks stand round you, and admire.
> Wit, past thro' thee, no longer is the same,
> As Meat digested takes a diff'rent Name;
> But Sense must sure thy safest Plunder be,
> Since no Reprizals can be made on thee.
> Thus thou may'st Rise, and in thy daring Flight
> (Tho' ne'er so weighty) reach a wondrous height;

So, forc'd from Engines, Lead it self can fly,
And pondrous Slugs move nimbly thro' the Sky.
Sure *Bavius* copy'd *Mævius* to the full,
And *Chærilus* taught *Codrus* to be dull;
Therefore, dear Friend, at my Advice give o'er
This needless Labour, and contend no more,
To prove a dull *Succession* to be true,
Since 'tis enough we find it so in You.

These would be competent verses at any age, but clearly more
so at fourteen than at twenty-four. The shift of grammatical
person is awkward, the metaphoric sequence unsteady, the
parenthesis fuzzy, the irony listless, and the squint of "content" (v. 22) more disconcerting than clever. Though Pope
would later transplant some of the lines to other poems,[8] what
we have here is in all probability a fairly primitive text, less
impressive as a composition than as a token of Pope's early
attraction to satire and politics. One suspects that Pope was
drawn to publish it at all chiefly for its Hanoverian glance,
which by 1712 was *de rigueur* in Tory polemics. As for revision, whatever that may have amounted to, and it seems little
enough, it is unlikely to have affected subject. We may be
safe in assuming therefore that by fourteen Pope was warming
to the theme of dullness, getting the hang of technique (the
fictitious name, insect imagery, scatology), and committing
himself to political argument in verse.

The existence, in the next case, of two manuscripts, one an
autograph, enables us to be more confident of the early state
of the poem. *On Silence*, an imitation of Rochester's *Upon
Nothing*, was also published in 1712, but its manuscripts date
from 1702–3.[9] Rochester's poem consists of seventeen stanzas,
reduced in Pope's manuscript versions to sixteen and in the
printed text to fourteen. While the ultimate product is a better,
more Popeian poem, it retains a surprising balance of the earlier
working. The changes are principally verbal, though four
stanzas of the manuscript version are dropped in the published
text and two are added. Still the survival rate is considerable:
just under one-third (fifteen lines) of the autograph. If we
count seven other verses in which only one word is altered (in

one instance two), the rate of survival mounts to just under one-half, or twenty-three lines.

To trace out all the changes would be tedious and pointless. One example will serve to illustrate the increasing nicety of Pope's satiric touch. What is now stanza 13 originally read thus:

> The Country's witt the Policy o'th Town
> A Courtiers learning, Citts Religion
> Are best by thee expressed and shine in thee alone.[10]

By 1712 it read as follows:

> The Country Wit, Religion of the Town,
> The Courtier's Learning, Policy o' th' Gown
> Are best by thee express'd, and shine in thee alone.

We may suppose the change from *Country's witt* to *Country Wit* was dictated by Pope's recognition that the possessive implies *national* rather than *rural*, which he obviously intended. The other changes may have taken rise from his recognition that *religion* does not make a very good rhyme with *town*, prompting him to the satiric addendum of *gown*, with adjustments for meter. Perhaps it was then he fell upon the idea of shifting the ousted *religion* to line one, consummating in the process a happy irony in the place of what was originally mere statement. *Policy*, he may have then perceived, could be salvaged to equally ironic advantage by moving it down to *religion's* old place and joining it oxymoronically with *gown*. There remained but to change *a* courtier's learning to *the*, and the job was done. Whether this is how it came about is purely speculative of course, but the important thing is the ingenuity, thriftiness, and satiric alertness of the alteration.[11] Pope was not everywhere so effective, either in the retouching or in the original.

As for Rochester's poem, it is enough to say that Pope worked freely with it, conflating, adapting, omitting, adding. Satirically he is less subtle than Rochester, more impatient of the satiric advertisement. Where Rochester husbands the disclosure, Pope hurries it; where Rochester can be content with bare substantive, Pope invokes the surety of epithet: "gawdy Science," "noisy witt," and the like. Rochester's satire runs a course from theological premise-reduction through a restrained moral but pronounced political indictment to a conclusion catching up a variety of human follies. Pope's, partly by virtue of the change of subject, runs a course from general rhetorical folly through dullness and vice to religio-political censure. For the theological, or philosophical, burden of Rochester's poem, Pope—his subject not lending to that, nor probably his interest—substitutes a rhetorical counterpart: the birth of speech out of primal silence. Rochester's various notice of vice (moral fault) Pope distills to a single stanza:

> *Silence*, the Knave's Repute, the Whore's good Name,
> The only Honour of the wishing Dame;
> Thy very want of Tongue makes thee a kind of Fame.[12]

Rochester is mordant on the theme of politics, as he is everywhere:

> But Nothing, why does Something still permit
> That sacred monarchs should in council sit
> With persons highly thought at best for nothing fit,
>
> While weighty Something modestly abstains
> From princes' coffers, and from statesmen's brains,
> And Nothing there like stately Nothing reigns?

Though political failure haunted Rochester more than it did his still youthful imitator, Pope was by no means insensitive to it, especially as it affected the Catholic plight:

> Yet speech thy Foe [i.e., the foe of silence] submissively
>   withdraws
> From Rights of Subjects and the Poor mans Cause
> And Silence then in Pomp sits nodding ore the Laws.[13]

Nor is Pope's canvass of general folly negligible, though again less sweeping than Rochester's. It includes the senate and the bar, the bumpkin, lawyer, courtier, cit; and by 1712, besides the national debt, peculation in high place, ingratitude, clerics, and critics.[14]

On Silence shows Pope turning early to one of the most passionate and political of Restoration satirists, throwing himself with more vigor than discretion into the emulation, adapting his model to the theme of rhetorical vice and folly, revisiting dullness, paying his respects to clericalism and city piety, and, if not with equal resonance, still with promise, following his mentor onto the rostrum of political discontent.

ii

When he turns next to the translation and imitation of the classics, Pope does not so much leave satire and politics as take them underground. If not in every instance, in most neither is far behind, and in some they are directly beneath the stage, uttering a ghostly but audible summons.

At about the same time he was imitating Dorset and Rochester, Pope tried his hand at Ovid and, perhaps a little after, Statius. Although not satiric, the Ovid (with one exception) afforded him exercise in characters and situations available to satire and in the comic spirit that seasons it. In the *Polyphemus and Acis* he is given the opportunity of painting a clownish lover, and in the *Vertumnus and Pomona* that of dramatizing an Olympian seducer of the *carpe diem* school, experiences which, if carried over visibly, affect the later prose more than the verse. *The Fable of Dryope*, on the other hand, is wholly pathetic, remote from either the comic or the satiric. *The First Book of Statius his Thebais*, begun in this period, does not apparently take on at this time the political coloration it will assume by 1709. Pope may have sensed its political potential by the earlier date, but if so he did little or nothing about it. Its discussion will, in any case, better fit the later date.

Sometime between 1704, the date Pope assigned to them, and 1705–6 Pope wrote his *Pastorals*.[15] Their significance to this history lies as much in the notice they brought Pope as in any satirico-political drift they disclose. The persons attracted by the poems were figures of political and satiric consequence, most of whom sooner or later affected Pope's education in such matters. According to Pope's own note, the *Pastorals* were seen in manuscript and applauded by Walsh, Wycherley, Granville (later Lansdowne), Trumbull, Garth, Halifax, Somers, Mainwaring, "and others."[16] Pope dedicated to three of these: Trumbull, Garth, and Wycherley. A fourth pastoral was dedicated at Walsh's behest and so in effect to him.

Satire per se has of course no place in the pastoral, at least as Pope understood it, but his dedication of *Spring* to Trumbull, a retired politician and mentor to the young poet, is indicative of Pope's tendency to see almost every enterprise in some relationship to that motive:

> *You*, that too Wise for Pride, too Good for Pow'r,
> Enjoy the Glory to be Great no more,
> And carrying with you all the World can boast,
> To all the World Illustriously are lost!
>
> (vv. 7–10)

This is the retirement motif satirically promulgated which we have remarked earlier. As for Sir William, it is not likely that in their rides together Pope learned from him only about "the classics." He must have learned something too about politics and King William, though he may not have heeded all he heard.

Pope found at least two other opportunities for political allusion in *Spring*. Together they constitute no very equivocal expression of political sympathies. Taking off from the *nomina regum* of Virgil's riddle in the third *Eclogue* (v. 106) he devises an allusion to the Royal Oak of Charles: "Say, *Daphnis*, say in what glad Soil appears / A wondrous *Tree* that Sacred *Monarchs* bears?" Then, following the lead of Virgil's *quibus in terris* (*Eclogue* III, 104), he alludes to the House of Stuart and the English mastery of France: "Nay tell me first, in what more happy Fields / The *Thistle* springs, to which the *Lilly* yields?" The Twickenham editors associate this with Anne's revival of the Order of the Thistle in 1703 and suggest in the "*Lilly*" an allusion to the Battle of Blenheim (1704), the date to which Pope assigns the composition of the poem.[17] But the primary allusion may extend beyond Anne. Pope could scarcely have been unaware that his contemporaries would be apt to read James II into it as well, for it was he who founded the Order in the first place. Coupled with the reference to Charles, such an allusion to Anne's symbolic act of family tie amounts to something like a declaration of Stuart loyalty.

Except perhaps for the dedication to Wycherley, with its celebration of his comic wit, the *Pastorals* yield no further hint of satiric or political motive. Given the pastoral decorum, that comes as no surprise. It would be surprising, however, if the first version of *Windsor Forest*, assigned to the same year (1704), did not reveal more than a passing political turn. One cannot be sure of course, because the earliest manuscript of the poem dates from 1712 or early 1713, and the earliest reference to the poem from late 1707. Such evidence as we have points to extensive revision of the poem before its publication and the unlikelihood therefore of ever deducing a primitive text. It is nevertheless neither impossible nor unlikely that, as Professor J.R. Moore suspects, the original poem included the Williamite allusion as we now find it.[18] Two lines suppressed in the early editions and restored in 1736 read, in fact, like a youthful descant on the Stuart surcease of Williamite sorrow:

> Oh may no more a foreign master's rage
> With wrongs yet legal, curse a future age!

Pope may have withheld this couplet, as the Twickenham editors suggest, "because it was too pointed an allusion to William III."[19] But it is not necessary to suppose, as they do, that the "wrongs yet legal" refer to the forest laws, at least not exclusively. Pope's petition seems aimed at a larger constituency than huntsmen and to describe a despotism more extensive than that of the chase. It is more likely that the lines refer to the Catholic disabilities and penalties associated with William's reign. Exactly what, if not Protestant spite, invasion, and war-like reputation in general, Pope had in mind by William's "rage" is not apparent, though it could be an allusion to William's implication in the Glencoe massacre of 1692.

In any event, whatever its vintage, the case against William

the Conqueror in *Windsor Forest* is clearly intended to pass
for that against William III, namely,

> . . . hostility to the Church, contempt for the agricultural in-
> terests, heartless indifference to the rights of the people, callous-
> ness toward the shedding of human blood.[20]

As Pope pursues the analogy his lines bristle with resentment
of savage laws, slavery, tyrants and tyranny, crime and despotism, oppressor and oppression. One passage stands out as
preeminently transferable from the Norman William to the
Dutch:

> Aw'd by his Nobles, by his Commons curst,
> Th' Oppressor rul'd Tyrannick where he *durst*,
> Stretch'd o'er the Poor, and Church, his Iron Rod,
> And serv'd alike his Vassals and his God.
>
> (vv. 73–76)

The application is unmistakable: the parliamentary resistance
to William's bid for prerogative, the burden of Williamite taxation (especially on Catholics), and the heretical tendencies of
Dutch theology, aggravated by William through such latitudi-
narian appointments to the episcopate as Gilbert Burnet and
John Tillotson.[21]

The celebration of Utrecht is demonstrably of later vintage,
as well no doubt as much of the patently Tory line, both of
which are already a matter of record. But Pope was under no
necessity of awaiting the Peace or the Tory fellowship to strike
out at William and tyranny. He was born and bred to that.

iii

In 1704/5 Pope set himself to school in a different academy,
that of Chaucer, translating or modernizing the *Merchant's
Tale* and the Prologue to *The Wife of Bath's Tale*.[22] The former
afforded Pope his first opportunity to exercise his wit in what
he later came to excel in, the satiric appraisal of sexual vanity,

hypocrisy, and folly. The results are emphatic and prophetic. January would "try that Christian Comfort, call'd a Wife." His counsellors pontificate upon the subject, "Each wondrous positive, and wondrous wise." The wedding party proceeds to church, "At once with carnal and devout Intent." Later, after a dubious bridal plunder, "Honest and dull, in Nuptial Bed they lay, / 'Till the Bell toll'd, and All arose to Pray." And so they end at last, "A fruitful Wife, and a believing Spouse."[23] Such vein and manner are those occasionally of *The Rape of the Lock* and frequently of the *Ethic Epistles.*

In the spirit of the former, at its bawdy level, is the pun in Justin's Scriptural consolation, as Pope embellishes it:

> Then be not, Sir, abandon'd to Despair;
> Seek, and perhaps you'll find, among the Fair,
> One, that may do your Business to a Hair.
>   (vv. 283–85)

More in the spirit of the *Ethic Epistles* is the surprisingly fine line which Pope introduces into Chaucer's brief parade of candidates for January's favor:

> Still one by one, in swift Succession, pass
> The gliding Shadows o'er the polish'd Glass.
> This Lady's Charms the Nicest cou'd not blame,
> But vile Suspicions had aspers'd her Fame;
> That one with Sense, but not with Virtue blest;
> And one had Grace, that wanted all the rest.
>   (vv. 236–41)

Scarcely anything in the passage would be unworthy the company of the portraits in *To a Lady,* but the last line is beyond dispute. In it Pope has already struck that pathetic chord which seems to sound only when his satire touches women. The effect is remarkable in one so young.

The Merchant's Tale also lent itself to exercise in the treatment of courtly folly, and there Pope's satire becomes more businesslike. The adaptation of Placebo's assent to January's marital plans is a good illustration of Pope's satiric downrightness at this stage. The passages can be found adjacent in the Twickenham edition, where it may be conveniently observed how Pope drives his speaker to the brevity and point of satiric priority over the ironical and self-characterizing behavior of Chaucer's speaker.

Chaucer's Placebo speaks with the leisure of dramatic personality and, though not without irony, more in the spirit of a man of the world than of a satirist. Pope's Placebo is satirist through and through, and when he turns the reproof on January it is not, as in Chaucer, masked and louting, but, like the brazen irony of the *Epistle to Augustus*, forthright and merciless.

Brother mine, says Chaucer's man, "Of me taak this motyf, / I have now been a court-man al my lyf." "Sir," says Pope's, "I have liv'd a Courtier all my Days, / And study'd Men, their Manners, and their Ways."[24] Chaucer's consultant lingers over his experience:

> And God it woot, though I unworthy be,
> I have stonden in ful greet degree
> Abouten lordes of ful heigh estaat.

Pope hurries to the point:

> And have observ'd this useful Maxim still,
> To let my Betters always have their Will.
> Nay, if my Lord affirm'd that Black was White,
> My Word was this; *Your Honour's in the right.*
> (vv. 158–61)

The Chaucerian Placebo is Socratically ingratiating and devious. We learn as much about him as we do about courtiers in the gross and tend, perhaps more even than Chaucer could wish, to become absorbed in his personality rather than his profession. Pope has no such interest in personality and does not risk its interference in the satiric mission. Compare his treatment of what follows in Chaucer:

> A ful greet fool is any counseillour
> That serveth any lord of heigh honour,
> That dar presume, or elles thenken it,
> That his counseil shoude passe his lordes wit.
> Nay, lordes been no fooles, by my fay!

This is the satire of Chaucerian archness, ironically self-depre-
cating while it passes judgment on another. Pope learned something from it, though curiously enough not in this place.
Impatient of hide-and-seek, he goes for the dispatch of sarcasm:

> Th'assuming Wit, who deems himself so wise
> As his mistaken Patron to advise,
> Let him not dare to vent his dang'rous Thought;
> A Noble Fool was never in a Fault.
>
> (vv. 162–65)

When Chaucer's Placebo turns at last to January's case, he
does so in apparent dissociation from what he has said before.
He declares January's argument one of "heigh sentence" and
confesses himself quite persuaded by it. The supposition is that
January will not see through the equivocation. Pope sacrifices
the dramatic irony of this toying by giving his speaker language too obvious to sustain poetic faith in January's obtuse-
ness:

> This Sir affects not you, whose ev'ry Word
> Is weigh'd with Judgment, and befits a Lord.
>
> (vv. 166–67)

Where Pope settles for irony at all, it is, as this illustrates, much
more declarative than Chaucer's. We see this difference again
in the conclusion of Placebo's speech. Having pronounced it an
act of "heigh corage" in January to take on a young bride at
his age, Chaucer's speaker contents himself with predicting a
"joly pyn" and bidding his brother do as he wish, with his
blessing. Pope maintains the more overt stance. Let, says his
Placebo,

> . . . grey Fools be Indolently good;
> Who past all Pleasure, damn the Joys of Sense,
> With rev'rend Dulness, and grave Impotence.
>
> (vv. 173–75)

If this is ironical at all, it is but barely so. Only an idiot could
fail to catch the insult. But that is precisely the point where
Pope is concerned. He saw January in just such terms, not as a

character worthy of manipulation by a clever ironist. For his purposes therefore the head-on approach is appropriate, however untrue to Chaucer, or unequal. Still, Chaucer has enabled him to begin taking the measure of the courtly fool: ignorant, vain, arrogant, and besotted.

With Justin's advice, in the passage following, the satiric occasion is again brought round to the sex, where Pope is more proficient. This is especially apparent in his brisk transformation of Justin's catalogue of marital risks—whether a prospective bride is apt to prove

> wys, or sobre, or dronkelewe,
> Or proud, or elles ootherweys a shrewe,
> A chidestere, or wastour of thy good,
> Or riche, or poore, or elles mannyssh wood.

Still ignoring dramatic propriety, though now perhaps less blamably, Pope converts Justin's almost pedantic catalog into a witty parade of saints and sinners:

> Whether she's chast or rampant, proud or civil;
> Meek as a Saint, or haughty as the Devil;
> Whether an easie, fond, familiar *Fool*,
> Or such a *Wit* as no Man e'er can rule?
>
> (vv. 186–89)

However he missed or ignored the Chaucerian design and flavor, Pope found much in *The Merchant's Tale* to whet the satiric appetite and educate it in ways and topics congenial to his own palate. The Prologue to the *Wife of Bath's Tale*, on the other hand, while it undoubtedly afforded him something, seems not to have lent itself so readily to his talents. The Wife is rather too complex for Pope's tastes, too ambivalent for his sensibilities, too much an enigma for the satiric disposition. Pope will later engage, and with stunning results, characters of contradictory makeup and appeal—

> 'Twas thus Calypso once each heart alarm'd,
> Aw'd without Virtue, without Beauty charm'd;
>
> · · · · · · ·

> . . . ne'er so sure our passion to create,
> As when she touch'd the brink of all we hate.
> *(Epistle to a Lady,* vv. 45–46, 51–52)

—but he does so as a superb satiric observer, not as a dramatist, and therein lies his problem with the Wife of Bath. It is the same problem we have remarked in his treatment of *The Merchant's Tale,* only more overpowering, and without the benefit of themes and situations more readily adaptable and compensatory.

In the one passage where Pope did have such an opportunity as he met so wittily in *January and May,* he fails here, with one exception, to rise to the occasion:

> If poor (you say) she drains her Husband's Purse;
> If rich, she keeps her Priest, or something worse;
> If highly born, intolerably vain;
> Vapours and Pride by turns possess her Brain:
> Now gayly Mad, now sow'rly Splenatick,
> Freakish when well, and fretful when she's Sick.
> If fair, then Chast she cannot long abide,
> By pressing Youth attack'd on ev'ry side.
> If foul, her Wealth the lusty Lover lures,
> Or else her Wit some Fool-Gallant procures,
> Or else she Dances with becoming Grace,
> Or Shape excuses the Defects of Face.
> There swims no Goose so gray, but, soon or late,
> She finds some honest Gander for her Mate.
> (vv. 86–99)

This is not Chaucer's Wife, but neither is it Pope. It is some isthmus of a middling state, out of which the translator seems all but powerless to move. Only in the final couplet does he take command and, on the strength of that perhaps, musters two more couplets of Popeian show:

> Horses (thou say'st) and Asses, Men may try,
> And ring suspected Vessels ere they buy,
> But Wives, a random Choice, untry'd they take;
> They dream in Courtship, but in Wedlock wake.
> (vv. 100–3)

Only occasionally in the Prologue does Pope thus wrestle Chaucer to a draw.

Though the effort was not a total loss, Pope, like the Pardoner, must have felt uneasy in the presence of so formidable a creature as the Wife, and one cannot but wonder why he chose to "sippe / Of thilke tonne." Perhaps he saw it as an opportunity to practice, under the license of Chaucer, the bawdy his age found so palatable. Probably it never occurred to him, nor to the age, to seek for more. With *January and May* it was different; there was a bawdy he could convert into high wit and a court satire he could warm to. The benefits may have begun to accrue as early as the *Epistle to Miss Blount, with the Works of Voiture.*

Written according to Pope in 1705, the epistle anticipates *The Rape of the Lock* in theme and *To a Lady* in portraiture. Following a tribute to Voiture which is at once an announcement of theme ("wisely careless, innocently gay") Pope analyzes the Sex in its various modes of slavery, bidding his lady settle for nothing short of freedom and content, unlike Pamela, who settled for, and got, something less:

> The Gods, to curse *Pamela* with her Pray'rs,
> Gave the gilt Coach and dappled *Flanders* Mares,
> The shining Robes, rich Jewels, Beds of State,
> And to compleat her Bliss, a Fool for Mate.
> She glares in *Balls, Front-boxes,* and the *Ring,*
> A vain, unquiet, glitt'ring, wretched Thing!
> Pride, Pomp, and State but reach her outward Part,
> She sighs, and is no *Dutchess* at her Heart.

If, in view of this sad spectacle, the Fates still destine the poet's lady for marriage, let her not rely upon frail beauty, but repose her hopes in the only durable charm, good humor. The poem is a shapely miniature of more ambitious things to come. In it Pope has already mastered the structural nicety, the tonal modulation and sureness of verse, the blend of wit and grace, the art of didactic resonance, satiric portraiture, and the gift of conferring enduring value through understanding that mark him at his maturest and best.

A second epistle, *To Henry Cromwell, Esq.*, is an exercise in a different key, with different satiric aims.[25] It is in the short meter and burlesque rhyme familiar in Swift, with something too of the drollery of his household lampoon. But unless we date it later than 1707, it can hardly be regarded as owing anything to that hand, since Swift had not as yet published anything of the sort. How Pope came by the idiom, especially so well, is not easy to imagine. There is nothing like it in his previous work and very little like it in his later. Perhaps he imbibed it in the coffeehouse ambiance, but whatever its derivation, it reveals a poet more than competent in octosyllables, adept at macaronic and broken rhyme, and altogether at home in the easy style of familiar address:

> And pardon me a little Fooling,
> —Just while your Coffee stands a Cooling.

> Just as a Still, with Simples in it,
> Betwixt each Drop stays half a Minute.[26]

> I hope, you think me none of those
> Who shew their Parts as *Pentlow* does.

> To end with News—the best I know,
> Is, I've been well a Week, or so.
> The Season of green Pease is fled,
> And Artichoaks reign in their Stead.
> Th'Allies to bomb *Toulon* prepare;
> G—d save the pretty Lady's there!
> One of our Dogs is dead and gone,
> And I, unhappy! left alone.

The satire moves effortlessly between badinage and amiable lampoon, witty aside and domestic *causerie*. It shows Pope already free with omber, snuff, and playgoing; with the political press, poetasters, sexual deviance, Whig Jacobitical malaise, the war and Marlborough, the Union, the "Nymphs of Drury," and the amours of the poets and wits; with Cervantes, Rabelais, and Aristophanes; and with his own health, his garden, and his dogs—all in a spirit of shared detachment and reflecting a widening range of satiric reconnaissance.

The *Letter to Cromwell*, 1708, while not so striking, repre-

sents a further experimentation in the same idiom. Consisting
of two parts separated by the "plain prose" of the containing
correspondence, it is not so much a poem as two sallies of verse,
in the later Scriblerian manner. In them, especially the first,
Pope experiments richly in metrical variation and rhyme pattern. The mood is lively and chummy:

> The Business of it is t'express,
> From me and from my Holiness,
> To you and to your Gentleness,
> How much I wish you Health and Happiness;
> And much good News, and little Spleen as may be;
> A hearty Stomach, and sound Lady;
> And ev'ry Day a double Dose of Coffee,
> To make you look as sage as any Sophy.

This is followed by some bawdy in defense of the earlier epistle's reference to "Nymphs of *Drury*, not of *Drury*-Lane,"
rounded off with a quaint adieu:

> To *Baker* first my Service, pray;
> To *Tydcomb* eke,
> And Mr. *Cheek;*
> Last to *yourself* my best Respects I pay,
> And so remain, for ever and for ay.[27]

This is impromptu verse of no mean order, and, like its predecessor, reflects Pope's aptitude for every call of poetry.

iv

Pope's earliest poetical acquaintance of stature, and his earliest sponsor of literary repute, was the then aging Wycherley,
whom Pope apparently met in 1704 and with whom he immediately struck up a correspondence on the subject of wit
and poetry and Pope. It was through Wycherley apparently
that Pope met Walsh and perhaps Cromwell and others of the
society at Will's, from all of whom he learned much about the
ways of the world and the life of letters. Writing to Wycherley
26 October 1705 Pope reports that he has just returned from

the company at Will's to that of the Forest, and, in a manner doubtless acquired in the coffeehouse, delivers himself of a comparison of the wits of the country with the fools of the town. Posed as all this must have been, it doubtless reflects some very real impressions breeding on the subject of "the gentle Reign of Dulness."[28] Wycherley responds to the invitation to visit the country by inviting Pope to visit *his* forest in town, "where the Beasts that inhabit, tame or wild, of long Ears or Horns, pursue one another either out of Love or Hatred," all of which he embellishes with the usual satirical wit, concluding that Pope must "leave your Forest of Beasts, for ours of Brutes, call'd Men, who now in full Cry, (pack'd by the Court or Country) run down in the House of Commons, a deserted horned Beast of the Court, to the satisfaction of their Spectators."[29] By February-March of the following year Wycherley, who had already engaged Pope to correct his *Epistle to Mr. Dryden*, proposes now to convey his entire stock of verses into Pope's hands for brushing up. From this point on Pope struggles with Wycherley's muse and vanity, along with his own zeal and circumspection, until, by 1710, the burden proves too much and they fall out, to make up later but imperfectly.

In the meanwhile the epistolary record is interesting. In November of 1707 Pope writes two letters describing the extensive modifications and additions he has made to Wycherley's *Panegyrick on Dulness* along with his plans for proceeding upon "the Poems of *Solitude,* on the *publick,* and on the *mixt Life; the Bill of Fare; the Praises of Avarice,* and some others."[30] Early in 1707/8 Wycherley expresses pleasure in being memorialized in the *Pastorals* and announces his intention of honoring his young friend with commendatory verses. In May of the following year he writes of "a whimsical new Newspaper, from and to the Coffee houses, called the Tatler."[31] Later in the same month he resumes a theme by now no doubt familiar between them, namely "the Coffee-house Wits, or rather Anti-wits, the Criticks."[32] From such as this, one can surmise Wycherley's contributions, both witting and unwitting, to Pope's satiric nurture. If, in this period between 1705 and 1710, Walsh taught Pope the need and art of correctness, and Cromwell the world (if not the flesh) of mistresses, Wycherley, for all the superannuation of his muse—perhaps on account of it—taught him much about dullness, the critics, and the resources of the satiric profession.

Here and there in his correspondence and notes Pope identifies some of his additions to Wycherley's poems, now brought together by Norman Ault in the Twickenham edition of the *Minor Poems*. The earliest of these are some lines on dullness, appended to Wycherley's poem on that theme. As Pope explained in a letter already noted, they constitute a "Climax" to Wycherley's *Panegyrick*, summing up "all the *praise, advantage,* and *happiness* of Dulness in a few words, and [strengthening] them by all the opposition of the *disgrace, disadvantage,* and *unhappiness* of Wit, with which it concludes." Whatever seeds Wycherley had planted either did not or could not flourish in this ground; the lines are few and undistinguished.

The similitude added to *The Various Mix'd Life* says nothing to our inquiry, but the additions to *On Solitude and Retirement* and *The Bill of Fare* merit notice. The first represent a descant on the theme of Pope's own *Ode* on that subject. A few lines will show how the theme continues to affiliate itself with satire:

> Alone, remov'd from Grandeur and from Strife,
> And ev'ry Curse that loads a publick Life,
> In Safety, Innocence, and full Repose,
> Man the true Worth of his Creation knows.
>
> . . . .
>
> To him, with humble Privacy content,
> Life is, in Courts, and gawdy Pride, mis-spent.
> To him, the Rural Cottage does afford
> What he prefers to the *Patrician* Board.
>
> (vv.16–25)

The additions to *The Bill of Fare* capture the spirit of the times and foreshadow times and tidings to come. The scene is the *cena* of Menippean derivation. Toward the end the celebrants fall to talking of this and that:

74

Some, over each Orac'lous Glass, fore-doom
The Fate of Realms, and Conquests yet to come;
What Lawrels *Marlbro'* next shall reap, decree,
And swifter than *His* Arms, give *Victory*.[33]

Well in their cups, the tipplers fall next upon literary reputa-
tions, comparing Defoe to Dryden, Ozell to Butler, and Rowe
to Wycherley. At last they turn upon the host himself and
drink him quite under the table, whereupon the poet leaves
them with this admonition:

Soft be his Slumbers! But may this suffice
Our Friends the Wits and Poets to advise,
(Tho' Dinners oft they want and Suppers too)
Rather to starve, as they are us'd to do,
Than dine with Fools, that on their Guests will force
Mixt Wine, mixt Company, and mixt Discourse:
Since not much Wine, much Company, much Food,
Make Entertainments please us as they shou'd;
But 'tis of each, the *Little*, and the *Good*.[34]

Toward the end of 1708 Pope took up the epigram in defense
of his mentor, who had been dealt with rather irreverently in
John Ozell's translation of *Le Lutrin*, published in June of that
year. The spirit is again that of *The Dunciad:*

OZELL, at *Sanger's* Call, invok'd his Muse,
For who to sing for *Sanger* could refuse?
His Numbers such, as *Sanger's* self might use.
Reviving *Perault*, murd'ring *Boileau*, he
Slander'd the Ancients first, then *Wycherley;*
Not that it much that Author's Anger rais'd,
For those were slander'd most whom *Ozell* prais'd:
Nor had the toothless Satyr caus'd complaining,
Had not sage *Rowe* pronounc'd it *Entertaining*.
How great, how just, the Judgment of that Writer!
Who the *Plain-dealer* damns, and prints the *Biter*.[35]

For all the eventual awkwardness of their fellowship, Pope
was much beholden to Wycherley. Wycherley introduced him
to the town and the society of wits, lent him a valuable literary
patronage, made him acquainted with dullness in politics and
the press, and just possibly first inspired him to think of satire

as a profession. Wycherley was after all, despite his decline, still the foremost living satirist, a fact which Pope obviously took pride in and which must have helped confirm him in his own leanings. Pope was commemorating more than a friendship when later he declared of Wycherley, "*poeta morum scientia clarus, ille meos primus qui habebat amores.*"[36]

v

In 1707/8 Pope returned to the ancients, translating Ovid's *Sapho to Phaon*, Homer's *Episode of Sarpedon* and *The Arrival of Ulysses in Ithaca*, and resuming his work on Statius. Except for the first, these, like his other translations, touch in one way or another the satiric motive. *The Episode of Sarpedon* (published 1709) looks ahead, not just to the Homer, but to *The Rape of the Lock* and perhaps Pope's growing sense of satiric mission as well.

In the "Postscript" to the *Odyssey*, Pope is at pains to distinguish that poem as "a moral and political work, instructive to all degrees of men, and filled with images, examples and precepts of civil and domestick life."[37] *The Arrival of Ulysses in Ithaca*, which with slight revision was later incorporated in the translation of the *Odyssey*, is indicative of this understanding from the beginning. In addition to love of country and dedication to its well-being, implicit in the homecoming, there is the theme of rural and agricultural virtue, something real and deep-seated in Pope's conscience and experience. Here it is put in the mouth of Pallas, who identifies the homeland Ulysses cannot yet recognize:

> The rugged Soil allows no level Space
> For flying Chariots, or the rapid Race;
> Yet not ungrateful to the Peasant's Pain,
> Suffices Fulness to the swelling Grain;
> The loaded Trees their various Fruits produce,
> The clustring Grapes afford a gen'rous Juice;
> Woods crown our Mountains, and in ev'ry Grove
> The bounding Goats and frisking Heyfers rove;
> Soft Rains and kindly Dews refresh the Field,
> And rising Springs Eternal Verdure yield.   (vv. 122–31)

This is as much Windsor as Ithaca, and will reappear in the *Burlington* and *Bethel* of later vintage. This much of Pallas's speech Pope takes to heart, but not her counsel regarding "Domestick Woes," the "Pride of Fools," and "Slaves insulting Scorn":

> But thou be Silent, nor reveal thy State,
> Yield to the Force of unresisted Fate,
> And bear unmov'd the Wrongs of base Mankind,
> The last and hardest Conquest of the Mind.
>
> (vv. 182–87)

Though he will not be silent in the face of such wrong, he will, as we see when we consult his Statius, be circumspect.

vi

We have already noted how Pope's satire is no respecter of genre. That the same is true of his politics is nowhere perhaps more evident than in his admission of it into the *Ode for Music*, written according to Pope in 1708, but apparently reworked before publication in 1713. Though neither the theme nor the Drydenian precedent warrants, Pope cannot forbear a glance at English history and politics:

> Intestine War no more our *Passions* wage,
> Ev'n giddy *Factions* hear away their Rage.
>
> (vv. 34–35)

In 1730, when the *Ode* was published in a Cambridge memorial volume, there appeared, directly following this couplet, a stanza unprinted before or after in Pope's lifetime:

> *Amphion* thus bad wild Dissention cease,
> And soften'd Mortals learn'd the Arts of Peace.
> *Amphion* taught contending Kings,
> From various Discords to create
> The Musick of a well-tun'd State,
> Nor slack nor strain the tender Strings;
> Those useful Touches to impart
> That strike the Subjects answ'ring Heart;
> And the soft, silent Harmony, that springs
> From Sacred Union and consent of Things.[38]

Though the "Musick of a well-tun'd State" might suggest a dating closer to the third epistle of *An Essay on Man*, the idea is present in Dryden's *Song for St. Cecilia's Day* (1687), and Pope's "contending Kings" suggests a date closer to the Statius, perhaps the very 1708 that Pope claimed for the composition of the ode. If so, the stanza might have been withheld from the 1713 edition because of its proximity to the Statius, published only the year before. By 1730 "contending Kings," which smacks more of England than of Amphion, would scarcely have been a topic of urgency for Pope, though he might have been willing by then to retrieve a once lively allusion for the embellishment of the Cambridge performance and publication of his ode.

Among Pope's early imitations of English poets, declared in 1736 to have been "Done by the Author in his Youth," some "at fourteen or fifteen Years old," are a group of six that can safely be dated no more precisely than Ault's "before 1709." They include the ribald takeoff on Chaucer (the "Schole-boy's Tale of fayre Irelond"), the burlesque of Spenser called *The Alley*, the sprightly imitation of Waller titled *On a Fan*, the sober imitation of Cowley called *The Garden*, and two portraits of the Sex—*Artimesia* and *Phryne,* in the manner of Dorset. The Chaucer is a piece of barefaced bawdy, clever enough but little more. *The Alley* is an interesting, though not especially impressive, specimen of the vogue of Spenserian travesty and, depending upon the accuracy of the dating or the degree of revision, an interesting anticipation or reflection of Swift's *Description of the Morning* and *Description of a City Shower*.[39]

By far the most impressive satirically are the imitations of Dorset, looking, as they do, backward to that licentious muse and forward to the portraiture of *To a Lady* and other pieces. It is not easy, however, to speak of the *Artimesia* as the product of ante 1709. It, along with *Phryne*, was not published until 1727 and then with no suggestion of Dorset or of imitation, these designations being first applied in 1736. The problem is compounded by the claim and apparency of allusion to Queen

Caroline in the *Artimesia*.[40] If Artimesia is Caroline, the poem cannot date from before 1709 unless between then and publication it was reshaped to fit the Queen. One would like to think that its subject, with her *"Malebranche, Boyle,* and *Locke"* and her need of *"cleaner Smock,"* was an early exercise in the Rufa and Sappho of *To a Lady,* but she may have been no more than a half-dozen years the senior of those. But there is that *huge* and *haughty* "High-Dutch Bride," *dauntless, proud,* and "theatrically loud," who simply has to be Caroline of Anspach, however overdrawn.

Phryne is more in the sexual vein of the Restoration wits, though more restrained than that usually encountered in the earlier school.

> PHRYNE had Talents for Mankind,
> Open she was, and unconfin'd,
> Like some free Port of Trade.

Having trafficked in all nationalities, religions, and climes, Phryne at last paces forth a bride, "the first of batter'd Jades," at which point Pope invokes an insect image which suggests the possibility of Hanoverian adaptation:

> So have I known those Insects fair,
> (Which curious *Germans* hold so rare,)
> Still vary Shapes and Dyes;
> Still gain new Titles with new Forms;
> First Grubs obscene, then wriggling Worms,
> Then painted Butterflies.[41]

A not unrelated vein is to be found in Pope's version of Voiture's *Où vous savez,* included in a letter to Cromwell in 1710, an instance it would seem of Pope's early readiness to turn his own physical deficiencies to advantage:

> You know where you did despise
> (T'other day) my little eyes,
> Little legs, and little thighs,
> And some things of little size,
>   You know where.

> You, 'tis true, have fine black eyes,
> Taper legs, and tempting thighs,
> Yet what more than all we prize
> Is a thing of little size,
>   You know where.[42]

Except for the Statius and *An Essay on Criticism*, which require separate treatment, this chapter in Pope's politics and satire concludes with another series of translations. Though not canonically beyond question, they are I think rightly attributed to Pope by Norman Ault and dated by him "not later than 1710."[43] From these we gather evidence not so much of politics and satire as of the philosophical mind behind the political satirist.

Little is to be made of the first, *On the Statue of Cleopatra*, which is in the tradition of the Ovidian *heroides*. Nor, except for its "bright *Militia* of the sky," should we attach more than straightforward significance to the rendition of Psalm 91 (*Qui habitat*), with its declaration of faith in the protection of God against enemies and evil.

Stanzas From the french of Malherbe is a version of Malherbe's *Paraphrase du Psaume Cent Quarante-Cinquième*, which, in Pope's hand, describes the "treach'rous world" and its vanity, especially in high place:

> In vain, for all that empty greatness brings,
> We lose our lives amidst the courts of kings,
> And suffer scorn, and bend the supple knee;
> The monarch dies—one moment's turn destroys
> Long future prospects, and short present joys:
> Oh unperforming, false mortality!

"Th'impartial worms" feed on kings and lesser mortals alike:

> The lofty styles of happy, glorious great,
> The Lords of fortune, Arbiters of fate,
> And Gods of war, lye lost within the grave!
> Their mighty minions then come tumbling down,
> They lose their flatt'rers as they lose their crown,
> Forgot of ev'ry friend, and ev'ry slave!

Pope's hand is to be seen in the rendition of "arbitres de la paix" as "Arbiters of fate," of "serviteurs" as "slave," in his introduction of "minions," and in the satirico-pathetic quality of the last two lines, which in Malherbe read simply:

> Tous ceux que leur fortune
> Faisait leurs serviteurs.

The last of this group of translations, *From Boetius, de cons. Philos.*, celebrates, with its source, the governance of Reason in Creator and creation, and anticipates in some of its language passages of *An Essay on Man*.[44]

From the distance of the thirties Pope himself may not have recalled how little in fact he ever wandered in "Fancy's Maze," or how early he "stoop'd to Truth, and moraliz'd his Song."[45] If in terms of the earlier period *moraliz'd* seems not quite the word, we may say instead *satiriz'd* or *politiciz'd*, either of which amounts to much the same thing. Certainly we cannot take him literally when he says, in the conclusion of *An Essay on Man*, that it was the Bolingbroke of the twenties and thirties who turned his poetry from "sounds to things, from fancy to the heart."[46] Pope had lisped in satire and politics, as we shall see further in the chapter to follow.

V

THE CHANGE OF SCEPTERS
AND IMPENDING WOE

·

POPE DID NOT have to await Horace and the thirties to hit upon the idea of adapting translation to the uses of political satire. He was, we may suppose, groping for something of the sort as early as the *Ode on Solitude* and the *Pastorals*. He was certainly into "imitation" of a satiric, if not political, import by 1709, the date of his version of *The Merchant's Tale*. When he turned to translation as such, on a substantial scale, he perceived soon enough its usefulness as a satiric vehicle and screen, and he never thereafter failed to take advantage of the discovery. It seems likely, in fact, that his choice of works to translate was everywhere, in one degree or another, at one point or another, influenced by his perception of their adaptability to English political application.

His first venture of this kind was the translation of *The First Book of Statius his Thebais*, published in 1712, but begun according to Pope in 1703 and apparently completed by 1709. The allusion is the governing one of the whole period: the once and future kings—William (and the Stuarts before) on the one hand, Hanover on the other.

In January of 1708 Pope wrote to Cromwell enclosing a copy of his translation for comment. He explains that the version is not complete, wanting vv. 128–43, 168–310, and 408–81 of the original.[1] In May of the year following he wrote again, of his resumption of the work, declaring, "I had I know not what extraordinary Flux of Rhyme upon me for three days together, in which time all the Verses you see added, have been written."[2] It is reasonable to assume that the verses added were those said earlier to have been wanting and that Pope had by then essentially finished the Book. The additions represent a crucial alteration in the character of the undertaking—an attempt to bend it to the present state of affairs in England.

Although Pope's resort to Cromwell was undoubtedly prompted in no small part by literary concerns, there is reason to believe that it was intended to sound other questions as well. In 1735 he told Spence that his "letters to Cromwell were written with a design that does not generally appear. They were not written in sober sadness."[3] Some have taken this remark as hinting a "cryptic significance,"[4] though Sherburn discounts such a view. "If," he says, "there was any hidden design in these letters . . . it would seem to have been that of practising his learning so as to see if it could pass muster."[5] Of the letters as a whole Sherburn may be right, but of those relating to the Statius he may have missed the mark. There is reason to believe that by the time of his first letter to Cromwell, Pope had already recognized the possibilities of adapting Statius to English politics. If that is so, his appeals for advice and consent may have been intended not simply to elicit critical comment but to draw Cromwell out on the subject of political allusion. Even if it had not yet occurred to him to tamper with Statius, it must have occurred to him that the Theban story was ticklishly close to the history and politics of his own time and place. That alone would have been grounds for apprehension, but Pope had added cause to be concerned, for he was pressing the likeness. That he could plead translation was still an untested hypothesis, and he would want to try it out before venturing into print. To come right out and ask would be both risky and self-defeating; he needed to know to what extent the allusion would announce itself and at the same time recede convincingly into its background if challenged. That there is no record of Cromwell's response to the probe need signify no more than that the trial was a failure or that the record is incomplete.

In view of the story we can appreciate Pope's concern. Its

subject is civil war, contending royal claimants, and an expedition by a foreign state in behalf of one of these. As Statius handles it, it is a highly charged account of a people visited by discord, treachery, violence, and ruin. Usurpation, tyranny, banishment, and lowering fate round out the parallel. Out of this welter of analogy Pope was at pains to shape a careful but unmistakable commentary on England past, present, and future: its civil war, revolution, and struggle between pretender and incumbent; its suspension between Williamite disappointment and Hanoverian omen; its blows to constitutional kingship; its party strife; and its fickle and venal people.[6]

The translation commences innocently enough, making Statius speak the spirited English of a youthful probationer to fame. But it is not long before Pope begins to press the allusion, rendering *geminis sceptrum exitiale tyrannis* "A fatal Throne to two contending Kings" and adding to the troubled sleep of Eteocles and Polynices such non-Statian passions as "sacred Thirst of Sway," "impotent Desire to Reign alone," and scorn of "the dull Reversion of a Throne."[7] These are from the lines we know Pope to have added sometime in 1709. Taken with the others, a little farther on, it is apparent that, for whatever reason—whether of sudden inspiration or resolve to venture at last what had been in the back of his mind all along—Pope had by now decided to force the analogy and try his hand at satire under the cover of translation. The full disclosure of this intent comes in vv. 224–72, which, despite their length, must be quoted if we are to follow the argument:

> But the vile Vulgar, ever discontent,
> Their growing Fears in secret Murmurs vent,   225
> Still prone to change, tho' still the Slaves of State,
> And sure the Monarch whom they have, to hate;
> New Lords they madly make, then tamely bear,
> And softly curse the Tyrants whom they fear.
> And one of those who groan beneath the Sway   230
> Of Kings impos'd, and grudgingly obey,
> (Whom Envy to the Great, and vulgar Spight
> With Scandal arm'd, th'Ignoble Mind's Delight,)
> Exclaim'd—O *Thebes!* for thee what Fates remain,

84

What Woes attend this inauspicious Reign?   235
Must we, alas! our doubtful Necks prepare,
Each haughty Master's Yoke by turns to bear,
And still to change whom chang'd we still must fear?
These now controul a wretched People's Fate,
These can divide, and these reverse the State;   240
Ev'n Fortune rules no more:—Oh servile Land,
Where exil'd Tyrants still by turns command!
Thou Sire of Gods and Men, Imperial *Jove!*
Is this th'Eternal Doom decreed above?
On thy own Offspring hast thou fix'd this Fate,   245
From the first Birth of our unhappy State;
When banish'd *Cadmus* wandring o'er the Main,
For lost *Europa* search'd the World in vain,
And fated in *Bœotian* Fields to found
A rising Empire on a foreign Ground,   250
First rais'd our Walls on that ill-omen'd Plain
Where Earth-born Brothers were by Brothers slain?
What lofty Looks th'unrival'd Monarch bears!
How all the Tyrant in his Face appears!
What sullen Fury clowds his scornful Brow!   255
Gods! how his Eyes with threatning Ardour glow!
Can this Imperious Lord forget to Reign,
Quit all his State, descend, and serve again?
Yet who, before, more popularly bow'd,
Who more propitious to the suppliant Crowd,   260
Patient of Right, familiar in the Throne?
What Wonder then? he was not then Alone.
Oh wretched we, a vile submissive Train,
Fortune's tame Fools, and Slaves in ev'ry Reign!
     As when two Winds . . .   265
         · · · · · · ·

Thus on each side, alas! our tott'ring State
Feels all the Fury of resistless Fate,   270
And doubtful still, and still distracted stands,
While that Prince Threatens, and while this Commands.

A comparison of these lines with their counterparts in Statius and Thomas Stephens, the translator whom Pope read as a boy and apparently consulted in shaping his own version, will leave little room to doubt that Pope was aiming for more than poetry in his translation.[8]

The drift is evident at once, with the bending of Statius in the direction of Drydenian and Restoration contempt for the mob. What Pope calls the "vile Vulgar, ever discontent," Statius called only *"plebis Echioniae"* (Echionian people), *"qui mos populis"* (as a crowd will). Stephens, the intermediate translator, says simply "the commons . . . as they use." Although Statius (and Stephens after him) acknowledges a measure of depravity in the people, neither makes much of it, tending rather to sympathize than to reproach. Pope is drawn, on the other hand, not to see them as victims so much as pawns to their own capriciousness, like Dryden's "giddy *Jews*," who "once in twenty Years, their Scribes Record, / By natural Instinct . . . change their Lord."[9] These, not Statius, are the source of Pope's *vulgar:*

> Still prone to change, tho' still the Slaves of State,
> And sure the Monarch whom they have to hate;
> New Lords they madly make, then tamely bear,
> And softly curse the Tyrants whom they fear.[10]

But Pope has extended Dryden too, making his *hoi polloi* the committee of invitation and the Revolution Convention which brought William over and installed him as monarch.[11] As for William himself, he is greeted both here and in the lines hard following. Of the spokesman who gives voice to these sentiments (vv. 234 ff.), Statius says only, "And one of them, whose mind it was mainly to insult by mean and hurtful speech and never to bow the neck to the yoke of rulers, said." Stephens renders it, "And one amongst the rest (whose mind was set / To blast the Scepter, and could never yet / With patience bear commands) cries out." Though Pope will conclude his characterization on this note of "vulgar Spight," he introduces it on grounds more relevant, the Williamite experience (italics mine):

> And one of those who groan beneath the Sway
> Of *Kings impos'd,* and grudgingly obey.

He plays off too in "O *Thebes!* for thee what Fates remain, / What Woes attend this inauspicious Reign?" Statius had spoken only of the lot of *Ogygia,* Stephens of the vexation of "th'*Ogygian* State." Pope has in effect already looked ahead to the extension of the Williamite shadow:

> Must we, alas! our doubtful necks prepare,
> Each haughty Master's Yoke by turns to bear,
> And still to change whom chang'd we still must fear?

The glance would have been Hanoverian with no more than the Statius of the lines, but the intrusion of "Each haughty Master's yoke" renders it unmistakable. What follows is a plague o' both the houses:

> These now controul a wretched People's Fate,
> These can divide, and these reverse the State;
> Ev'n Fortune rules no more:—Oh servile Land,
> Where exil'd Tyrants still by turns command!

That the plague is Pope's, and English, is apparent in the drift from Statius, where the speaker says, "From hand to hand they toss the destinies of peoples [*partiti versant populorum fata manuque*] and make fortune fickle [*fortunam fecere levem*]." "Th'ave," he says in Stephens, "made division of our lives, th'ave weaken'd / The hand of Fortune." Pope has added *control, wretchedness,* the *state* and *servility;* he has incorporated Stephens's *division* (wherein I think he looks back to William) and read *reversal* (and with it, I suspect, Hanoverian turnabout of the Stuart restoration under Anne) into *versant,* which signifies in Statius no more than sequential change of hands. All this is too much and too pointed to be put down to translational enthusiasm. Pope has made Statius a witness for the prosecution.

Statius concludes the passage with a question: "Am I always to serve princes that take their turn of exile?" (*semperne vicissim / exsulibus servire dabor?*) "Shall I," says the speaker in Stephens, "still be reckon'd / A bond-slave rul'd by banish'd spirits?" Pope's version is not a question, but an exclamation, and looks before as well as after. Between the two is not the Thebes of Statius, but the "unhappy State" of England.[12]

Though what follows could easily pass for simple transla-

tion, the force of allusion already set in motion excites the
expectation (not disappointed) of continued allegory. By it one
is encouraged to associate the Cadmus of these lines (245 ff.)
now with Charles, now with James, now with the current pretender, as the application fits or allows. Either exiled king—
Charles or James—would fit the opening lines. The "rising Empire of a Foreign Ground" will pass for a St. Germain, and the
brothers that were by brothers slain is palpable civil war at
home. At this stage Pope does not have to force the issue; he
can count on the analogies to do their own work. That they
do, and in ways I have suggested, is important to his argument,
providing the Stuart, even Jacobitical, premises necessary to
define his grounds of discontent and confirm his charges of
miscarriage and misfortune.[13]

In altering the portrait of Eteocles to fit William, Pope needed
no more than commonplace to hint the royal likeness—*tyrant,
sullen, threatning, imperious.* But when it came to picturing
the *prince,* the candidate for power, he turned to Dryden again.
Statius says of the earlier Eteocles, "Yet was he [before king-
ship] gentle to our prayers, affable of speech, and more patient
of the right."[14] Pope, no doubt reminded of Dryden and determined his readers should be as well, described him thus:

> Yet who, before, more popularly bow'd,
> Who more propitious to the suppliant Crowd,
> Patient of Right, familiar in the Throne?

The borrowing is more than merely verbal. It includes Dryden's
prince himself, and the paupers. "Fir'd with near possession of
a Crown," Absalom courts the people:

> Th'admiring Croud are dazled with surprize,
> And on his good person feed their eyes;
> His joy conceal'd, he sets himself to show;
> On each side *bowing popularly* low:
> His looks, his gestures, and his words he frames,
> And with familiar ease repeats their Names.
>   (vv. 686–91. Italics mine)

This conjured Dryden would serve to recall William's court-

ship of English favor in the months before the takeover, but
also his implication, along with Monmouth, in the Exclusion
movement. "Patient of Right, familiar in the Throne," on the
other hand, is both something and nothing of either Dryden
or Statius. The latter says nothing of familiarity in the throne,
but it would not require the aid of Dryden for a perceptive
reader to associate that and patience of the right with William's
relationship to and expectations of the English crown. Given
the Dryden already invoked, these strokes would tar William as well with the hypocrisy and filial ingratitude of Absalom.

Though something of both translational sources figures in
the outcry that follows, Pope still manages the impression of
immediacy:

> Oh wretched we, a vile submissive Train,
> Fortune's tame Fools, and Slaves in ev'ry Reign!

Stephens commiserates with the crowd: "But we're contrould
by all; Poor, abject men." Statius indicts them: "We are worth-
less in the gross, ready for any chance, open to any lord and
master."[15] Pope is not insensitive to the plight of the subject
(he has been a wretched one himself), but he deplores the sort
that conspires in its own undoing and then submits in apathy
to the consequences. "Slaves in ev'ry Reign," not explicit in
either Statius or Stephens, smacks again of once and future
kings "impos'd."

In concluding the passage, Pope leans rather to Stephens
than to Statius, following the former's emphasis now on the
state as against the *sors populis*. Statius reads, "Alas! for the
cruel, intolerable lot of the people, suspended between doubt
and fear, this prince commanding, the other threatening."[16]
Stephens puts it thus:

> ... such fate
> Hangs o're this doubtful, this distracted State.
> One Prince commands obedience, whilst t'other
> Threatens as much if they obey his brother.

Though in part a "very bad hand,"[17] this comes closer to what

Pope wanted to testify, and so he draws on it for his own farewell and prophecy:

> Thus on each side, alas! our tott'ring State
> Feels all the Fury of resistless Fate,
> And doubtful still, and still distracted stands,
> While that Prince Threatens, and while this Commands.

In one point Pope, of course, does not follow Stephens. He does
not invoke the term *brother*. By avoiding that he is able once
more, and finally, to link the prospect of things to come with
the remembrance of things past.

There is little else in *The First Book* that Pope could bend to
his purpose, but allusive echo continues to the very end: the
speech of Jove, with its reminiscences of David's speech in *Absalom and Achitophel;* Juno's complaint of "barb'rous Kings";
and most clearly that part of the closing prayer that speaks of
the "Change of Scepters, and impending Woe." In the Statius
Pope is doing more than "preparing to become the translator
of Homer."[18] He is preparing to become the imitator of Horace.
And his translation belongs as much to Hanoverian opposition
literature as to any other.

ii

Pope did not abandon the practice of covert satire with the
Statius, nor did he wait until the Horatian period to pick it up
again. He resumed it almost at once with his modernization of
the third book of Chaucer's *Hous of Fame*. Though published
in 1715—a dangerous year—the *Temple of Fame* was written,
according to later statements, "in the Year 1711," or even
earlier, "before the Author was 22 Years old."[19] Either date
would put its inception hard on the heels of Statius and suggest a carryover of the smuggling device hit upon there. Like
the earlier experiment, moreover, it would appear that *The
Temple of Fame* began innocently enough and only later, between 1712 and 1715, took on the political coloration evident
in its printed form.

Professor Tillotson, who edited the poem in the Twickenham edition, though not unaware of certain satiric and political contingencies, seems not to have found or felt them especially significant. He calls attention to Dilke's suggestion that some of Pope's illustrations are taken "from King William & the revolution party," but only in connection with Pope's departure from the Chaucerian parallel.[20] Observing that "Pope's choice of heroes . . . was necessarily determined by his age," he discounts as irrelevant Elwin's complaint that Pope includes "no English king, warrior, statesman, or patriot."[21] Finally, though he acknowledges that satire in Pope, as in Dryden, "will have Room, where e'er [they] write" and that *The Temple of Fame* combines the descriptive and the moral (including the satirical) modes,[22] Tillotson does not follow up on the implications of his own reconnaissance. But then neither, as far as I know, has anyone else. And that is curious, for the poem is deep in political play.

The opening of the poem has the look of original, unrevised composition, but what follows seems less certain. The account of heroes (vv. 151–77) is commonplace enough, but its want of counterpart in Chaucer makes it tempting to find it topical as well, shadowing forth persons and events in the war and peace of Anne, the rise and fall of ministries, and the Hanoverian scales of justice. While the portraits will pass the prima facie test, certain strokes hint of contemporary allusion. Thus Marlborough, though no youth, even in his finest hour afield, aspired, like Alexander, beyond himself, and "all things but himself subdu'd."[23] Oxford and Bolingbroke are, by the same token, discernible in the account of the soldiery of national interest (v. 159 ff.): "those who not for Empire fought, / But with their Toils their People's Safety bought." These, the shapers of Utrecht, are the soldiers of peace; not, like Marlborough, soldiers of fortune.

To the original catalog of heroes in the national defense—Epaminondas, Timoleon, Scipio—Pope added in 1717 one suited for the role of *amicus curiae*, Marcus Aurelius, whose reputation for political mercy, whose power joined with virtue, and

whose patronage of "Mankind" could have been calculated to
bespeak the clemency of Hanover. The case is all but openly
pleaded in the verses that follow:

> Much suff'ring Heroes next their Honours claim,
> Those of noisy, and guilty Fame,
> Fair Virtue's silent Train: Supreme of these
> Here ever shines the Godlike *Socrates*:
> He whom ungrateful *Athens* cou'd expel,
> At all times Just, but when he sign'd the Shell.
> Here his Abode the martyr'd *Phocion* claims,
> With *Agis*, not the last of *Spartan* Names:
> Unconquer'd *Cato* shews the Wound he tore,
> And *Brutus* his ill Genius meets no more.
>
> (vv. 168–77)

The present wit of this, as Pope well knew, would shine through
the safe cadence of that ancient line. The English equivalents
are not far to seek—the Tory leaders of the last four years of
Anne; the Treaty of Utrecht (the shell they signed) and the hue
and cry of an ungrateful nation; the English Phocions (the
same Oxford and Bolingbroke) on the verge of impeachment
for aiding, as alleged, the French Macedonians; and the Cato
who, in Addison's tragedy, was, like Brutus, claimed by Tories
and Whigs alike as the defender of British liberties. The inclusion of Agis may have been intended to add an implied complaint to this writ of grievance. Dryden's Plutarch, familiar to
Pope's audience, would have furnished the clue:

> For they [Agis and Cleomenes], being desirous also to raise the
> people, and to restore the noble and just form of government, now
> long fallen into disuse, incurred the hatred of the rich and power-
> ful. . . .
> When the love of gold and silver had once gained admittance
> into the Lacedaemonian commonwealth, it was quickly followed
> by avarice and baseness of spirit in the pursuit of it, and by lux-
> ury, effeminacy, and prodigality in the use. Then Sparta fell
> from almost all her former virtue and repute, and so continued till
> the days of Agis and Leonidas, who both together were kings of
> the Lacedaemonians.[24]

For those qualified to recall, this account would spell Whig and
Tory politics: not only the Tory mission to rescue an England

fallen on evil times under Whig mismanagement, but the Tory complaint of Whig moneyed morality and politics, a charge abundantly published by Swift and Bolingbroke.[25]

That part of the poem treating of great literary figures (vv. 178–243) probably dates in essence from the time of first working, though it may have undergone some stylistic touching up. The same may be inferred of the passage following, with its account of the seat of Fame itself, and the Goddess. But at her Sessions there is considerable evidence of later and political recasting. The first such, perhaps, appears at v. 297, where the poet says that *Fortune* "undiscerning, scatters Crowns and Chains." Since Chaucer has nothing to say of this, it is not too much to suspect a passing glance at arbitrary, misguided, and hence unjust behavior on the part of court and ministry under the new regime. Next comes what in Chaucer is simply a "thridde company" (v. 1657), "Folk that han ful trewely / Deserved fame ryghtfully," but which Pope identifies as "the Good and Just," who, observing (independently of Chaucer) that "the best Men are treated like the worst" (v. 321), beg their due of Fame. Given the tendentiousness already at work, this departure reads like another brief in behalf of the embattled Oxford and Bolingbroke.[26]

There is no Chaucerian parallel for Pope's next suppliants, the royal conquerors, and, while it is possible to see these as commonplace types, their "proud Defiance" of aspect and their admission of vanity rather than virtue as their true motives of conduct suggest another glance at William and, with Fame's sentence of "Oblivion," a tacit admonition to George I. Two other groups of petitioners follow before Pope brings on his most palpable English counterparts thus far:

> . . . those who boast of mighty Mischiefs done,
> Enslave their Country, or usurp a Throne;
> Or who their Glory's dire Foundation laid,
> On Sovereigns ruin'd, or on Friends betray'd,
> Calm, thinking Villains, whom no Faith cou'd fix,
> Of crooked Counsels and dark Politicks.
>
> (vv. 406–11)

Dilke first remarked the drift of this passage, though he associated it with an earlier significance only:

> No one, I think, can doubt that these illustrations
> are from King William & the revolution party—Usurper
> of a throne &c &c[.] Pope was at the time of writing
> deep in with Swift & the tories—had . . . naturally
> quarreled with Addison—& here is something like
> proof that he was willing to go all lengths with the
> tories. The death of the Queen & the accession of
> the Whigs, probably cooled his ardor.[27]

If the lines are indeed, as I agree, an allusion to Williamite Whiggism and takeover, they must also be an allusion to the consequences thereof, and it is not easy to see how, since Pope published them in 1715 (and again in 1717), they could be thought of as reflecting any cooling of his ardor. I suspect in fact that the lines were written later than Dilke seems to imply, that is, after, not before, the death of the Queen; and that the passage, like others we have encountered, looks two ways—backward to William and ahead (or at hand) to George. If the Whigs are to be supposed to have usurped a throne in 1688, they may likewise be thought to have usurped it again in 1714. If they enslaved a nation then, they bid (unless dissuaded) to do it again. If they "ruin'd" a James, they later bedeviled an Anne.[28] It is, in short, inconceivable that the allusion could have been dissociated from its date of publication. "Calm, thinking Villains" would have spelled *Whig* as readily in 1715 as before.[29] Far from cooling in ardor, Pope seems almost reckless in its display, for beyond the word "trayterye" (v. 1818) there is nothing he could appeal the passage to in Chaucer.

He is equally bold in embellishing Chaucer at one point in the temple of Rumor, where there is noise

> Of Turns of Fortune, Changes in the State,
> The Falls of Fav'rites, Projects of the Great,
> Of old Mismanagements, Taxations new—
> All neither wholly false, nor wholly true.[30]

Tillotson acknowledged the reflection here—whether fortuitous or deliberate he is not sure—"of the events of 1714:

Oxford's dismissal, Queen Anne's death, the Hanoverian succession, and Bolingbroke's impeachment."[31] If there is fortuity
in the allusion, it is to developments between 1715 and 1717
rather than to the events of 1714;[32] and the fortuity is to be
associated with such subsequent lines as "Hosts rais'd by Fear,
and Phantoms of a day" (v. 461), "home-born Lyes, or Tales
from foreign Lands" (v. 465), and their ensuing text: rumors
of insurrections, charges of treason, and the like. But I do not
believe in fortuity in Pope anyway. I believe the allusion there
by design, and I think it twofold: glancing at the debacle of
1714 and at the apprehensions and threats of 1715 and after.

Pope's own views on fame, with which he ends the poem,
also bear traces of later vintage: his situation in the fact and
fancy of the Hanoverian succession:

> Nor Fame I slight, nor for her Favours call;
> She comes unlook'd for, if she comes at all:
> But if the Purchase costs so dear a Price,
> As soothing Folly, or exalting Vice:
> Oh! if the Muse must flatter lawless Sway,
> And follow still where Fortune leads the way;
> Or if no Basis bear my rising Name,
> But the fall'n Ruins of Another's Fame:
> Then teach me, Heaven! to scorn the guilty Bays;
> Drive from my Breast that wretched Lust of Praise;
> Unblemish'd let me live, or die unknown,
> Oh grant an honest Fame, or grant me none!
>
> (vv. 513–24)

Norman Ault associates these lines with Pope's disaffection
with Addison—his strictures on "Envy and Detraction" in the
opening of his review of *An Essay on Criticism* in the *Spectator*
for 20 December 1711.[33] In Pope's way of differential allusion,
as I may call it, this might well be one face of these Janus lines,
but their Addisonian burden seems strong for the slight of 1711
and not "Homeric" enough for that of 1715. There are, besides,
elements that do not accord. Addison surely cannot be thought
to have provoked Pope to disclaim the praise of "Vice," nor
is it easy to see how he could have prompted the rejection of
flattery to "lawless Sway." Whatever the little Senate was, it

was scarcely that. Nor is Addison likely to have provoked the rejection of Fortune's beck. The last three couplets have perhaps an Addisonian flavor, but the first three smack more of grave expectations than of pride and prejudice. Even the couplet on "the fall'n Ruins of Another's Fame," as Addisonian as any, more nearly fits, in the gravity of its complaint, the poet's refusal to climb a Whiggish ladder at the expense of a fallen Bolingbroke or Oxford. On balance it appears that the "Vice," the "lawless Sway," the "Fortune," and the "fall'n Ruins" of this valediction point to a cause more somber than Addisonian grievance, that they point, like other parts of the poem, to the crisis in politics and the state, to the plight of friends, and to the hopes and fears at hand and in the days ahead.

VI

SATIRE AS ORDONNANCE
An Essay on Criticism

·

IT IS NOT GENERALLY ACKNOWLEDGED, I believe, that Pope's *Essay on Criticism* is as much a satire as it is an art of criticism. Published in 1711, the *Essay* was composed during the period of satiric experimentation already touched upon and represents both a continuation and extension of that activity. Though his target is now principally literary and critical, Pope avails himself of the same opportunities for political aside that he has taken throughout the work of the early period.[1]

It is possible that the failure to think of the *Essay* satirically is related to a tendency to overlook the satiric character of the whole tradition of the versified *ars*. Horace, with whom it all began, is unmistakable, if modest, in setting the precedent. He opens the *Epistle to the Pisos* with notice of the absurdities that disfigure the poetic art, and in the course of the letter takes occasion to advert satirically to the boaster and his labored mouse, the unpared, unshorn, and unwashed poets of Democritean suffrage, the scorners of learning and discipline, the Bufos of the flattery mart, and the mad poet of public nuisance. With one exception the tendency ever since has been to augment the satiric component.

The exception is Vida. A distressingly humorless critic, he is the least satiric of all the writers of versified arts of poetry. Only two or three times in a very tedious treatise (*De Arte Poetica*) does he resort to satire: once on the teacher of bombast (I, 96 ff.), once on the brutal schoolmaster (I, 246 ff.), and once on the "learned blockhead" (II, 191–202).[2] Whatever influence he may have had on Pope, it was not satirical.

Though Boileau invites "l'oreille à mes *instructions*,"[3] he restores to the art of poetry "un trait de satire" which undoubtedly affected Pope, whether directly or indirectly. Boileau's most notable innovations were his introduction of names into the account of literary success and failure and his readiness to call a spade a spade—"vers monstreux," "insipides plaisants, buffons infortunés," "une muse grossière," "un sot orgueil," and the like. Even so, Boileau does not entirely escape the heavy hand of didactic sobriety, and the impression finally left by the *Art poétique* is perhaps more nearly doctrinaire than satiric.

It remained for the English to capitalize the satiric potential of the genre, largely, but not exclusively, through translations of Horace and Boileau. The Soame–Dryden translation of the latter intensifies its satiric vein conspicuously, and there can be little doubt that the precedent leading directly to Pope takes its rise there. Not just the English ear, but Pope's more assertive temperament, would have attracted him more readily to the "Cant of Belingsgate" than to *le langage des halles*, to "Boundless and Mad, disorder'd Rhyme was seen" than to *La Licence à rimer alors n'eut plus de frein*, to "dullest Scriblers" than to *plus mauvais plaisant*, and to "this low stuff" than to *ce style*.[4]

Other English antecedents include Oldham, Rochester, Mulgrave, and Roscommon. Oldham modernized the *Epistle to the Pisos* in 1681, conferring upon it a downright English bluster. Where Horace, speaking of the decorum of dramatic speech, declares it necessary to determine who is speaking, an old man or a budding youth (*senex . . . florente iuventa*), a matron or a nurse (*matrone . . . nutrix*), trader or tiller, Colchian or Assyrian, Theban or Argive (vv. 114–18), Oldham takes to the streets:

> Whether a Man that's elderly in growth,
> Or a brisk Hotspur in his boiling Youth:
> A roaring Bully, or a shirking Cheat,
> A Court-bred Lady, or a tawdry Cit;

> A prating Gossip, or a jilting Whore,
> A travell'd Merchant, or an home spun Boor:
> *Spaniard,* or *French* . . . .[5]

Horace's complaint (vv. 355–58) of the poet who consistently errs, like the harpist who always blunders over the same string, Oldham vulgarizes with characteristic rasp:

> Yet he, who having oft been taught to mend
> A Fault, will still pursue it to the end,
> Is like that scraping Fool, who the same Note
> Is ever playing, and is ever out;
> And silly as that bubble every whit,
> Who at the self-same blot is always hit.
> When such a lewd incorrigible Sot
> Lucks by meer chance upon some happy thought;
> Among such filthy Trash, I vex to see't,
> And wonder how (the Devil!) he came by't.[6]

More Popeian (at least in theme) is Oldham's version of the poet who advertises his genius and scorns to admit his ignorance (Hor., vv. 417–18): a "conceited Dunce, without pretence / To the least grain of Learning, Parts, or Sense, / Or any thing but harden'd Impudence." Pope, we know, judged Oldham "too much like Billingsgate,"[7] but he learned something from that quarter and certainly found precedent for invigorating the satiric reprimand.

Rochester's *Allusion to Horace* (1680), though not an art of poetry, is not unrelated to the genre, being a canvass of the Restoration literary scene modeled on Horace's *Sat. I. x.* In it, mixed with an urbanity not unworthy of Horace, is a satiric candor equally Horatian:

> Well, Sir, 'tis granted I said Dryden's rhymes
> Were stol'n, unequal, nay dull, many times.
> What foolish patron is there found of his
> So blindly partial to deny me this?[8]

Rochester continues to give plain English for honest Latin, bringing Dryden off no better than Horace did Lucilius, and scoring the "tedious scenes" of Crowne, the "blund'ring" of Settle, the "jaded Muse" of Flatman, the "hot-brain'd fustian" of Lee and others, while dispensing laurels to such as Shadwell, Wycherley, Waller, Buckhurst, and Sedley.

Mulgrave's *Essay upon Satire* (1680), which Pope was later to edit, though it disclaims lampoon, engages that style shamelessly, as we have seen. Pope, who may have read the poem as early as 1702, would have been drawn to its theory if not its practice:

> Satire has always shin'd amongst the rest,
> And is the boldest way, if not the best,
> To tell men freely of their foulest faults,
> To laugh at their vain deeds and vainer thoughts.
>
> . . . .
>
> Some did all follies with just sharpness blame,
> While others laugh'd and scorn'd them into shame;
> But of these two the last succeeded best,
> As men aim rightest when they shoot in jest.[9]

Mulgrave disclaims certain types and levels of subject for satire, but his inclusion of "wits" in politics as well as letters must have given encouragement to Pope's tendency that way. There is also Mulgrave's authority for the use of satire in teaching.

But it is Mulgrave's *Essay upon Poetry* (1682) that is of most relevance to this particular history. In it for the first time, so far as I know, satire is explicitly associated with the arts of poetry as motive and vehicle. After lamenting that Horace has left so little for the modern critic to say, Mulgrave declares:

> Yet modern Laws are made for later Faults,
> And new Absurdities inspire new thoughts;
> What need has *Satyr* then to live on theft,
> When so much fresh occasion still is left?
> Folly abounds, nay, flourishes at Court,
> Where on its sphere it finds a kind support;
> But hold, *White-Hall* has nothing now to fear,
> 'Tis Wit and Sence that is the Subject here,
> Defects of witty Men deserve a Cure,
> And those who are so will the worst endure.[10]

Here, if Pope needed it, is not only immediate authorization for approaching the art of poetry (criticism) via satire, but for extending that satire to grounds courtly and political. Mulgrave himself proceeds freely after this fashion, singling out the "Fop" at song, "Bawdry bare-fac'd," "Noisy Nonsense," "some Lumpish Minister of State," "That silly thing men call sheer Wit," and other faults of poets and poesy, courtiers and politicians.[11] On satire itself, Mulgrave discourses as he did in the *Essay upon Satire,* still preaching better than he practiced, but affording another text for the value of satire to didactics:

> Of all the ways that Wisest Men could find
> To mend the Age, and mortify Mankind,
> *Satyr* well writ has most successful prov'd
> And cures because the remedy is lov'd.[12]

Roscommon's *Essay on Translated Verse* (1684), both saluted and echoed in the *Essay on Criticism,* rings the satiric changes from Horace through Boileau and adds a few of its own: pedantry, bombast, pride, flattery, sottishness, "*Holy Garbage* tho by *Homer Cookt,*" the *vox populi* ("alwayes in the Wrong"), "Pompilian, Wealthy, pamper'd Heirs," and "*Absur'd Expressions, crude, Abortive Thoughts,* / All the lewd *Legion* of *Exploded fau'ts.*"[13]

In 1701 George Granville, later Lord Lansdowne, published his *Essay upon Unnatural Flights in Poetry,* versified largely from Bouhour's *La Manière de bien penser.* Though brief and neither especially good nor much satirical, the poem seems to have left an impression on Pope. It almost certainly enters the *Essay on Criticism* and may have affected the *Peri Bathous* and *Epistle to a Lady* as well. Its opening image of the painter consulting "each beauteous line, / Adjusting to his Object his design" and winning fame as his portrait mirrors nature (else failing) is close to Pope's lines in the *Essay* on right drawing and ill coloring (20–25), the "joint Force and full *Result* of *all*" (243–52), and the "*bright Idea* of the Master's Mind" (484–93). It is almost certain that Pope's

> But *you* who seek to *give* and *merit* Fame,
> And justly bear a Critick's noble Name,

owes something to Granville's

Who seek from Poetry a lasting Name,
May in their Lessons learn the road to Fame;

and that Granville's "*Roscommon* first, Then *Mulgrave* rose"
played a part in Pope's catalog of critics in the conclusion of
the *Essay on Criticism*. But more to the point, Granville's reference to the Restoration of Charles and "banisht Peace" gave
added license for the introduction of political allusion in this
species of writing.[14]

Blackmore's *Satyr against Wit* (1700) could hardly be called
an art of poetry, or of anything else for that matter, but it does
engage in the literary controversy lying back of Pope's *Essay*
and provides another example, certain to have been well known
to Pope, of satire in the service of critical homiletics.[15]

When Pope undertook the *Essay on Criticism* he had before
him a well-established tradition of satirical enforcement of the
didactic intent. He not only proceeded to augment that role but
to articulate it more perfectly into the whole, adjusting the end
and means with great skill, invoking satire as the teaching warrants or invites, laying it aside where it does not. In Part I the
satire is finely trimmed to the instructive motive, with which,
while it participates, it never becomes competitive. In Part II,
by virtue of the subject (causes hindering sound judgment), it
is brought to the fore and made climactic to a rising and falling
censoriousness throughout. With Part III it is carefully modu-
lated to the rhetorical need for a laudatory and ethically modest peroration.

The poem commences with a nice balance of the instructive
and the admonitory:

> 'Tis hard to say, if greater Want of Skill
> Appear in *Writing* or in *Judging* ill;
> But, of the two, less dang'rous is th'Offence,
> To tire our *Patience*, than mis-lead our *Sense*:
> Some few in *that*, but Numbers err in *this*,
> Ten Censure wrong for one who Writes amiss;
> A *Fool* might once *himself* alone expose,
> Now *One* in *Verse* makes many more in *Prose*.

More witty than cutting, this vein gives way quickly to the expository requirement:

> In *Poets* as true *Genius* is but rare,
> True *Taste* as seldom is the *Critick's* Share;

and there it holds essentially until the subject of "*false learning*" excites a burst of sarcasm:

> Some are bewilder'd in the Maze of Schools,
> And some made *Coxcombs* Nature meant but *Fools*.

The tone remains quickened through the "*Eunuch's* spite," the "Itching to deride," and the Maevian disgrace, until it peaks at last in the scornful account of the geniture of critics:

> Some have at first for *Wits*, then *Poets* past,
> Turn'd *Criticks* next, and prov'd plain *Fools* at last;
> Some neither can for *Wits* nor *Criticks* pass,
> As heavy Mules are neither *Horse* nor *Ass*.
> Those half-learn'd Witlings, num'rous in our Isle,
> As half-form'd Insects on the Banks of *Nile*;
> Unfinish'd Things, one knows not what to call,
> Their Generation's so *equivocal*.
>
> (vv. 36–43)

With this contemptuous note satire gives way again to the instructive voice and, save for an occasional admonitory turn, Pope proceeds to set forth the conditions of sound criticism and illustrate its rise and triumph in ancient Greece. Its fall thereafter is occasion for the resumption of satiric comment:

> But following Wits from that Intention stray'd;
> Who cou'd not win the Mistress, woo'd the Maid;
> Against the Poets *their own Arms* they turn'd,
> Sure to hate most the Men from whom they *learn'd*.
>
> . . . .
>
> *Some* on the Leaves of ancient Authors prey,
> Nor Time nor Moths e'er spoil'd so much as they:
> Some dryly plain, without Invention's Aid,
> Write dull *Receits* how Poems may be made:
> These leave the Sense, their Learning to display,
> And those explain the Meaning quite away.
>
> (vv. 104–17)

Both here and in the earlier glance at education Pope anticipates the Scriblerian war with pedantry and *The Dunciad* beyond. Meanwhile, except for an occasional frown, Pope lays
by the rod and concludes Part I in the teaching voice, not, to be
sure, without moments of eloquence.

When he resumes the rod in the second lecture, he not only
applies it more vigorously but more extensively, calling up, in
addition to writers, religious bigots and royal offenders. Beginning with pride, "the *never-failing* Vice *of Fools*," he turns in
more tutorial vein to the dangers of "*little Learning*," the necessity of judging by the whole, and of refusing, except "in such
Lays as neither *ebb*, nor *flow*," the "malignant dull Delight" of
mere fault-finding. Dispatching the "*Verbal Critick*" with the
reminder that "*not* to know some Trifles, is a Praise," he then
turns to those who "talk of *Principles*, but Notions prize" and
relates the story of "*La Mancha's* Knight," a drollery on critics
by the book, with Dennis as the prime exhibit. This comic
touch, enlivened with dialogue, serves as relief between the
sarcasm going before and some even sterner stuff ahead.

When he comes to the fault of "*Love to Parts*," Pope scores
both critics and poets alike, beginning with the Metaphysicals
and the cult of the conceit. True wit, as he remarks (soberly),
is "*Nature* to Advantage drest," not, as he observes satirically,
"One *glaring Chaos* and *wild Heap* of *Wit*." False eloquence
receives like treatment until the two are caught up together,
along with kindred folly, in a fine parade of sarcasm:

> A vile Conceit in pompous Words exprest,
> Is like a Clown in regal Purple drest;
> For diff'rent *Styles* with diff'rent *Subjects* sort,
> As several Garbs with Country, Town, and Court.
> Some by *Old Words* to Fame have made Pretence;
> Ancients in *Phrase*, meer Moderns in their *Sense!*
> Some *labour'd Nothings*, in so *strange* a Style,
> *Amaze* th'unlearn'd, and make the Learned *Smile.*
> Unlucky, as *Fungoso* in the Play,
> These Sparks with aukward Vanity display
> What the Fine Gentleman wore *Yesterday!*
> (vv. 320–30)

The moral briefly drawn ("Be not the *first* ... Nor yet the *last*"), Pope turns to the "tuneful" set, who "haunt *Parnassus* but to please their Ear." Here the satire grows facetious again, though hardly less pointed. In it Pope resorts to mimicry, imitating the bathetics of hiatus, expletive, monosyllabics, hackneyed rhyme, and the "*needless*" Alexandrine. Then follows a serious illustration of sound as echo to the sense, which, after some notice of the folly of judgment by extremes, gives way to a satiric attack on sectarian criticism, with liberal notice to its religious counterpart. This is the opening volley in what proves an almost unrelieved satiric takeover for the remainder of Part II.

Beginning with the charge,

> Some *foreign* Writers, some our *own* despise;
> The *Ancients* only, or the *Moderns* prize:

Pope translates it at once in terms of religious sectarianism:

> Thus *Wit*, like *Faith*, by each Man is apply'd
> To *one small Sect*, and All are *damn'd beside*.[16]

As we know, such reflections on religious bigotry cost Pope no little embarrassment among his Catholic friends; but his protestations, admirable as they are,[17] do not—perhaps could not —touch the rhetorical justification: the discrediting of critical prejudice by the most telling analogy available to his time and place.[18]

After a few lines on the general implications of such sectarianism, Pope aims some well-trimmed barbs at the first of several literary offenders in this kind, the Pollyanna, ad hominem, and sycophantic critics:

> Some ne'er advance a Judgment of their own,
> But *catch* the *spreading Notion* of the Town;
> They reason and conclude by *Precedent*,
> And own *stale Nonsense* which they ne'er invent.
> Some judge of Author's *Names*, not *Works*, and then
> Nor praise nor blame the *Writings*, but the *Men*.
> Of all this *Servile Herd* the worst is He
> That in *proud Dulness* joins with *Quality*,
> A constant Critick at the Great-man's Board,

> To *fetch and carry* Nonsense for my Lord.
> What *woful stuff* this Madrigal wou'd be,
> In some starv'd Hackny Sonneteer, or me?
> But let a *Lord* once own the *happy Lines,*
> How the *Wit brightens!* How the *Style refines!*
>
> (vv. 408–21)

Pope is already on the scent of Bufo and his "undistinguish'd race," the tribe of Scriblerus, and the sons of Mother Dulness.

When he turns to inconstancy in criticism, Pope takes the illustration again to the disgraces of churchmanship: the unreason, contentiousness, ignorance, sophistry, and sterility of school theology—

> Once *School-Divines* this zealous Isle o'erspread;
> Who knew most *Sentences* was *deepest read;*
> Faith, Gospel, All, seem'd made to be *disputed,*
> And none had *Sense enough to be Confuted.*
> *Scotists* and *Thomists,* now, in Peace remain,
> Amidst their *kindred Cobwebs* in *Duck-Lane.*
>
> (vv. 440–45)

In what follows the religious analogy has the force, not just of explication, but of bad (corrupting) example, the effect of the greater upon the lesser:

> If *Faith* it self has *diff'rent Dresses* worn,
> What wonder *Modes* in *Wit* shou'd take their turn?

With partisan criticism Pope completes the web of interrelationship, adding politics to church and letters:

> Parties in *Wit* attend on those of *State,*
> And publick Faction doubles private Hate.
> *Pride, Malice, Folly,* against *Dryden* rose,
> In various Shapes of *Parsons, Criticks, Beaus.*
>
> (vv. 456–59)

Pope will have more to say later of the "Poetical Church and State."[19] Meanwhile he remits of the satire briefly, commenting on the fragility of language as the depository of poetry and, now seriously, now facetiously, on the plight of Wit. The latter, however, provokes him again to the strap, and he defines Wit finally and in disgust as

. . . what the *Vicious fear,* the *Virtuous shun;*
By *Fools . . . hated,* and by *Knaves undone!*

"If *Wit,*" he pleads, "so much from *Ign'rance* undergo, / Ah let not *Learning* too commence its Foe!" Poets were once encouraged and rewarded:

> *Now,* they who reach *Parnassus'* lofty Crown,
> Employ their Pains to spurn some others down.
>
> (vv. 514–15 ff.)

It seems likely enough that Blackmore and other neo-puritans on the literary scene are involved in this complaint,[20] but it is also possible that Pope, recalling some rebuff (Dennis?), is issuing a warning of restraint against others similarly inclined.

If, says Pope, such a critic must indulge his spleen, let him rather

> Discharge that Rage on more Provoking Crimes,
> Nor fear a Dearth in these Flagitious Times.

But there is something disingenuous in this counsel, for Pope seems in fact to be preparing the way for more than "vile Obscenity." The age of Anne was scarcely flagitious, nor much in need of scourge for steaming ordures of the page. Pope's true object, it would appear, was a time before, and not the "fat Age of Pleasure, Wealth, and Ease" with which, discreetly, he began, but that of the doctrinal decline of Williamite importation:

> The following Licence of a Foreign Reign
> Did all the Dregs of bold *Socinus* drain;
> Then Unbelieving Priests reform'd the Nation,
> And taught more *Pleasant* Methods of Salvation;
> Where Heav'ns Free Subjects might their *Rights* dispute,
> Lest God himself shou'd seem too *Absolute.*
> *Pulpits* their *Sacred* Satire learn'd to spare,
> And Vice *admir'd* to find a *Flatt'rer* there!
>
> (vv. 544–51)

This is as close as Pope comes in the *Essay* to fetching his satire afar. Though not unrelated to his convictions, already implied, about the interdependence of all parts of the moral fabric, Pope is obviously at some pains to bring William to trial again and just possibly, under the brand of "Foreign Reign," to hint of risks ahead. In the first version of these lines appeared a couplet, since removed, that added to the articles of complaint that of Dutch profiteering at English expense:

> Then *first* the *Belgian Morals* were extoll'd;
> We their *Religion* had, and they our *Gold*.[21]

The charge savors of the Tory case against the Dutch alliance during the war then still in progress. If that is the case, it adds to the evidence that Pope was already well on his way to Tory alignment before its leaders—Swift, Bolingbroke, and the Scriblerians—took him into that fellowship.

As I suspect that Pope led up to the Williamite *exemplum* by way of Charles for reasons of prudence as much as anything else, so, I believe, he followed it with a caveat calculated to answer the same need:

> Yet shun their Fault, who, *Scandalously nice*,
> Will needs *mistake* an Author *into Vice;*
> All seems Infected that th'Infected spy,
> As all looks yellow to the Jaundic'd Eye.

Actually Pope accommodates several things in these concluding lines: he closes the lecture on a dispassionate note while maintaining the continuity of his immediate argument, and he warns the auditor not to count on reading him into trouble.

Though Part III, like I, more nearly balances the interplay of satire and instruction, it maintains, in respect of the former, the more quickened tone of Part II. It begins with instruction, counseling "Truth and Candor" in the critic, silence when in doubt, and modesty when sure. Only a glance at "Some positive persisting Fops" ruffles the surface of the lecture until, having counseled liberality in advice (nor fear of stirring anger), the poet—perhaps remembering a personal experience—points to an example of the risks involved:

> 'Twere well, might Criticks still this Freedom take;
> But *Appius* reddens at each Word you speak,

And *stares, Tremendous!* with a *threatning Eye,*
Like some *fierce Tyrant* in *Old Tapestry!*

(vv. 584–87)

For all their aftermath in Dennis diatribe, the lines are comic in spirit and illustrate again how Pope graduates into the satiric voice. What follows is much more biting, though Dennis may not have thought so:

> Fear most to tax an *Honourable* Fool,
> Whose Right it is, *uncensur'd* to be dull.

These claim poetry by right of peerage, and their censure is best left to the satiricaster, their flattery to "fulsome *Dedicators.*" But Pope cannot resist the temptation to have at them on his own:

> 'Tis best sometimes your Censure to restrain,
> And *charitably* let the Dull be *vain:*
> Your Silence there is better than your *Spite,*
> For who can *rail* so long as they can *write?*
> Still humming on, their drowzy Course they keep,
> And *lash'd* so long, like *Tops,* are lash'd *asleep.*
> *False Steps* but help them to renew the Race,
> As after *Stumbling,* Jades will *mend* their Pace.
> What Crouds of these, impenitently bold,
> In *Sounds* and jingling *Syllables* grown old,
> Still *run on* Poets in a raging Vein,
> Ev'n to the Dregs and *Squeezings* of the Brain;
> Strain out the last, dull droppings of their Sense,
> And Rhyme with all the *Rage* of *Impotence!*
>
> (vv. 596–609)

The scatology, no doubt partly derivative,[22] is an increment to Pope's satiric rhetoric and a signal, as nearly always hereafter, of his arousal. He turns next to the "Bookful Blockhead," whose portrait also builds to a climax:

> No Place so Sacred from such Fops is barr'd,
> Nor is *Paul's Church* more safe than *Paul's Church-yard:*
> Nay, fly to *Altars; there* they'll talk you dead;
> For *Fools* rush in where *Angels* fear to tread.
>
> (vv. 622–25)

With one or two exceptions, this is the poet's last volley, as he moves on through the portrait of the ideal critic to the roll call of the great critics. When he reaches Horace he takes occasion to compare the Roman with the English:

> *Our Criticks* take a contrary Extream,
> They *judge* with *Fury,* but they *write* with *Fle'me:*

and, of course, they mistranslate and misquote most shamefully. The catalog continues until the fall of Rome provokes a final censure, scoring the tyranny and superstition of the mind:

> A *second* Deluge Learning thus o'er-run,
> And the *Monks* finish'd what the *Goths* begun.

With this reflection Pope lays down the rod and concludes the catalog of worthies: Vida, Boileau, Roscommon, Walsh, and —by modest implication—Mr. Pope himself.

On incidence alone the *Essay on Criticism* would have to rate high as satire. But what distinguishes the performance is its economy, not degree. Never simply random, malicious, or abusive (even in its political glance) the satire serves to promote the rhetoric, to structure and enforce the argument. It is this coordination of satire with the didactic intent, along with the variety in the satiric voice, that sets Pope's performance apart from almost every other essay of its kind.

VII

IN THE MANNER OF SCRIBLERUS

·

Off and on during his second literary decade Pope took occasion to indulge in what Sherburn has aptly called "holiday efforts."[1] These include among other things his prose satires—greater or less in satiric intensity, often (but not always) arising out of the Scriblerian agenda, all fairly brief, some better than others, and taking a variety of forms. Mainly literary in theme and dedicated to the requital of his detractors, they represent satire in a new key, the serio-comics of Menippeanism. Though no longer much noticed they reflect an interesting side of Pope's literary life and make up an important part of the record of satire and politics in the early career. In considering them it will be useful to allow for certain groupings.

i. The Dennis Lampoons

Although his satiric impulse was assuredly given encouragement and Menippean bent by his Scriblerian association, Pope was scarcely dependent on that fellowship for his discovery of the mode or for his aptitude in it. Before he had met any of the Scriblerians or the club itself had been formed, he had given earnest of his qualification for Menippean satire in *The Critical Specimen*, a retort upon Dennis's *Reflections* on his *Essay on Criticism*.[2]

The *Specimen* is a takeoff on Dennis in general and his

Grounds of Criticism in Poetry in particular, itself a "specimen" of a magnum opus which Dennis offered to undertake by subscription. Pope's parody of this aborted enterprise consists of "A Specimen of the Preface" and "A Specimen of A Treatise in *Folio*, to be printed by Subscription, Entituled, *The Mirror of Criticisme:* Or, The History of the Renown'd *Rinaldo Furioso,* Critick of the Woful Countenance."[3] The completed work, we are told, "will be publish'd either by single Chapters, or in the whole, as the Majority of Subscribers shall please to Appoint; who are desir'd to pay half a Guinea down, and the other half when the Book is delivered."[4] Though the *Specimen* is essentially literary in its aim, it pays its respects as well to Dennis's political paranoia, something Pope obviously found beneficial as well as amusing to advertise.

In the Preface, Pope sports with Dennis's fondness for blank verse, Milton, and the Christian epic. He had (says Pope's persona) first thought to cast the story in the form of an epic, but gave over in view of problems relative to the unities and to truth. He does, however, reprint a simile salvaged from that abandoned scheme, wherein there is no mistaking the Dennisian Pope:

> A baneful *Hunch-back'd Toad*, with Look Maligne,
> Glares on some Traveller's unwary steps,
> Whether by Chance, or by Misfortune led
> To tread those dark unwholesome, misty Fens,
> Rage strait Collects his Venom all at once,
> And swells his bloated Corps to largest size.

The specimen of the life itself consists of a sample chapter and headings for the rest. The former treats "Of the *Critick's* first Extravagance, How he took a *Hobby-Horse* for *Pegasus*, with some other Conceits, not unworthy attention, being the shortest Chapter in the whole Book." Glancing as much perhaps at Dennis's Longinian fancy as at his self-delusion, the chapter compares the "height of Imagination" in Rinaldo and Don Quixote and gives the palm to Rinaldo, at least in respect to horses, *Rosinante* being after all merely real. But what for a lesser soul would prove a drawback proved none for Rinaldo, who, we are told, boldly bestrode his hobby-horse of a day, in emulation of Bellerophon,[5] and bare-back "thrice scamper'd o'er the Floor," trailing his stick behind him and repeating "with great vehemence" a Rhapsody proclaiming his Parnassian destiny, especially as restorer of the Ancients. Having repeated this rhapsody several times over, "he put himself into distorted Figures, and screw'd his Visage into New Grimaces, crying aloud, s'*Death*, I'm *Roscius*, I'm *Roscius*, I'm *Roscius*."

Returning to Dennis's dislike of rhyme, the author recounts how one day it came into Rinaldo's head that he had never read in Milton or the Ancients that Pegasus wore bells, whereupon he tore away those from his hobby-horse and has ridden it so ever since. After some additional comment on Rinaldo's "Chimaerical Notions" of the Muses—as a homely, hoarse, hobbling band of "Rural Hoydens"—the specimen chapter concludes and the others are given in headings only.

These are richly and archly allusive, making fun of Dennis's obsession with Longinus and Milton, his insistence on religion as the touchstone of true poetry, his literary fiascos, dislike of opera, resentment of criticism, irascibility and brow-beating, and, along with much else, his delusions of conspiracy against his person on the part of the French. Chapter 2 treats "Of his Education, Person, Parts, and *other inconsiderable Matters*." Chapter 12 tells of his "mortal aversion to the *Catt-call*," Chapter 24 "Of the Difficulties he found in attaining to a C[la]p," and Chapters 32–33 how he was nearly lured aboard ship for transportation to France and of the French King's desire to have him in the Bastille.

The sport concludes in a flurry of bookmaking parody, which may or may not owe something to Swift. An *N.B.* regarding the print to be used indicates Elzevir for the Critick's virtues and a "Noble large Letter" for his excesses. This is followed by an *au lecteur*, annotations on chapter 4, and an ADVERTISEMENT announcing "speedily to be publish'd" a dissertation by Bentley proving the author of Æsop not *Crooked* but *Strait* and another by Dennis proving the author of *An Essay on Criticism* not *Strait* but *Crooked*, and giving the price of the *Speci-*

men: 2p. or 20s. per hundred to any who would undertake to give it about gratis.

The *Specimen* is a skillful riposte to the broadsword assault by Dennis, but even more impressive, and just as certainly Pope's, is *The Narrative of Dr. Robert Norris, Concerning the strange and deplorable Frenzy of Mr. John Denn[is]*, 1713, a reply to Dennis's *Remarks upon Cato*, published just a few weeks before.[6] Whatever additional motives Pope may have had for launching this takedown, he must have reasoned Dennis mad to attack Addison, especially on so popular a play, regardless of its actual merits. But whatever the vintage of the madness, Pope fell upon the perfect device for publishing it— an advertisement in *The Guardian* by one Robert Norris advising the public of his services in the cure of the lunatic.[7] On 28 July Pope advertised in the *Post Boy* the publication of *The Narrative of Dr. Robert Norris.*

In his account the doctor reports how he was visited lately by an old woman begging his assistance for her master (Dennis), who, she explained, had been "taken ill of a violent Frenzy last *April*" [the date of *Cato*] and had continued in a state of disturbance ever since, staring, raving, and muttering *"Cator"* over and over. When anyone would knock at his door, he would run to the window crying, *"S'death! a Messenger from the French King! I shall die in the* Bastile."

Repairing to the gentleman's quarters, the doctor found him seated on his bed in the company of the publisher Lintot and "a grave elderly Gentleman . . . who, as I have since learnt, calls himself a Grammarian."[8] Upon the doctor's appearance Dennis cried out, *"S'Death, a Frenchman!"* His eye was "fiery" and rolling, his beard unshaven, nightcap awry, breeches agape, and stockings adroop. The room was hung about with old tapestry from which Dennis had cut "the Heads of divers *Tyrants*," and on all sides were pinned sheets of *Cato* variously glossed *"Absurd, Monstrous, Execrable."* There was some small-coal in a *Spectator*, other copies of which the nurse had hidden because of their effect upon her master. The floor was littered with manuscripts, the table with "Ends of Verse and of Candles; a Gallipot of Ink with a yellow Pen in it, and a Pot of half-dead Ale cover'd with a *Longinus*."

Dennis declaring that he suffered from nothing more than a swelling in his legs, the doctor proceeded to question him, with the result that Dennis became more and more irrational:

> *Denn.* O I am sick, sick to Death!
> *Dr.* . . . Pray, Sir, of what are you sick?
> *Denn.* Of every thing, Of every thing. I am sick of the *Sentiments*, of the *Diction*, of the *Protasis*, of the *Epitasis*, and the *Catastrophe*—Alas, what is become of the *Drama*, the *Drama?*
>
> . . . .
>
> *Denn.* O shameful Want, scandalous Omission! By all the Immortals, here is no *Peripaetia*, no Change of Fortune . . . Z——— no Change at all.
>
> . . . . . .
>
> Mr. *Lintott.* Plague on't! I am damnably afraid they are in the right of it, and he is mad in earnest, if he should be really mad, who the Devil will buy the *Remarks?*
> (*Here Mr.* Lintott *scratched his Head*.)
>
> *Denn.* Caitiffs stand off; unhand me, Miscreants! Is the Man whose whole Endeavours are to bring the Town to Reason mad? Is the Man who settles Poetry on the Basis of Antiquity mad? Dares any one assert there is a *Peripaetia* in that vile Piece that's foisted upon the Town for a Dramatick Poem? That Man is mad, the Town is mad, the World is mad. See *Longinus* in my right Hand, and *Aristotle* in my left; I am the only Man among the Moderns that support them. Am I to be assassinated? and shall a Bookseller, who hath liv'd upon my Labours, take away that Life to which he owes his Support?

An attempt to cup the patient results in a free-for-all from which the cupper, Lintot, and the doctor take a hasty retreat. Lintot later furnishes the doctor with further particulars regarding Dennis's behavior: how the year before, on coming into his shop and opening a volume of the *Spectator*, Dennis violently tore out and threw into the street the essay on poetical justice; how, shortly before that, finding in his shop *An Essay on Criticism* and reading therein the lines "Some have at first for Wits, then Poets past, / Turn'd Criticks next, and prov'd plain Fools at last," he bellowed, "*By G—— he means*

Me"; how, upon being told Shakespeare was of a contrary opinion to his, he "swore the said *Shakespear* was a *Rascal*," and how, not two months since, coming into his shop and seeing a stranger, and being told he was a new author about to be published, he drew his sword upon the fellow and, but for restraint, would have infallibly dispatched him.

To these the doctor adds more of his own. He was driven, says the doctor, to publishing his *Narrative* because Dennis had reported that he had forced his way into his lodgings either to take his life or his *Coriolanus*,[9] given out that the doctor was in league with Lintot to steal some of his papers without paying copy-money, had called him a "Mountebank," and spread it about town that he was a spy in the employ of the French out to deliver him over for imprisonment in the Bastille.

The *Narrative* is the brightest of all Pope's Menippean sallies. Wholly comic, it is untouched by anything that could detract from or diminish its high spirits and infectious gaiety. Both the Dennis lampoons, in fact, differ in this respect from the Curll lampoons to follow, some few years later. Meanwhile, not necessarily out of choice, Pope would continue working the sprightly vein, though not in lampoon.

ii. Periodical Satire

During 1712 and 1713 Pope tried his hand at periodical satire, contributing modestly to *The Spectator* and *The Guardian*. In these his satire was compelled to adapt itself to the scruples of Addison and Steele, and it may be for this reason, as well as others, that his contributions of this kind were so few. Of some dozen essays he contributed to *The Spectator* only two, Nos. 452 and 457 (8 and 14 August 1712), are of a satirical turn, and these in the humorous style set by Mr. Spec.[10] The first is a facetious proposal to "make some Amends for that Dearth of Intelligence, which we may justly apprehend from times of Peace" by publishing a daily of remarkable occurrences in towns, villages, and hamlets round about London, featuring such notices as that

> Letters from *Paddington* bring little more, than that *William Squeak*, the Sow-gelder, passed through that Place the 5th Instant

and that

> They advise from *Fulham*, that things remained there in the same State they were. They had Intelligence, just as the Letters came away, of a Tub of excellent Ale just set abroach at *Parsons Green;* but this wanted Confirmation. (*PW*, p. 58)

The second piece is a follow-up, proposing two further projects, one for a *News-Letter of Whispers*, to be supplied by Peter Hush and Lady Blast, and to consist of such disclosures as

> Sickness of Persons in high Posts, Twilight Visits paid and received by Ministers of State, Clandestine Courtships and Marriages, Secret Amours, Losses at Play, Applications for Places, with their respective Successes or Repulses. (*PW*, p. 59)

The other project, one which proved momentous for Pope's career, was for a "Monthly Pamphlet" on the order of the European *Account of the Works of the Learned,* this one to be called *An Account of the Works of the Unlearned.* When, better than a year later, Pope communicated this, or a similar idea, to Swift, along with Parnell and Gay, it was warmly embraced and gave rise to the Scriblerian club and program.

When the Scriblerians called themselves to order in early 1714, the idea for a *Works of the Unlearned* gave way to that of the *Memoirs* and other lucubrations of Martinus Scriblerus, but events of that year prevented the development of the principal work in any but a tentative form, and before the year was out the club members were scattered.[11] Even so, spin-offs from the scheme appeared from the next year on, including *A Key to the Lock, The What D'ye Call It, God's Revenge Against Punning, Three Hours after Marriage, Gulliver's Travels, The Beggar's Opera,* and *The Dunciad.* Pope was in the thick of it all, and it undoubtedly afforded him as much fun as he ever had with satire.

Meanwhile, in 1713, he was contributing to *The Guardian*. Steele eventually attributed to Pope Nos. 4, 61, 78, 91–92, 173, "and some others," which, whatever else that may imply, most certainly includes No. 40 on the pastorals of Pope and Philips. The first of Pope's contributions (No. 4) is a humorous essay on dedications and dedicators, a piece, like most of his periodical endeavors, in the humorous style made obligatory by editorial taste. Its most amusing touch is the invention, with example, of a dedication to oneself. No. 11, on the *Grand Elixir*, said by Steele to have been contributed by Gay, but attributed to Pope from Warburton on, is in the same whimsical vein, offering a nostrum to restore anyone who had come to his senses to his original state of madness or folly. Among other uses, the *Restorative* is recommended for any who "have been stung with Satyr," fortifying, as it does, "the Heart against the Rancour of Pamphlets, the Inveteracy of Epigrams, and the mortification of Lampoons." Pope undoubtedly penned that part with mixed emotions.

Guardian 40 is of course Pope's revenge against the Buttonians for slighting his pastorals in favor of those of Ambrose Philips. It is a cheeky piece of irony and, as Sherburn says, so "obvious" that it is difficult to believe anyone was really taken in by it. The author, purporting to be the same who had authored earlier numbers on the subject, alleges that complaint of partiality has compelled him to reopen the question with some comments on another gentleman (Pope) who had published pastorals in the same volume with Mr. Philips. By his own definition, says the author, the better part of the eclogues of Theocritus and Virgil must be allowed to fall short of the purity of those of Mr. Philips. Virgil especially is too courtly, and Mr. Pope has obviously fallen into the same error, just as he has erred in following classical precedent in regard to names like Daphnis, Alexis, and so on. Philips, on the other hand, "who hath the strictest Regard to Propriety, makes choice of Names peculiar to the Country . . . such as *Hobbinol, Lobbin, Cuddy,* and *Colin Clout*."

After some observations on Philips's more happiness than care in regard to the niceties of animal and floral usage, the author proceeds to a comparison of passages, showing how, in one instance, Mr. Pope "deviates into downright Poetry." Eventually he turns to those things in Philips "in which no Man can compare with him," as for example the *"beautiful Rusticity"* of such as the following:

> O woful Day! O Day of Woe, quoth he,
> And woful I, who live the Day to see!

In view of Philips's many virtues, including his *"Elegant Dialect,"* the author hopes none will think it an injustice that he had forborne earlier to mention Mr. Pope,

> since upon the whole, he is of the same class with *Moschus* and *Bion,* whom we have excluded from that Rank; and of whose Eclogues, as well as some of *Virgil's,* it may be said, that according to the Description we have given of this sort of Poetry, they are by no means *Pastorals,* but *something Better.*
>
> (*PW,* p. 106)

Guardian 40 is the most Popeian of all Pope's contributions to the periodicals, and it is still a wonder how it got by. In No. 78 appeared his "Receit to make an *Epick Poem,*" a takeoff on the "Mechanick" treatises then so much in vogue, like Le Bossu's *Traité du Poëme Épique.*[12] There Pope offers a formula for writing epic poems *"without a Genius,* nay without Learning or much Reading." Running the gamut of parts—fable, episode, moral, and so forth—he applies to each the meiotic language of cookery. For fable he advises culling such adventures out of history or romance as will best admit of "long Descriptions" and throwing the same together around a hero chosen for the sound of his name, who should then be allowed to simmer for twelve books. For the moral and allegory, these may be extracted "out of the Fable afterwards at your Leisure," only taking care to "strain them sufficiently"—

and so on, through manners, machines, and descriptions, concluding with the advice not to hesitate at *"too much Fire"* because the "warmest Thoughts" have been observed "to cool before they are read."

The essays on the Club of Little Men (Nos. 91, 92) illustrate Pope's willingness (which never deserted him) to have fun at his own expense. The first tells of the formation of the society, its meeting place, rules of membership (no one over five feet tall), and the penalties for anyone caught trying "to get above his Size" by whatever device. The second gives an account of the members and the topics of club discourse. The president, almost certainly a takeoff on Pope himself, is *Dick Distick*, a poet, accorded the office not only because the shortest of the fellowship but because he stoops when he walks and resembles a "Spider." He has a great talent in poetry and has promised "a long Work in *short Verse*" to celebrate the heroes of diminutive stature. He is a great admirer of Statius, chiefly on account of one verse—*Major in exiguo regnabat corpore virtus*—and he once designed to translate the whole of the *Thebaid* for the sake of *Tydeus*.[13] The Club's gallant is Tom Tiptoe and its politician a fellow "of *real Gravity*, and *professed Wisdom*," pale and meager from "much watching and studying for the Welfare of *Europe*." The hero is *Tim. Tuck*, whose chief pride it is "that in all the Campaigns he has made, he never once *Duck'd* at the whizz of a Cannon Ball." Conversation in the club turns on the adventures and misadventures occasioned by smallness, whether of the members themselves, or of history or legend, like the story of "little *David*" and "mighty *Goliah*."

Guardian 173, on gardening, though serious in the main, concludes on a facetious note, ridiculing artificial practices then in vogue, especially the topiary craze. For those so inclined the author offers a catalog of such bargains as "The Tower of *Babel*, not yet finished"; "A Pair of Giants, *stunted*, to be sold cheap"; "Divers eminent Modern Poets in Bays, somewhat blighted, to be disposed of a Pennyworth"; and "A Pair of *Maidenheads* in Firr, in great forwardness."

Though Pope got the hang of periodical humor and performed well in it, the medium, at least as watched over by Addison and Steele, was not the best outlet for his satiric talent. Only two of his contributions, those on the pastoral and the epic, stand out, and of those by far the more impressive is the former, in which he managed to slip past the editorial outpost something fairly lethal. Politics also being against the house-rules, nothing of that sort was probably ever ventured.[14]

iii. *A Key to the Lock*

With the *Key to the Lock* (1715) the resort to politics may not have been a matter of choice, but something forced on Pope by an indiscretion in an otherwise innocent poem. With one exception, *The Rape of the Lock* was a playful and politically blameless excursion into social satire, going no further in politics than a compliment to Anne, a harmless mimicry of Partridge on "the Fall of *Rome*," and a witticism on the benefits of coffee to the politician. The exception is a couplet in the third canto:

> And now, (as oft in some distemper'd State)
> On one nice *Trick* depends the gen'ral Fate.
> (vv. 93–94)

Pope's simile has all the marks of an allusion to the emerging polarization of loyalties and passions surrounding the failing health of Anne and the looming prospect of Hanover.[15] Because of it Pope may have felt the need to take advantage of the innocence of the rest of the poem to do what he doubtless found congenial anyway, namely, to spoof the practice of reading sinister intent into any and everything of Tory or Catholic extraction.[16] Now that Hanover was installed Pope was more than ever vulnerable, and he was doubtless right in assuming, if he did, that some form of disclaimer would be prudent, especially if he could devise a way of doing so that would mock his stalkers and compound the impeachment all at the same time.

To enhance the impression of absurdity in any such accusatory view of his muse, Pope prefixed to the second edition of the *Key* four commendatory poems on its putative begetter, Esdras Barnivelt. The first of these is attributed to Nathaniel Casleton, who had himself been taken to task for gratuitous allegorizing in *Spectator* 595. His commendatory verses, anagrammatic of Barnivelt's name, consist of a series of Grubaean changes on "Barrels," including the exhortation to "Extract from *Tory* Barrels all *French* Juice." The second is signed by the High German Doctor and salutes Barnivelt as the "Censor of Tories," his "Pestle braining all the Sons of *Rome*." The third is from the Grumbler (Burnet), who asks the question, "Can Popish Writings do the Nations good?"

> Each drop of Ink demands a Drop of Blood.
> A Papist wear the Lawrel! is it fit?
> O *Button!* summon all thy Sons of Wit!
>
> . . . .
>
> If all this fail, let Faggot, Cart, and Rope,
> Revenge our Wits and Statesmen on a *Pope*.[17]

The last poem is signed by James Baker, Knt., who eludes identification. Sir James has a hit at the "Papist" who "masques his Treason in a Joke," and wishes for Barnivelt a knighthood like that conferred upon himself and Sir William Read, quondam quack and sometime oculist to Queen Anne.[18]

But Pope will have it both ways, however dangerous, and even as he thus argues his innocence he engages (as he does in the *Epistle to Augustus*) in the very mischief to which he is pleading not guilty. In the *Key* he has the benefit of an unwitting collaborator in his persona, whom he manipulates much in the same fashion he does those in the Horatian poems of later date. Barnivelt is after all a Dutchman, with all that implies of the Dutch stake in his exposé and, by extension, of William and his legacy of war and Barrier Treaty, the breach of which Barnivelt sees as the basic cipher of *The Rape of the*

Lock.[19] Between all this and Barnivelt's friendship with the High German Doctor, the allusion borders on impertinence before the very bench of appeal.

Associating the *Rape* with a rash of political allegories and fables, Barnivelt declares the Lock a figure of the Barrier Treaty and identifies Belinda as Great Britain (or Anne), the Baron as the Earl of Oxford, Clarissa as Lady Masham, Thalestris as the Duchess of Marlborough, and Sir Plume as Prince Eugene, all of which, and more, he demonstrates upon such grounds as the resemblance of the altar of French romances to Oxford's "Love of France" and of Sir Plume's "clouded Cane" to the "Ensign of a General." The sylphs and gnomes are "heads of Parties." Ariel, whose *"Azure Wand"* plainly stands for the ensign of the Treasury, is Oxford, and Ariel's position on the mast a figure of Oxford's presiding over the South Sea venture. Umbriel is associated with "some grave and worthy Minister," maliciously said to have given *"Belinda* the Spleen."[20] The inmates of the House of Spleen are those "called the *Whimsical,"* that is, the Hanoverian Tories, while the sylph cut in half is "undoubtedly ... my L[or]d To[*wnshen*]d," who signed the first Barrier Treaty. Shock is Sacheverell, who "awaken'd *Great Britain* with his *Tongue,"* and the "Steel" that "did the Labours of the Gods destroy" (III, 173 ff.) is Sir Richard, who urged the demolition of Dunkirk.

It is under "Episodes" that Barnivelt touches the sore spot. Sniffing the war in the game of omber, Marlborough in "mighty Pam, that Kings and Queens o'erthrew," and the Peace Council in the tea-table, he finally takes notice of the passage we have mentioned. According to Barnivelt, "That the Author here had an Eye to our modern Transactions, is very plain from an unguarded Stroke towards the End of this Game.

> *And now, as oft in some* distemper'd State,
> *On* one nice Trick *depends the gen'ral Fate.*

This observation is clearly not of a piece with the others Barnivelt has made. This one holds water, and that is why, I suspect, Pope led him to it. It is just possible that it was this couplet which prompted the *Key to the Lock* in the first place. Sensible of its vulnerability, especially in 1715, and of the liability of his other work to date, Pope may have decided the time had come to take the Scriblerian way out, dropping the couplet in the middle of much madness on either side in the hope of its being taken with the same grain of salt as the rest.

Among the madness on the other side are Barnivelt's popish findings, the Romish flavor in the machinery of guardian angels and patron saints; the allegory of the Mass, image-worship, and incense pots in the *Toilette*; the worship of the Cross; the identification of the "Lunar Sphere" as purgatory, and so on.

Like most Menippean narrators, Barnivelt damns himself and his cause at every turn, especially in his muddled thinking and zealotry. His self-incrimination is egregious: equating Belinda now with Anne (England), now with the Whore of Babylon; interpreting the descent of the Bodkin (= the British Scepter) as an "open Satyr upon *Hereditary Right*"; and explaining the stellification of the Lock as "the Old Barrier Treaty [turned] into a new and glorious *Peace*," to say nothing of what else we have observed of his ludicrous and self-defeating mentality. Though he serves Pope both in fun and in earnest, it is not improbably the latter with which Pope began. If so, the episode proves once again that where Pope is concerned politics as well as satire will have room where'er he writes.

iv. The Curll Lampoons

Curll first fell seriously afoul of Pope in 1716 with his publication of *Court Poems*, in which he implicated not only Pope but Gay and Lady Mary.[21] Offended on all scores, but particularly, it would appear, on behalf of Lady Mary, Pope took immediate revenge, administering an emetic by sleight and then publishing *A Full and True Account of a Horrid and Barbarous Revenge by Poison on the Body of Mr. Edmund Curll, Book-*

seller, With a faithful copy of his Last Will and Testament.
The *Full and True Account* is a high spirited scatalogical
takedown, beginning with a frank admission of Pope's part in
the episode and the reasons therefor. Lintot having invited
Curll to what we should now call a business luncheon, Pope
joined them on pretense of consulting with Lintot about the
Homer, contriving the while to slip an emetic into Curll's drink.
Upon his return home, Curll's wife, observing his color, asked
if he were sick, to which he replied, *"Bloody Sick,"* and fell to
vomiting and straining most desperately.

Believing his hour at hand, Curll sends for his partner to
help make his will. Praying forgiveness for new-titling old
books, falsely attributing others, publishing private quarrels,
and other offenses, he pleads at least impartiality in vilifying
political figures:

> I hope it will be considered, that if I have vilify'd his Grace the
> Duke of M[arlborou]gh, I have likewise aspers'd the late Duke of
> O[rmon]d; if I have abused the honourable Mr. W[alpo]le, I
> have also libell'd the late Lord B[olingbro]ke. (PW, p. 262)

All he has done, contends Curll, has been out of charity, "having made it wholly my Business to print for poor disconsolate
Authors, whom all other Booksellers refuse: Only God bless
Sir *Richard Bl[ackmo]re;* you know he takes no Copy Money."
Oldmixon having come in, Curll exclaims, *"Ah! Mr. Oldmixon . . . to what a Condition have your Works reduced me!
I die a Martyr to that unlucky Preface* [to *Court Poems*]. However . . . you shall have your Third Share . . . as was* stipu-
lated."[22] Turning then to his partner, Curll tells him he has
"several *Taking Title Pages"* that want only "Treatises to be
wrote to them," whereupon, falling into a fit of "Grippings,"
he sends for the Prayer Book. Reading somewhat,

> He clos'd the Book, fetch'd a Groan, and recommended to Mrs.
> *Curll* to give Forty Shillings to the Poor of the Parish of St. *Dun-
> stan's,* and a Week's Wages Advance to each of his Gentlemen
> Authors, with some small Gratuity in Particular to Mrs. *Cent-
> livre.* (PW, p. 265)

And thus he continued for some while until, of a sudden, he was relieved "by a plentiful foetid Stool, which obliged them all to retire out of the Room." Even so, according to the *Account,* Sir Richard Blackmore judges the poison still latent and certain to bring him down within the month.

Pope returned to the attack, not without added provocation, toward the end of the year with *A Further Account of the most Deplorable Condition of Mr. Edmund Curll.*[23] Since the first lampoon, Curll had published Pope's satiric verses on John Moore, "Author of the Celebrated Worm-Powder," a profane burlesque of the First Psalm, and had sponsored and published such libels on Pope as Oldmixon's *The Catholick Poet* and Dennis's *A True Character of Mr. Pope.* But what most excited resumption of the attack apparently was Curll's advertisement in *The Evening Post* of 15 September of *More Court Poems,* again implicating Lady Mary along with Pope himself.

The *Further Account* is a more elaborate and versatile piece than its predecessor, "a Three-Penny sticht Book," as its author says, by comparison with the "Sheet and half" that preceded it. Pope is warming to the sport and, as we shall see, touching base with politics again.

Curll is presented as having gone from bad to worse since his poisoning. From speaking civilly to his customers, saying his prayers, singeing a pig with a new purchased libel, and refusing two and nine pence for Sir Richard Blackmore's essays, he has begun "to *void his Excrements in his Bed, read* Rochester's *bawdy Poems to his Wife,* [give] *Oldmixon* a *slap* on the *Chops,* and wou'd have kiss'd Mr. *Pemberton's* A—*by Violence.*" At last his wife is driven to bespeak prayers for him at various churches and finally to write to Mr. Lintot.

Her husband's condition, she reports, "is the greatest Adversity that ever befel [him] since he lost *one Testicle* at School by the bite of a black Boar." Should he die, she wonders how she would ever dispose of his stock. After more in the same vein, she says she hears her husband's cane upon the counter and so must give over and "put his Son out of the way for fear of Mischief."

The narrative resuming, we are told that Curll, in a *"lucid Interval,"* sent a summons to his authors with a Bill of Directions how to find them, as for example,

> At the Bedsted and Bolster, a Musick House in *Morefields,* two Translators in a Bed together.
> At a Blacksmith's Shop in the *Friars,* a Pindarick Writer [Ambrose Philips] in red Stockings.

Others include Curll's "best Writer against *reveal'd Religion,"* his *"Index-maker,"* and an "old Beetle-brow'd Critick" in the Mint, almost certainly Dennis. These gentlemen being gathered, in no great spirit of charity one for the other, Curll addresses them from his close-stool:

> *"Whores* and *Authors* must be paid beforehand to put them in good Humour; therefore here is half a Crown a piece for you to drink your own Healths, and Confusion to Mr. *Addison,* and all other successful Writers.
> "Ah Gentlemen! What have I not done, what have I not suffer'd, rather than the World should be depriv'd of your Lucubrations? I have taken involuntary Purges, I have been vomited, three Times have I been can'd, once was I hunted, twice was my Head broke by a Grenadier, twice was I toss'd in a Blanket; I have had Boxes on the Ear, Slaps on the Chops; I have been frighted, pump'd, kick'd, slander'd and beshitten. ——— I hope, Gentlemen, you are all convinc'd that this Author of Mr. *Lintott's* [Pope] could mean nothing else but starving you by poisoning me. It remains for us to consult the best and speediest Methods of Revenge." (*PW*, pp. 280–81)

Out of this "great consult" (the passage suggests Milton as well as Swift) comes a series of Resolutions, as that

> . . . towards the Libelling of the said Mr. *Pope,* there be a Summ employ'd not exceeding Six Pounds Sixteen Shillings and Nine Pence (not including Advertisements.)
> . . . he has on Purpose in several Passages perverted the true ancient *Heathen* Sense of *Homer,* for the more effectual Propagation of the *Popish* Religion.
> . . . the Printing of *Homer's* Battles at this Juncture, has been the Occasion of all the Disturbances of this Kingdom.
> . . . Mr. *Barnivelt* be invited to be a Member of this Society, in order to make further Discoveries.

And so on, to various effect, not the least interesting of which, for our purposes, being the resumption of the strategy of *A Key to the Lock* with respect to Pope's political posture.

This business dispatched, and the authors having given parting advice how to drive the "*Pope* out of his *Belly*," a pile of essays falls suddenly upon the bookseller's head, whereupon, having involuntarily committed a natural atrocity upon the essays, he falls to railing at his books:

> Now *G—d damn* all *Folio's Quarto's, Octavo's and Duodecimo's!* ungrateful Varlets that you are, who have so long taken up my House without paying for your Lodging? . . . And have I not . . . sent you into the World with the Names of *Persons of Quality?* . . . Damn ye . . . *Rags ye were, and to Rags ye shall return.* . . . To my Shop at *Tunbridge* ye shall go, by *G—* and thence be drawn like the rest of your Predecessors, bit by bit, to the *Passage-House:* For in this present Emotion of my Bowels, how do I compassionate those who have great need, and nothing to wipe their Breech with? (*PW,* pp. 284–85)

At which, recalling his own unfinished business, the poor fellow "abated of his Fury, and with Great Gravity" wiped his own breech with the "unfinish'd Sheets of the Conduct of the E[arl] of N[ottingha]m."

Here endeth the *Further Account.* But Pope was not done yet. Norman Ault makes a good case for dating his next lampoon in early April 1720, though the only surviving text dates from 1732.[24] This, Pope's last word to Curll in prose, is *A Strange but True Relation How Edmund Curll . . . was converted from the Christian Religion . . . And how he was circumsis'd,* and so forth. It too may have been provoked by another Curllian advertisement reflecting on Lady Mary. It certainly carries the revenge to its crudest extremity, though it begins humorously enough, with illustrations out of the history of avarice and its wretched consequences (for example, Scylla, who "shot *Alcibiades* the Senator with a Pistol, and robb'd him of several *Bank Bills* and *Chequer Notes*"), after which, says the author, is it any wonder that "Mr. *Edmund Curll* the Stationer, should renounce the *Christian Religion* for the *Mammon* of Unrighteousness"?

The story tells how Curll, fallen in with the Jews out of envy, found himself importuned by them to convert, promising him many benefits and citing examples of their greatness in such persons as Solomon and David. Having thought all along that these were "*Roman Catholicks,*" Curll at first resisted, but when the Jews offered, if he would poison his wife and give up pork, to marry him to a wealthy Jewess, they began to make "some Impression on him." Little by little Curll bartered away his faith until, save for giving up black-pudding (sausage) and being circumcised, he was "a perfect Jew." The details of the surgical consummation of his conversion are best left to Pope, but they make for high farce and Rabelaisian laughter. The *Relation* concludes with a prayer for protection against avarice, which sooner or later draws all "*into the cruel Clutches of* Satan, Papists, Jews, and Stock-jobbers."[25]

v. *God's Revenge and a Clue to the Non-Juror*

God's Revenge against Punning (1716), which Sherburn explicitly lists among the "holiday efforts," is now well established in the Popeian canon. It is a slight piece, printed on both sides of a single sheet, and aimed at showing the "*miserable Fates*" of those addicted to the crying sin of punning. Citing divine judgments on the English sins of the past—the Plague, Fire, playhouse bawdy, and, after "Whoring and Popery were driven hence by the Happy *Revolution,*" Socinianism, Arianism, and Whistonism—the author (none other than J. Baker, Knt.) points to the latest evil, "more Epidemical, and of consequence more Fatal" than all the others, to wit, "the woful Practice of PUNNING," for which, as a deterrent, he offers examples of "God's Revenge against *Punsters.*" There are first off, in the words of the Curllean advertisement of "*Pope on the Stool of Repentance,*"[26] three "*Noble and Illustrious Patriots*" who fell into one or another misfortune—a "wry'd Nose," the "Displeasure of [an] Aged Grandmother," and a "*Dalilah*"— for their flagitious punning.[27] The list goes on to include, among others, *Eustace* Esq., probably Budgell; *Daniel Button* of the Whig coffeehouse, who for punning was (in pun upon pun) "depriv'd of all his Wits"; "Divers eminent Clergymen of . . . *Cambridge* . . . [become]great Drunkards and Tories"; and a *Devonshire* wit (Gay), who, for punning, fell from his horse "and broke his Snuff-box and Neck."

God's Revenge is short if not sweet, and were it not for its naming of names could scarcely have excited the interest it did at the time. For us its chief interest is in the evidence it affords of Pope's continuing asides on popery, the Revolution, Whiggery and the Buttonians, Tories, and, perhaps, the introduction of the Hervey family into the ken of Popeian satiric notice.[28]

Early in 1718, apparently in requital of some lines Cibber had smuggled into the role of Bays in a revival of *The Rehearsal*,[29] Pope published *A Clue to the Comedy of the Non-Juror*, a squib *à la* Barnivelt on Cibber's adaptation of Molière's *Tartuffe*. Pope's reprisal, as Sherburn says, is "ingenious," but it is neither so witty nor so lively as some of Pope's other prose frolics. It does, however, maintain the political glance, harking to the *Key to the Lock* in parodic design.

The *Clue* is addressed as a letter to Nicholas Rowe, purporting to oblige his request that the writer set down on paper certain hints he had conveyed earlier in conversation. In essence the letter charges that *The Non-Juror* is Bangorian in drift and hence anti-Anglican establishment. According to the epistolist, Dr. Wolf (Tartuffe) represents not only a Presbyterian, but a Bishop, who, though protesting a "great Zeal for the *Church*," is clearly busy about its betrayal, as Sir John Woodvil's son, the colonel, makes plain when he tells his father that "*Tho' I have always honour'd your Concern for the Church, I little thought it was for a Church that is Establish'd no where,*" that is, as the commentator says, "*No visible Church.*" In further evidence the epistolist points out that Dr. Wolf argues against tediousness in prayer and "pretends a mighty Regard to *tender Consciences.*" The political drift of the doctor's machinations is apparent in his reply to the colonel's objection of the constitution to the doctor's way of thinking: *"there may come a Time,"* replies the doctor, *"when this Constitution you talk so much of, may be overturned."* On top of all this, the doctor turns out to be a Jesuit. Well, this prelatical Jesuit and his "Gang" set out to "contrive the *Ruin*" of the Woodvil family, as the epistolist demonstrates from certain episodes in the play, including that in which Dr. Wolf tries to bring Sir John *"into a Scheme of Church Comprehension."*

The writer concludes by remarking, as an afterthought, the poor English of the dialogue in the play, scarce any of the characters talking "at all like *English Folks;* but perpetually [making] use of an uncorrect, *Foreign, Jargon.* What his drift is in this [says the epistolist] I cannot imagine."

Pope no doubt took more pleasure and comfort in all this than we do, for whom it is likely to be more durable as a record of Pope's satire and politics than anything else.

We need say nothing of Pope's hand, whatever it was, in such fairly uninspiring and unpolitical pieces as *Stradling versus Stiles,* a parody of legalese probably the work, or at least suggestion, of Pope's friend Fortescue; or of the *Memoirs of P. P. Clerk of this Parish,* a somewhat heavyhanded spoof between Pope and Gay on Bishop Burnet. Nor is it necessary to add anything to what has been said in passing of Pope's collaboration with Gay and Arbuthnot in *Three Hours after Marriage* (1717), satirizing such targets as Woodward the antiquarian, Dennis (Sir Tremendous), just possibly Cibber, the Countess of Winchelsea or Susanna Centlivre, and who knows what others.

For all its unevenness Pope's prose satire deserves better than it has enjoyed at the hands of Prince Posterity. Though sometimes labored and meager of fancy, it is on the whole witty, vigorous, and satirically imaginative. If it is occasionally smutty, it is, at its best, facetious and eminently comic. As for politics, though that does not loom, it is, characteristically, always lurking. The prose satire shows Pope still countering, and discrediting by *argumentum ad personam*, those busy at tarring him with Catholic and Jacobitical sympathies; taking pot shots at the Buttonian cabal; baiting, as well as subtly petitioning, Hanover; and dropping names both Whig and Tory with serio-comic mixture of motive.

VIII

DEEP WHIMSIES

·

BETWEEN 1711 and the last volume of the Pope-Swift *Miscellanies* (1727), besides all else he was doing, Pope was busy about a variety of occasional verse now unfortunately relegated to the dustbin of minor poems, though indifferent in neither literary nor other interest. Most of these pieces touch, in one way or another, upon the political motive, either as that relates to the Catholic or Jacobitical issue, the Buttonian conspiracy, or the Whig and Tory showdown. Of two dealing with the Sex, only one is politically oriented and that facetiously. These we may consider first and then the others, in the order named.

The *Epilogue to Jane Shore,* composed sometime before the performance of the play in February 1713, though it addresses the Sex essentially in the patronizing style then popular in prologues and epilogues, manages in at least one instance something better, a foretaste of the sophistication and discernment of *To a Lady:*

> There are, 'tis true, who tell another tale,
> That virtuous ladies envy while they rail;
> Such rage without betrays the fire within;
> In some close corner of the soul, they sin:
> Still hoarding up, most scandalously nice,
> Amidst their virtues, a reserve of vice.
> The godly dame who fleshly failings damns,
> Scolds with her maid, or with her chaplain crams.
> Wou'd you enjoy soft nights and solid dinners?
> Faith, gallants, board with saints, and bed with sinners.[1]

This is the cutting edge and psychological insight of another satirist than the author of *The Rape of the Lock*. "In some close corner of the soul, they sin" is as consummate Pope as one could seek.

Pope brings the ladies to politics in a breezy lampoon on the maids of honor at Court, published (on the connivance of Curll) in 1717. Pope never acknowledged the *Court Ballad*, but it is unquestionably his, and would probably have done him no harm had he chosen to own it.[2] Perhaps he felt there were those who might attach a sinister construction to his references to the Townshend-Sunderland quarrel, the Prince's household in Leicester Square, the King's return from Hanover, and standing armies, though the last is plainly a bawdy pun:

> And thus fair Maids, my ballad ends,
> God send the K. safe landing,
> And make all honest ladies friends,
> To Armies that are Standing.
> Preserve the Limits of these nations,
> And take off Ladies Limitations.
>> With a fa.

This may be as casual as Pope ever was on the subject of Court and politics. He is certainly not casual in the pieces that follow.

Though he does not much advert to the issue of Catholicism in these poems, when he does so it is with a soberness and Jacobitical candor that suggest the earnestness and concern with which he nearly always faced that question. His *Epitaph. On John Lord Caryll*, except for six lines adapted to the epitaph on Trumbull, was not published in Pope's lifetime. It reflects first, no doubt, Pope's friendship for Lord Caryll's nephew, John Caryll, but also, we may suppose, his readiness to pay tribute to (perhaps even to advertise) an exemplary Jacobite and at the same time say something, however implicit, about the Revolution. The elder Caryll had quitted England for France in 1689 and become Secretary of State to James II in exile, in which service he was granted his title. Pope's epitaph, probably written soon after the Earl's death in September 1711, has this to say of the old Jacobite's political and personal character:

> Honour unchang'd; a Principle profest;
> Fix'd to one side, but mod'rate to the rest;
> An honest Courtier, and a Patriot too;
> Just to his Prince, and to his Country true.

That these lines were subsequently transferred to Trumbull need not be taken to imply indifference of political import.[3] Both men served their prince and their country as loyalty dictated, and both were politically honorable and just; but the fact remains that as originally conceived the tribute was Jacobitical and the implications less than gloriously revolutionary.[4]

In 1713, perhaps at the instance of Harley, Pope turned his hand to the modernization of Donne. Though the performance is not otherwise remarkable, it does show Pope experimenting with the kind of thing he was to practice so effectively in the *Imitations of Horace* and touching base, as he could, with the Catholic issue. Canvassing corruptions in poetry and law alike, Donne's *Second Satire* would have commended itself to Pope at this juncture with or without encouragement from another.[5]

Pope follows the original closely enough, both in wording and sequence, though he does not hesitate occasionally to transpose lines and words, omit certain (mostly indelicate) expressions, and even to embellish. He clearly responded to, found useful, and so retained Donne's excuse for the sin of poetry and its perpetrators, which he expresses thus:

> ... poor, disarm'd and helpless is their State
> Like that of Papists, now not worth their Hate.[6]

He follows Donne closely on the various kinds of poetasters and may have carried over something from Donne's account of the parasite to his own (later) simile of the Westphaly hogs in the *Epilogue to the Satires*.[7] When the satire turns to law and its exemplar, Coscus, Pope in one instance at least rises above his occasion, improving upon Donne's account of the breeding of that professional:

Whom time, (which rots all, and makes botches pox,
And plodding on, must make a calf an ox)
Hath made a Lawyer . . . .

(Donne, vv. 41–43)

Whom ripening Time, that Turns a Clap to Pox
That plodding on must make a Calf an Ox
And brings all Natural Events to pass:
Has made of late a Lawyer of an Asse.

(Pope, vv. 53–56)

One change suggests Pope's alertness to the political expedi-
ent: the alteration of Donne's bastardy in Kings (v. 74) to bastardy in nobles (vv. 86–87). Donne's Elizabethan allusion
would have been pointless, even "un-Patriotic" in 1713, and
Pope would certainly not have cared to raise the question of
the Pretender's ("Perkin's") birthright.

He no doubt found it congenial to hold with Donne on the
desolation of the land and hospitality and opportune to make
Donne's conclusion more pointed:

. . . But my words none draws
Within the vast reach of th'huge Statutes jawes.

This Pope renders,

Thus much I've said, I trust without Offence;
And hopes no *captious Fools* will wrest my sense
Nor *sly Informer* watch my Words to draw
In the vast reach of our huge Statute Law.

(Italics mine)

The adaptation is interesting enough in itself, as evidence
of Pope's satiric regimen under still another master and of his
continuing sensitivity to church and state; but perhaps its
principal interest lies in its reflection, along with the Statius
and other works, of his early resort to satire under the cover
of translation or modernization.

In the active arena (so to speak) Pope was devoting not a
little attention to the Buttonians. Though the falling out between him and that company was immediately related to the
pastoral and Homeric wars, it is ultimately traceable, one sus-

136

pects, to political difference. Pope clearly found the conditions of Buttonian fellowship too costly in terms of self-esteem, and probably of politics as well, for he cannot have been unaware of the political implications of such association. When, on top of that, he found the literary welcome so guarded and grudging (for example, Addison's notice of the *Essay on Criticism* in *Spectator* 253), it is not surprising that he should take up instead with the more congenial, respectful, and less demanding company of the Scriblerian Tories. The rebuff, which the Buttonians would have interpreted politically as much as any other way, called for requital on their part. For one so gifted as Pope, this meant if not silencing at least discrediting. Hence the pastoral snub and the battle of the *Iliads*. Still, the Buttonians were careful not to publicize the political complaint, which fact may account for Pope's withholding it as well and conducting his counterattack on purely literary grounds. No one would have failed to perceive the political issue anyway, on either part.

Pope begins his campaign (in verse) with *The Three Gentle Shepherds*, composed, it would appear, in 1713, hard on the heels of the conspiracy of silence greeting his pastorals as against those of Philips. A ten-line squib, the *Shepherds* expresses Pope's contempt for the blandness of the Buttonian muse and his preference for frank and telling satire:

> Of *gentle Philips* will I ever sing,
> With *gentle Philips* shall the Vallies ring.
> My Numbers too for ever will I vary,
> With *gentle Budgell*, and with *gentle Carey*.
>
> . . . .
>
> May *Satire* ne'er befool ye, or beknave ye,
> And from all Wits that have a Knack Gad save ye.[8]

With the verses *To Eustace Budgell . . . On his Translation of the Characters of Theophrastus*, Pope turns to the Homeric front. Composed probably on the appearance of the translation (May 1714), the verses are a snigger at Budgell and the whole Buttonian fraternity, tracing Budgell's progress (regress) from sonneteering and essay writing to translation; having a fling at the "arrant Whig," Abel Boyer,[9] along with Gildon and Ozell; and then turning, by way of the Theophrastian characters, to the little Senate:

> For me, I think (in spite of Blunders)
> You may, with *Addison*, do wonders.
> But faith I fear, some Folks beside
> These *smart, new Characters* supplyd.
> The *honest Fellow out at Heels*
> Pray between Friends, was not that *Steel's*?
> The *Rustic Lout* so like a Brute,
> Was *Philips's* beyond Dispute.
> And the *fond Fop* so clean contrary,
> Tis plain, tis very plain, was *Cary*.
> Howe're the *Coxcomb's* thy own Merit,
> That thou hast done, with *Life* and *Spirit*.[10]

The confrontation of *Iliads* reached its public climax in 1715, when Pope published Books I–IV and Tickell his Book I. But it reached a private climax with Pope's composition (and presentation to Addison) of the Atticus portrait, one of three such pieces he wrote at the same time, though none was published until later. Of these, *Macer* is another hit at Philips along the lines already registered in *Guardian* 40, with a contemptuous nod at his fellows in the society of Button's. The first half of the sketch states the case:

> When simple *Macer*, now of high Renown,
> First sought a Poet's Fortune in the Town:
> 'Twas all th'Ambition his great Soul could feel,
> To wear red Stockings, and to dine with *St—*
> Some Ends of Verse his Betters might afford,
> And gave the harmless Fellow a good Word.
> Set up with these, he ventur'd on the Town,
> And in a borrow'd Play, out-did poor *Cr—n*.
> There he stopt short, nor since has writ a tittle,
> But has the Wit to make the most of little:
>
> .   .   .   .
>
> Now he begs Verse, and what he gets commends,
> Not of the Wits his Foes, but Fools his Friends.

Umbra, either Carey or Budgell, is of less certain attribution, especially so as it has the "constant Index to all *Button's* Wits" cozying up, not only to Addison, Steele, and Tickell, but to Pope and Rowe as well.[11] There is no question of course about the *Atticus* lines, which appear to have been sketched in the summer of 1715 and sent to Addison in the spring of the next year, with the result that a truce was called.[12] The portrait is essentially the same that eventually found its way into the *Epistle to Arbuthnot,* with the exception of one couplet, referring to the Homer, and omitted in the later version: "Who when two Wits on rival themes contest, / Approves them both, but likes the worst the best."[13]

Whether the Buttonians scrupulously observed the truce or not, Pope himself did not entirely give over. He pays his compliments to them again, along with some others, in what was at the time taken to be a scandalous piece popularly styled *The Worms.* Apparently in revenge for the episode of the emetic, Curll secured and published in 1716 Pope's *To Mr. John Moore, Author of the Celebrated Worm-Powder,* a satiric ballad on Moore's remedy in which Pope argues the futility of the cure in view of the epidemic nature of the disorder. After all, says the poet, "All Humankind are Worms," which he proceeds to prove by a series of comic illustrations. But the witticism backfired, and the poem was taken as a satire on mankind.

Actually it is no such piece of misanthropy at all. The closest thing to Timonism is its second stanza, which is well within the framework of traditional Christian argument:

> Man is a very Worm by Birth,
> Vile Reptile, weak, and vain!
> A while he crawls upon the Earth,
> Then shrinks to Earth again.

The rest of the poem is plainly facetious, as the fourth stanza illustrates:

> The Learn'd themselves we Book-Worms name;
> The Blockhead is a Slow-worm;
> The Nymph whose Tail is all on Flame
> Is aptly term'd a Glow-worm.

Fops are "painted Butterflies," misers are "Muckworms," "Silk-worms Beaus," and so on. Pope finally addresses Moore himself, declaring his remedy futile, since worms shall even get him in the end. Then comes the greeting to Button:

> Our Fate thou only can'st adjourn
> Some few short Years, no more!
> Ev'n *Button's* Wits to Worms shall turn,
> Who Maggots were before.

Only malice could have made a satire on mankind out of such an obvious piece of mischief.[14]

Sandys' Ghost, if it is Pope's, as seems probable,[15] has another go at the Buttonians by way of a take-off on the appeal by Garth and Tonson (late 1716?) for translators for an edition of the *Metaporphoses*. It pokes fun at Budgell, Carey, Philips, Tickell, and Addison, along with others non-Buttonian, including Pope himself. Scarcely marked by brilliance, its best level may be seen in this:

> Ho! Master *Sam*, quoth *Sandys'* Sprite,
> Write on, nor let me scare ye;
> Forsooth, if Rhymes fall in not right,
> To *Budgel* seek, or *Carey*.

With this, except for the Atticus lines, published without authority in 1722, along with some occasional Duncical notice, Pope too gives over the battle.

If the *Prologue to Cato* is not exactly a part of the Whig and Tory showdown, it looks in that direction. With it, as Pope told Caryll, he "was clapped into a stanch Whig sore against his will."[16] The play itself, as we know, was made the property of both parties, the Whigs associating it with their lost leader Marlborough, the Tories with lost political virtues. While Pope was obviously not at liberty to introduce overtly into the *Prologue* just any sentiments he might have liked, it may be that he was less than ingenuous in such lines as these:

> Tyrants no more their savage nature kept. (v. 7)
>
> And wild ambition well deserves its woe. (v. 12)
>
> Here tears shall flow from a more gen'rous cause,

Such tears, as Patriots shed for dying Laws:
He bids your breasts with ancient ardour rise,
And calls forth *Roman* drops from *British* eyes.

(vv. 13–16)

Addison was not inattentive to such a danger apparently,
though he may not everywhere have been as alert as he was in
the incident reported by Warburton, according to whom the
verse beginning "*Britons*, attend" (v. 37) originally read "*Britons*, arise," whereupon Addison, "frighten'd at so *daring an
expression*, which, he thought, squinted at rebellion, would
have it alter'd . . . to *attend*."[17] But no one could secure or ob-
serve univocacy on such an occasion as this, and it would not
have been impossible for the appropriate audience to take the
following—

Who sees him act, but envies ev'ry deed?
Who hears him groan, and does not wish to bleed?

—as a reference to the Oxford of Utrecht, Guiscard, and the
Bandbox Plot. But whatever the extent of Pope's equivocation
in the *Prologue,* he was in the thick of the *Cato* politics and not,
obviously, on the Whig side.

He was at liberty to be more forthright in the first of the
Two Chorus's to the Tragedy of Brutus, published in 1717 but
composed perhaps as early as 1715.[18] The following lines point
clearly to the political unrest of the times and throw out broad
hints of tyranny and fallen patriotism:

When *Athens* sinks by fates unjust,
When wild *Barbarians* spurn her dust;
Perhaps ev'n *Britain*'s utmost shore
Shall cease to blush with stranger's gore,
See arts her savage sons controul,
And *Athens* rising near the pole!
'Till some new Tyrant lifts his purple hand,
And civil madness tears them from the land.

Ye Gods! what justice rules the ball?
Freedom and Arts together fall;
Fools grant whate'er ambition craves,
And men, once ignorant, are slaves.
Oh curs'd effects of civil hate,

In every age, in every state!
Still, when the lust of tryant pow'r succeeds,
Some *Athens* perishes, some *Tully* bleeds.

This is a reprise, scarcely disguised, of the Norman William of
Windsor Forest, the Dutch William of the Revolution, and the
Hanoverian succession (now come to pass), with its aftermath
of partisan rancor and persecution. The immediacy of the allusion is confirmed in the lamentation, reminiscent of that in
the Statius, over the "curs'd effects of civil hate."

Perhaps no poem of Pope's has ever missed more wide of
the mark than his *Farewell to London In the Year 1715*, written
on the occasion of his departure for Binfield to resume the
Homer. Politically sensitive, unflattering to some of his friends,
and potentially embarrassing at home, the poem was evidently
for these reasons sharply restricted in circulation, only Gay,
Jervas, and Edward Harley being known to have possessed
copies.[19] It is a curious mixture of joviality, ribaldry, and de-
spondency, in which, it would appear, Pope was uncertain
whether to laugh or weep. It both is and is not, at any rate, the
"light-hearted" *jeu d'esprit* it has been described as being.[20]

Pope begins offhandedly enough, bidding farewell to the
"Dear, dam'd, distracting Town," with its fools, critics, and
harlots, who may now enjoy a remission of his intrusions. He
nods to such as Jervas, Lintot, Philips, et al. and bids

> Farewell *Arbuthnot's* Raillery
> On every learned Sot;
> And *Garth*, the best good Christian he,
> Altho' he knows it not.

"Why should I stay?" he asks, and gives answer both grave
and gay:

> . . . Both parties rage;
> My vixen Mistress squalls;
> The Wits in envious feuds engage;
> And *Homer* (damn him!) calls.

Art's *amateur*, he says, "lies cold and dead / In *Halifax's* Urn,"
but more than that

> My Friends, by Turns, my Friends confound,
>   Betray, and are betray'd . . . .

What follows—the mention of two sister actresses fallen on evil days—has been taken, unfortunately, as appositional to these lines. But the lines clearly refer to the Tory crisis, both intramural and at large: the last days of Anne, the breach between Oxford and Bolingbroke, the vindictiveness of the new Whig Parliament, Bolingbroke's flight to France, Swift's well-advertised plans for deserting the ministerial mess for Letcombe, Oxford's prospect of impeachment, and all the other distresses attendant upon the "Change of Scepters," including the emergence of the Whimsicals, or Hanoverian Tories, who may be glanced at more overtly later on.[21] The mention of the actresses may have been intended as a rally upon the sober truth or as a shelter in event of need, but they are not the friends by friends betrayed. The appositive to that is made evident in the beginning of the next stanza—"Why make I Friendships with the Great, / When I no Favour seek?"—though once again Pope turns the thought aside with pretense of rakish drift: "Or follow Girls Seven Hours in Eight?— / I need but once a Week." Pope's friends by friends betrayed are the late heads of state and probably others in the Tory debacle as well.

Pope then offers the well-known but perhaps imperfectly understood portrait of himself:

> Still idle, with a busy Air,
>   Deep Whimsies to contrive;
> The gayest Valetudinaire,
>   Most thinking Rake alive.

The tendency to focus on the last two lines of this sketch and to ignore the rest may account for the failure not only to grasp their significance, but that of the poem as a whole. Engaging as the portrait is, it is far from a witty trifle. The oxymoronic statement, which should be the clue, apparently has proved the stumbling block. Pope invokes it not as a token of wit but of mixed emotion and knitted brow, busy at sorting the disorder.

There is the possibility, in the oxymoron of the second line, that Pope is playing upon the "Whimsicalls," whose Tory intransigence Swift complained of in *Some Free Thoughts upon the Present State of Affairs*, begun before he left London at the end of May 1714 and completed at Letcombe, where Pope and Parnell visited him in July. If Pope was playing with that counter, it is not necessary to suppose that he had anything more in mind than jogging as many associations, favorable or unfavorable, as his friends could and would attach to it: the mismanagement of the late ministry, the disloyalty of the Whimsicals themselves, or the capriciousness of fortune in the matter of Anne. Or, it may be, he was hinting his own whimsical frame of mind at this juncture or advertising whimsies of political intent he was contemplating for himself in the days ahead. All such ideas could of course have been excited without the *Whimsical* association, but that something more than fancy was at work is given reinforcement by the stanza following:

> Solicitous for other Ends,
> Tho' fond of dear Repose;
> Careless or drowsy with my Friends,
> And frolick with my Foes.

The "other ends" undoubtedly included the Homer, but they almost certainly included more than that, as the adieu to "frolick" with the enemy implies. Even the Homer, for that matter, was not (as Pope would know) without deep whimsies of its own.

It should not go unnoticed, either, that in the *Farewell* Pope's glance is less at Hanover and Whiggery than at Toryism itself and its failure. The *Farewell* may, in fact, be its own deep whimsey—Pope's own Whimsicall defection, however brief, from faith in the Tory leadership. His disappointment on that score is evident throughout, in the rage of *both* parties, in the friends by friends betrayed, and in the question about his own friendship with the great. His willingness at the close to bid farewell to all but Gay, who, "sincere and free, / Loves all

Mankind, but flatters none," reads indeed like a final reproach to the Tory household besides.

Whatever else it may be, the *Farewell* is not a frolic. It is a studied mingle of playfulness and gloom—in the last analysis a testament of political disillusionment and wry self-summoning in the face of disarray. It is the early counterpart of the later and grimmer *One Thousand Seven Hundred and Forty*.

Pope did not remain downcast of course, or disaffected. His love of Harley and awe of Bolingbroke survived the shock of failure and flowered again with the hopes that, for a short time at least, still sprang eternal. By 1721 he was ready to advertise his loyalty to the first of these fallen leaders in a dedicatory *Epistle to Robert Earl of Oxford, and Earl Mortimer*, printed with his edition of Parnell's *Poems on Several Occasions*.[22] The *Epistle* was a magnanimous gesture at a time when it was less than prudent to speak in such terms of such a man. As Geoffrey Tillotson says, it "is as much a political article in a newspaper as a poem: if it is an epistle, it is also an 'open letter.' " And he cites Henry Gratton to the effect that for Pope to write such a letter required "courage." It certainly required courage to print it.[23]

Pope is explicit in declaring Oxford's greatness and his ill use at the hands of party, and though he stresses the fallen hero's personal virtues, he is at pains to associate those with the Scriblerian, and hence Tory, fellowship. For Parnell, says Pope, Harley oft had "bid the World attend,"

> Fond to forget the Statesman in the Friend;
> For *Swift* and him, despis'd the Farce of State,
> The sober Follies of the Wise and Great.[24]

"And sure," says Pope, speaking of the fall from power, impeachment, and imprisonment,

> . . . if ought below the Seats Divine
> Can touch Immortals, 'tis a Soul like thine:
> A Soul supreme, in each hard Instance try'd,
> Above all Pain, all Passion, and all Pride,
> The Rage of Pow'r, the Blast of publick Breath,
> The Lust of Lucre, and the Dread of Death.

Harley's retreat from public life is vain though, for

> The Muse attends [him] to the Silent Shade:
> 'Tis hers, the brave Man's latest Steps to trace,
> Re-judge his Acts, and dignify Disgrace.

The Muse of course is Pope, who thus dares openly to vindicate his friend's statesmanship and honor. Though others, ungrateful, desert him, the Muse—"No Hireling she, no Prostitute to Praise"—

> Ev'n now, observant of the parting Ray,
> Eyes the calm Sun-set of thy Various Day,
> Thro' Fortune's Cloud One truly Great can see,
> *Nor fears to tell,* that MORTIMER is He.
>   (Italics mine)

Pope would have occasion, and courage, to witness such loyalty again in the trial of Atterbury and in the publication of Buckingham's *Works*.

IX

EVEN HOMER NODS

·

IT SHOULD BE EVIDENT by now that Pope undertook almost no literary enterprise in perfect innocence. The rule would appear to hold for the Homer as much as for anything else. While there can be no question that Pope was drawn to the Greek poet out of admiration, a desire to make him memorable in English and by so doing find for himself a place in the Temple of Fame, we know too that he was motivated by the desire and need of means:

> ... (thanks to *Homer*) ... I live and thrive.

But while these incentives were primary, they did not, apparently, preclude another, which must have occurred to Pope soon enough, and that is the political. If Statius had proved so amenable to the uses of adversity, the Homer must have seemed uncommonly opportune. Pope did not fail, at any rate, to draw it as far as he could or dared into the orbit of English allusion.[1]

Except for the Catholic-Jacobitical charges of his contemporaries, this political exploitation of the translation seems by and large to have gone unnoticed, or at best to have been but partially apprehended. The contemporary notice began at least as early as *The High German Doctor* (1714) and continued through the *Homerides* of 1715 and 1716, Oldmixon's *The Catholick Poet*, Dennis's *A True Character of Mr. Pope* (1716) and *Remarks Upon Mr. Pope's Translation of Homer*

(1717), *Madame Dacier's Remarks Upon Mr. Pope's Account of Homer* (1724), and *Pope Alexander's Supremacy and Infallibility examin'd* (1729).[2]

Though they rarely troubled to spell it out, Pope's contemporaries busied themselves alleging a political motive the actual extent of which, it is likely, even they did not perceive. Still, the assumption was rife. Subsequent students of Pope have been content to let the supposition pass, perhaps on the presumption, not altogether groundless, that the allegations were prompted by envy and spite, and not therefore to be credited. In the last quarter century, criticism of the Homer has concentrated its attention, by no means improperly, on the task of rehabilitating its reputation as a work of art. Douglas Knight has examined the question with much insight in *Pope and the Heroic Tradition*, though he concludes, with respect to the subject of the present inquiry, that Pope's *Iliad* is his "only nonsatiric narration of any length."[3] Although Reuben Brower is aware of Pope's moral, philosophical, and theological adaptation of Homer, he does not extend his notice to politics or indicate any awareness of political allusion.[4] More recently H. A. Mason has examined, both acutely and quixotically, Pope's success in catching the "nature" of Homer, but the closest he comes to the political question is in remarking that "Pope has made Agamemnon resemble a coarser Louis Quatorze rather than an Achaean chieftain."[5]

The prologomena of Maynard Mack and others to the Twickenham edition of Pope's Homer (1967) reveal an important, if somewhat tentative, advance in the modern awareness of the political dimension. Professor Mack speaks of Pope's desire to make Homer "contemporaneous and exemplary to the age, [to] use him (consciously or unconsciously) as an Ajax's shield under whose vast authority war might be waged on forces that deprecated poetic imagination and poetic worth." He sees certain bendings to accommodate Pope's own ethical, social, domestic, and personal sensibilities, though he tends to associate these with the spirit of the later Pope, the Pope of the *Essay on Man* and the Horatian imitations. The "treasury of allusion" discussed later by Professor Mack points, with little exception, backwards and forwards in literary, not political, directions. Professor Mack relates the Vice Triumphant passage of the *Epilogue to the Satires* to the memories of Hector's fate and the "intimations of the doom of England mirrored in the doom of Troy"; the seas of voyage and fields of battle of Achilles and Patroclus to the seas and fields ironically alleged of George II in the *Epistle to Augustus;* and the covetousness of Phoenops to the fate of Atossa and the Duke of Marlborough. Of the latter Professor Mack says, in his most explicit observation on political allusion, "it is possible that the Phoenops of the English Homer owes something to its creator's politics." Finally, he speaks briefly of the common ground of epic and satire in the defense of civilization against barbarism, but again he points the observation to Pope's later career.[6]

Norman Callan, discussing Pope's Greek and the learning available to him, reiterates the point that it "is his sense of the immediate relevance of the Homeric poems to his own day that gives Pope's translations their great urgency" and that Pope's was "an age where the dividing line between politics, religion, and social behaviour was almost non-existent." He adds, in connection with what he calls the translator's "diplomatic renderings," that Pope "often with remarkable brilliance, goes out of his way to embody two or more meanings in his translation of a passage." But he makes scant use of these insights as far as political allusion goes, remarking only Dennis's failure to recognize Pope's adaptation of Drydenian *murmur* for the expression of "political dissent" and Pope's tendency in adapting Homer to summon "the political consciousness of Juvenal (or, in this case, Horace) and all the perfectionist thinking of political satire since."[7]

William Frost, writing of Pope's English predecessors in translation, speaks of the "political lessons" that "can and have been deduced from the misfortunes of the Greeks after their leaders fall to quarreling among themselves" and remarks that "Pope writes a humanistic study of social, political, military, and psychological stress, rather than a religious or devotional epic," but says nothing further of either. Professor Knight, whose monograph has been mentioned already, writes that part of the introduction dealing with the literary achievement of the translation and, not surprisingly therefore, remarks of the political issue only "the preoccupation of Pope and Dryden with major problems of civic and personal order."[8]

Robert Fagles treats of the *Odyssey* and, though he does not come to particulars, gives perhaps the most discerning account of the political aspect of Pope's Homer. "While he worked at Homer," Professor Fagles observes,

> the subjects of his correspondence shuttled between a writer's problems and those of a citizen in "this miserable age . . . so sunk between animosities of party and those of religion . . . ." Faced with this situation, Pope made translation one of his main lines of defence. Swift saw in it "an Art where Faction has nothing to do"; he even envied Pope for what seemed his freedom from public controversy. But Pope saw something deeper: a way of serving society, open to one "deny'd all Posts of Profit or of Trust", by holding before it, under the prestigious name of Homer, all that it might yet be . . . . (TE, VII, ccxx)

Pope's Postscript to the *Odyssey*, says Professor Fagles,

> will summarize his strategy with Homer. Extending the *Iliad* and *Odyssey* beyond poetry and criticism to legislate ordered values to every aspect of his threatened society, Pope made translation a political act.[9]

But even Professor Fagles is content to take *political* in the *polite*, or philosophical, rather than practical sense, and so says nothing of Pope's application of his high argument to the facts of the English political scene.

It is my purpose to suggest how Pope specifically and in terms of real politics made of his translation "a political act." To have undertaken the whole would amount to a monograph in itself, and so I have limited the examination to a sampling, principally of the *Iliad*, taking one book from each of the five volumes of that translation and one (the last) from the translation of the *Odyssey*.[10] I would not pretend, even within those limits, to have exhausted the political allusion—am sure in fact that I have not—but I have tried to respect the danger Professor Mack remarked when he spoke of the difficulty (he says *impossibility*) of being sure "whether the tracks one thinks one sees are the poet's footprints or one's own."[11]

On that score perhaps some preliminary earnest and a caveat would be in order. Of the footprints I have taken to be Pope's I have tested them against the evidence of the Greek and of the translations in English up to Pope.[12] As for the caveat, insofar as my findings point to allegorical strategy in the allusion, they must be understood not to imply, nor to argue, anything like sustained, consistent, or point-by-point allegory. Anyone at all acquainted with Homer will recognize the impossibility of such a feat even if one were inclined to venture for it. The best Pope could hope for by way of specific allusion was occasion, and that of course is a variable as far as the story line goes. Even so, as Pope found, in Homer's house are many mansions in which to domicile English men and events, and he occupied as many of these as lent themselves to his purposes, even if it did mean changing address from time to time.

One final word. The burden of allusion in the Homer is essentially what it has been all along—Pope's once and future kings—though weighted now more on the Hanoverian than the Williamite side, and pointing more consistently to the Whig-Tory agon of roughly 1714–23 than heretofore or elsewhere. There is, not surprisingly in view of what has been said already, a variation in the density of allusion from book to book, but the glance is never wanting, nor the argument ever given over.

i. *Iliad* I (1715)

Two motifs dominate the allusion in Book I of the *Iliad*—kingship as tyranny and the poet (seer) as the public or social conscience in protest. Along with these are less recurrent, but no less apparent, allusions to lost leaders and better days. As in

Homer, Agamemnon is the villain of the piece, Achilles the injured and resentful hero, Calchas and Nestor the voices of reconciliation and comity. Pope is at pains to make the situation and the characters as much English as Greek—to suggest the Whig-Hanoverian stripping and humiliation of the Tory ministry and to reproach that policy in the names of reason and justice.

The principal clue to the royal indictment lies in the epithets Pope applies to Agamemnon, most conspicuously *tyrant*, but others as well. Agamemnon is nowhere I believe called tyrant in the Greek, though he is called very nearly everything else hateful. Pope's application of the epithet is not, I believe, simply to be attributed to change of linguistic habit in the post-Homeric world, or to prosodic considerations, but to his own disposition, abetted by Dryden and Mainwaring, to see certain kings under that rubric. Thus his Agamemnon repulses Chryses "with kingly Pride," where the Greek simply says, "yet the thing pleased not the heart of Agamemnon, son of Atreus, but he sent him away harshly, and laid upon him a stern command."[13] His Achilles addresses Agamemnon as "Insatiate King," where in the Greek he is styled "Most glorious son of Atreus, . . . most covetous of . . . men."[14]

The word *tyrant* first comes into play in vv. 161–62, along with a repetition of the idea of avarice or greed: "But to resume whate'er thy Av'rice craves, / (That trick of Tyrants) may be born by Slaves." Again the Greek is innocent: "it were not meet to gather these things back from the folk" (τὰ δέδασται, / λαοὺς δ' οὐκ ἐπέοικε παλίλλογα ταῦτ' ἐπαγείρειν. I, 125–26). Pope's alone among the various versions of this passage employs the word *tyrant* or associates avarice with it, though Pope follows Dryden, as Wakefield has noted, in associating the tolerance of tyranny with slavery.[15] To the extent that the avarice may also be considered English in glance, it may be so in reference to the confiscatory policies of William and the taxation under him and his German counterpart.

In addition to *tyrant*, which, with little or no textual authority, he uses on four other occasions in the first book,[16] Pope applies other expressions derogatory of royalty that are equally English in flavor. These—prompted in part, it would appear, by Dryden and, to a lesser extent, Mainwaring—include "a Monarch's Claim," "our Royal Pleasure," "Fraud, unworthy of a Royal Mind," "proud Monarch," "proud King," and "a Monarch's Right."[17] Agamemnon hurls the charge on Achilles when he bids him "Rule thy own Realms with arbitrary Sway," warning Achilles that he will rue the day he "stoodst a Rival of Imperial Pow'r." Pope is solely responsible for the language of these last two descriptions.[18]

Dennis, as we know, cited Agamemnon's claim "That Kings are subject to the Gods alone" as an instance of Pope's "Jacobitism,"[19] and, perverse as Dennis was, he may not have been altogether wide of the mark. Pope is certainly saying something other than Homer or his earlier translators, though it may be not so much a declaration of divine right as of royal obligation, something akin to what he had implied in the note—partly sermonic, partly ironic—to Homer's διοτρέφεων earlier in the same speech:

> In the Original it is Διοτρεφεῖς, or *nurst by Jove*. Homer often uses to call his Kings by such Epithets as Διογενεῖς, *born of the Gods*, or Διοτρεφεῖς, *bred by the Gods;* by which he points out to themselves, the Offices they were ordain'd for; and to their People, the Reverence that should be pay'd them. These Expressions are perfectly in the exalted Style of the Eastern Nations, and correspondent to those Places of holy Scripture where they are call'd *Gods*, and *the Sons of the most High*. (TE, VII, 98n)

Between this note and the verse Dennis suspected of Jacobitism there is more likely a lesson and an admonition for royalty newly incumbent. Pope might have been nearer to Jacobitical glance in putting the following in the mouth of Agamemnon: "What King can bear a Rival in his Sway?"—a question which has no real counterpart in any text preceding Pope's.[20]

As we see by Pope's note on διοτρέφεως, he is not only disposed to rebuke the misuses of kingship, but is given to appealing to the better instincts, if not the consciences, of royalty. The latter he may be doing when he has Nestor say, "Let Kings be just, and Sov'reign Pow'r preside." Again, Dryden may be the source: "Pow'r, self-restrain'd, the People best obey."[21] Some such idea as this may be all, in fact, that Pope had in mind in the passage that struck Dennis as smacking of Jacobitical intent.

Along with the royal glance and preachment, Pope manages to convey hints of domestic ills (factionalism), of a better day, and of the poet himself as gadfly. Though he is working well within the textual precedent, it is tempting to take his rendition of Nestor's remembrance of things past as a glance at the last four years of Anne: "A Godlike Race of Heroes once I knew, / Such, as no more these aged Eyes shall view!" Pope's eyes are not aged of course, but neither is he far enough along in the reign of George to suppose that he will ever see the likes of Harley, Bolingbroke, or Swift again.[22]

Jove's contempt for what I have called domestic ills is put in a noticeably contemporary way: "Ah why should *Jove* engage / In foreign Contests, and domestic Rage" (vv. 672–73). In the Greek Zeus complains that Thetis would propel him into domestic strife in the *household* sense, that is, with Hera, who already nags him for giving aid to the Trojans (I, 518–21). Chapman puts it essentially the same way, Ogilby skirts it, Hobbes repeats the husband-wife discomfort, and Dryden very nearly vulgarizes the nagging motif. Mainwaring's translation stops short of the passage, and OBO follows the others. Pope's "domestic Rage," on the other hand, especially when taken alongside the non-Homeric "foreign Contests," suggests more than Olympian household discord. It is a little early for it to point to Hanoverian household quarreling, but it could well allude to the partisan farce of state attendant on the accession of that house.[23]

Vulcan points to the same theme in his complaint:

> The wretched Quarrels of the mortal State
> Are far unworthy, Gods! of your Debate:
> Let Men their Days in senseless Strife employ,
> We, in eternal Peace and constant Joy.
>
> (vv. 742–45)

Pope noticeably sharpens the original, especially in the first and third lines,[24] and adds a note which may hint at his own designs while at the same time bidding for indulgence:

> This Quarrel of the Gods being come to its height, the Poet makes *Vulcan* interpose, who freely puts them in mind of Pleasure ... Homer had here his *Minerva* or *Wisdom* to interpose again, and every other Quality of the Mind resided in Heaven under the Appearance of some Deity: So that his introducing *Vulcan*, proceeded not from want of Choice, but an Insight into Nature. He knew that a Friend to Mirth often diverts or stops Quarrels, especially when he contrives to submit himself to the Laugh, and prevails on the angry to part in good Humour or in a Disposition to Friendship; when grave Representations are sometimes Reproaches, sometimes lengthen the Debate by occasioning Defences, and sometimes introduce new Parties into the Consequences of it.   (TE, VII, 122–23n)

Still, for all his circumspection, Pope is more at home in the role of gadfly—of censor or conscience—a part which he assumes early in the book. We see it first in the exchange between Calchas and Agamemnon. I must, says Calchas (bespeaking the protection of Achilles), declare what wisdom would conceal,

> And Truths, invidious to the Great, reveal.
> Bold is the Task, when Subjects grown too wise
> Instruct a Monarch where his error lies.
> (vv. 102–4)

These lines are not exactly Homeric or anything after Homer up to Pope. In the Greek, Calchas says, "methinks I shall make wroth a man who rules mightily over all the Argives, and whom the Achaeans obey. For mightier is a king, whenso he is wroth at a baser man." (I, 78–80). Chapman's Calchas bespeaks protection "because I well conceive / That he whose Empire governs all ... / ... will be mov'd, and find occasion of revenge." Ogilby's is more Machiavellian: "When Kings with meaner Persons are displeas'd, / Though for the time their Anger seems appeased, / Yet they within revengeful Rancour hide." Hobbes's Calchas also concentrates on the fear of revenge, though he says nothing of difference in rank.[25] Dryden, as usual, is nearer Pope:

> Plight first thy Faith [, Achilles] . . .
> To save me from those Ills, that may ensue.
> For I shall tell ungrateful Truths . . .
>
> . . . .
>
> And Sov'reigns ever jealous of their State,
> Forgive not those whom once they mark for Hate.
> (vv. 112–17)

Retribution is the burden in Mainwaring ("A Prince will be provok'd . . . / And still unequal is a Subject's Strife / Matched with a Monarch, who commands his Life"). OBO holds the line thus stretching from Homer: "for I shall utter disobliging Truths to him who holds the Reins of Government . . . An angry King is an unequal Match for any private Man."[26] While Pope does not depart from any of this in substance, he does so in emphasis: minimizing the elements of fear and disparity of rank, making his Calchas (that is, himself) more forthright and less apologetic, and, with Dryden and OBO, underscoring the issue of truth and instruction.[27]

Pope's Agamemnon collaborates in this turn when, in reply, he says, with little resemblance to the Greek:

> Augur accurst! denouncing Mischief still,
> Prophet of Plagues, forever boding Ill!
> Still must that Tongue some wounding Message bring,
> And still thy Priestly Pride provoke thy King?
> (vv.131–34)

In Homer it goes thus:

> Prophet of evil, never yet hast thou spoken to me the thing that is good; ever is evil dear to thy heart to prophesy, but a word of good hast thou never yet spoken, neither brought to pass.

Pope got his "Augur" from Dryden, but "accurst" and "King" are his own, by which he adds something to the image of royal displeasure in opposition. Ogilby may have furnished the "Mischief," which suits more nearly an annoyance Georgian and Whiggish than Atridean. "Plagues," which is entirely

Popeian, smacks of metaphor for foreign visitation on England's green and pleasant land. There is, however, another difference which suggests that Pope did not want to overplay the censor's role. He omits the charge, found in Homer, Chapman, Ogilby, and Mainwaring, of *delight* in ill boding. He would not have wished to have his role as counsellor imputed to motives dismissable or censurable as mere malice.[28]

Such a concern seems evident too in Agamemnon's next objection, a *charge* everywhere else, but in Pope a *question*, as if in invitation to the reader to look between the lines:

> For this are *Phoebus'* Oracles explor'd,
> To teach the *Greeks* to murmur at their Lord?
> (vv. 135–36)

Homer's Agamemnon says simply, "And now in the midst of the gathering of the Danaans thou utterest thy prophecies,"[29] to which he adds complaint of Calchas's attribution of their troubles to the wrath of Apollo. Chapman follows suit, as does Ogilby. Hobbes says nothing of Apollo, his Agamemnon complaining that Calchas blames *him* (compare OBO). Dryden and Mainwaring include both. Pope's version is the only one to speak of inciting discontent. Between this and his framing the complaint as question, it would seem evident that he is concerned with something beyond translation and that he means to be taken seriously.

In the first book Pope has in effect advertised the allusive dimension of his translation and defined the principal objects of its glance: vindictive kingship, partisan abuse, and the poet's role as historian, censor, mediator, and agitator all in one. Subsequent books repeat and add to these motifs.

ii. *Iliad* VIII (1716)

Book VIII describes the second battle between the Greeks and the Trojans, along with the efforts of Juno and Minerva to intervene in behalf of the former. Its introductory note signals the continuing allusive design:

> *Homer*, like most of the *Greeks*, is thought to have travell'd
> into *Ægypt*, and brought from the Priests there not only their
> Learning, but their manner of conveying it in Fables and Hiero-
> glyphicks. This is necessary to be consider'd by those who would
> thoroughly penetrate into the Beauty and Design of many Parts
> of this Author. For whoever reflects that this was the Mode of
> Learning in those Times, will make no doubt but there are sev-
> eral Mysteries both of Natural and Moral Philosophy involv'd in
> his Fictions, which otherwise in the literal Meaning appear too
> trivial or irrational; and it is but just, when these are not plain or
> immediately intelligible, to imagine that something of this kind
> may be hid under them.   (TE, VII, 394–95n)

Since Homeric allegory is a subject already touched upon, both
in the Preface and in Parnell's "Essay on Homer," it is hard
to imagine why Pope would repeat it here, especially without
reference to something specific, unless he felt the need, or desire, to alert his reader again to more than meets the eye.

The hieroglyph in this instance appears to be Pope's adaptation of the battle to the history of the Tory rout at the hands of
Hanover and the Whigs, with a foretelling of recovery in the
fullness of time. By that token, the Greeks become the Tories,
the Trojans the Whigs, and Jupiter (who favors the Trojans)
the Hanoverian monarch, not without resemblance at times
to his Trojan-Whiggish forebear, Cronos-William. Within that
framework Pope manages, not always without difficulty, to
work specific allusions to the ministerial crisis, to his own
role as Tory auxiliar, and to the subject of rebellion.

It is the first of these allusions that I had in mind when I
spoke of difficulty in connection with the allusive activity. Despite certain contextual problems, it is tempting to see the flee-
ing Ulysses (headed for ship) as Bolingbroke in flight from
Whig prosecution and possible execution. Such an inference is
not, obviously, without its awkwardness, not only because of
the imputation of cowardice, but because of Pope's note on
Diomedes's appeal to Ulysses, a note which raises the question
"whether *Ulysses* did not drop *Nestor* as one great minister
would do another, and fancy'd He should be the wise Man
when the other was gone?"[30] There is nothing as yet in the

annals of the new Whig ministry answerable to this aside, but there had been something in the Tory ministry. We know that Bolingbroke sought to "drop" Harley in the last days of Anne and that he regarded himself as the more qualified leader of the government. We know too that Swift was distressed and annoyed at the dissension between the two and that he must have communicated his sentiments to Pope, at Letcombe if not before. Unless, then, Pope's analogy was simply random, his note refers to Bolingbroke, and does the image of that statesman no very great honor. But even an allusion may bear more than meets the eye, and it is possible that Pope intended more than one commentary on Bolingbroke. He may well have meant to register a not especially soft impeachment of Bolingbroke's ministerial disloyalty and subsequent desertion (flight), while at the same time acknowledging the extenuating circumstances surrounding the latter and issuing a plea for his return,

> . . . [to] save from *Hector's* direful Rage
> The Glory of the *Greeks*, the *Pylian* Sage.
> (vv. 121–22)

One could then leave the matter at the rescue of Grecian glory and simply ignore the Pylian sage, though his exclusion, if we are on the right track at all, would only constitute another awkwardness and, what is more, run the risk of truncating Pope's dark conceit as well. According to the reading thus far, Nestor is already identified with Harley, an identification which in itself poses no problem—indeed fits perfectly—for Harley, whatever his faults, was (besides being at this juncture undoubtedly Pope's favorite) the most perceptive, deliberate, and judicious of all the Tory leaders, and he was, in addition, now in the Tower and in danger of his life.

The whole episode proves the futility of expecting, much less insisting upon, point-by-point analogy in Pope's allusions, for there are still problems under that rubric. For one thing, Bolingbroke could not return voluntarily even if he wanted to, and even if he could it is hard to imagine how he could rescue Harley, at least in the physical sense. For another, it is not easy to identify an English equivalent of Diomedes. It could hardly be Swift, who had left the scene himself. It could of course be Pope and doubtless is in part, but Pope figures later under a much more suitable guise. It might be better, if there is need to insist upon plenary equation, to think of Diomedes simply as "old England," or patriotism, or the Tory cause, now desperate. I do not believe, however, that such hard and fast thoroughness, and articulation, of allegorical reading is requisite for the perception and crediting of allusiveness in the medium of translation. It seems to me, for all the loose ends, that Pope is attempting in this episode something like a makeshift hieroglyph of Bolingbroke's flight, its culpability *and* its justification, the desire and need for his return, and meanwhile Harley's desolation in the absence of his one-time duumvir.

Whoever, if any but himself, Diomedes is—and he could, as I say, be the symbol of Tory desperation—he is advised by Nestor, who must now stand for common sense, to withdraw from the attempt at rescue in view of the odds against him:

> This Day, averse, the Sov'reign of the Skies
> Assists great *Hector,* and our Palm denies.
> Some other Sun may see the happier Hour,
> When *Greece* shall conquer by his heav'nly Pow'r.
> (vv. 171–74)

Here is Nestorian wisdom and, we may believe, Popeian hope— the consummation devoutly to be wished.

Who, then, is Hector? Surely not Townshend, the nominal head of the government at this time. Is he Walpole? Though the latter had not by this time achieved, or perhaps even approached, primacy in the government, he was not in 1715–16 inconsequential. He was First Lord of the Treasury and Chancellor of the Exchequer, and, though doomed to falter before he attained complete control, was well on his way to leadership. He was certainly foremost among those in hot pursuit of the Tory enemy. But again, specific identity need not be insisted upon. Hector, like Diomedes on the other side, may be no more allusively than the symbol of Whig vindictiveness. His exhortation of the Trojan warriors has about it a ring of partisan exultation and, if I read Pope's note aright, something of partisan overweening as well:

> Be mindful of the Wreaths your Arms have won,
> Your great Forefathers Glories, and your own.
> Heard ye the Voice of *Jove*? Success and Fame
> Await on *Troy*, on *Greece* eternal Shame.
>
> (vv. 212–15)

Pope's note to this excites suspicion:

> It was a noble and effectual manner of encouraging the Troops, by telling them that God was surely on their side: This, it seems, has been an ancient Practice, *as it has been used in modern Times by those who never read Homer.*   (TE, VII, 407n. Italics mine.)

Perhaps between the speech and the note upon it Pope is suggesting that the Whig victors might do well to reread their Homer, especially his version of it.

I have said that Pope figures in the hieroglyph under a part especially suited to him. That part is Teucer, the skillful archer, picking off the enemy from the safety of "the Telamonian Shield." Teucer's youth, his lesser stature, his darts, and his fighting from cover all fit and invite identification with Pope. The Telamonian shield is, by this token, Pope's translation and not just, we might add, that of the Homer, but of all the others from behind which Pope has already let fly his darts at the adversary: "Heaps . . . on Heaps, sad Trophies of his Art" (v. 335). Agamemnon's words to the young warrior seem especially applicable to Pope in the role he undoubtedly thought of himself as performing:

> Thus, always thus, thy early Worth be try'd.
> Thy brave Example shall retrieve our Host,
> Thy Country's Saviour, and thy Father's Boast.[31]

Teucer's reply is likewise noteworthy:

> . . . With Praise the rest inspire,
> Nor urge a Soul already fill'd with fire.
>
> (vv. 355–56)

Neither Homer nor the earlier translators say anything of inspiring others, and Pope is more distinct than any of them in his description of Teucer's mood as "fill'd with fire."

Teucer goes on to complain of having failed to bring Hector down:

> ... sure some God denies me to destroy
> This Fury of the Field, this Dog of *Troy*.
> (vv. 363–64)

Again there is no Homeric or other authority for Pope's reference to divine frustration, and his note on "this Dog of *Troy*" is suggestive of a present as well as Grecian passion:

> This is literal from the *Greek*, and I have ventured it as no improper Expression of the Rage of *Teucer* for having been so often disappointed in his Aim, and of his Passion against that Enemy who had so long prevented all the Hopes of the *Grecians*.
> (TE, VII, 414n)

Though less certain and more nearly random, allusion elsewhere in the book cannot be dismissed as a likelihood. Hector's pursuit of the retreating Greeks—leaving "many a Chief ... gasping on the Ground" (v. 414)—could well invite another glance at the Tory rout, especially in view of the fact that "chief" does not appear in the Greek or any of the earlier translations. A different version of the same thing may have been intended in Pope's wording of Juno's lament to Minerva:

> What Numbers fell! what Numbers yet shall fall!
> What Pow'r Divine shall *Hector's* Wrath asswage?
> Still swells the Slaughter, and still grows the Rage![32]

Minerva's complaint thereafter that Jupiter is ungrateful ("Forgets my Service and deserv'd Reward," v. 440) has the ring of Tory protest, and with Minerva's javelin, which "Proud Tyrants humbles" (v. 475), we are back to Pope's favorite epithet for kingship. He introduces it again in v. 575 and speaks, a few lines on, of Jove's "unmeasured Hate."[33]

Pope seems even to have found occasion to broach the issue of rebellion, in connection with the attempt by Juno and Mi-

nerva to thwart the will of Jove. Hobbes and OBO alone afford
precedence for his wording of Jove's rebuke:

My Light'ning these Rebellious shall confound.
(v. 494)

But even Hobbes and OBO are not this explicit, speaking only
in the infinitive form—against a father "to rebel" (Hobbes, v.
374; OBO, II, 208–9). In Homer, Chapman, and Ogilby, Jove
threatens his thunderbolt or lightning, but says nothing of rebellion or rebelling. The same is true of the repetition of his
threat in Iris's conveyance of it to Juno and Minerva.[34] When
later (v. 596) Pope returns to the expression—"With all thy
Rebel Force"—it is without precedent whatsoever. If Pope's
use of the term is allusive, we may be sure that his intention
was not to incite, but to discourage, such rebellions as that attempted in the Fifteen and still reverberating in stern reprisal.

iii. *Iliad* IX (1717)

In Book IX the Council of the Greeks and the embassy to
Achilles afford renewed opportunity for allusion to English
agony and injustice, the lecturing of kings and parties, and the
hinting of the poet's own emotions and role in what is past, or
passing, or to come. It may be useful to begin with the latter,
where Pope understudies, so to speak, the roles now of Ulysses,
now of Diomedes.

In the embassy to Achilles, Ulysses says, in terms that seem
more Popeian than Odyssean,

Heav'ns! how my Country's Woes distract my Mind!
(v. 316)

In Homer, who is followed by the other translators, the emotion expressed is not *distraction*, nor even love of country, but
fear, fear for the plight of the Achaeans waging war in Ilium.
Earlier, in the Council of the Greeks, Nestor had spoken to

Diomedes, who had just reproached Agamemnon for suggesting that the Greeks give up and retire. "Kings thou canst blame," says Nestor,

> . . . a bold, but prudent Youth;
> And blame ev'n Kings with praise, because with Truth.
>
> (vv. 79–80)

Neither Homer nor any of the translators save OBO says anything of *blame*, but only of counsel or advice; nor do any but OBO speak of boldness on the part of Diomedes. It is not improbable that Pope took advantage of OBO to suggest in this fashion his own courage and justness in satiric address to his own king.[35]

Along the same line should be counted Nestor's later words to the Council:

> Wise, weighty Counsels aid a State distrest,
> And such a Monarch as can chuse the best.
>
> (vv. 101–2)

What gives this its Popeian look is the "State distrest," which is found in none of the sources, including Homer.[36] The reasons for advice and counsel are certainly more English than Greek:

> Our Wealth, our People, and our Glory lost.
>
> (v. 30)

In Homer, Chapman, and Hobbes the reason is simply the loss of men; Ogilby and OBO do not translate the passage. Pope's "Wealth" is most likely a reference to the costliness of Williamite and Whig-supported wars, but it may also be a glance at the taxation imposed to subsidize those wars. The "Glory lost" would be that of Anne, especially her four last years.

With the Nestorian counsel the Popeian role begins to merge with the generalized allusive pattern, though Pope as an actor in the drama is never entirely absent, especially in the lecturing function. We see the thin partition in Nestor's reference (v. 144) to Achilles, which admits of Harleian interpretation:

You [Agamemnon] wrong'd the Man, by Men and Gods admir'd.

Pope has added nothing to the Greek or English history of this remonstrance; but falling as it does in the midst of allusion before and after, it is not difficult to feel the tremor of English intent.[37] The same is true of the handling of Nestor's rebuke of him who would promote dissension among his own people:

> Curs'd is the Man, and void of Law and Right,
> Unworthy Property, unworthy Light,
> Unfit for publick Rule, or private Care;
> That Wretch, that Monster, who delights in War:
> Whose Lust is Murder, and whose horrid Joy,
> To tear his Country, and his Kind destroy!
>
> (vv. 87–92)

Nowhere perhaps is Pope more visibly exercised in rendering the Greek, in intensifying and elaborating the Homeric statement:

> A clanless, lawless, hearthless man is he that
> loveth dread strife among his own folk.
>
> ἀφρήτωρ ἀθέμιστος ἀνέστιός ἐστιν ἐκεῖνος
> ὃς πολέμου ἔραται ἐπιδημίου ὀκρυόεντος.
>
> (vv. 63–64)

All the translators, it is true, except possibly Hobbes and Ogilby, respond to the Nestorian outburst, but none so much as Pope, whose verses fairly quiver with outrage and whose note, borrowed conveniently from Eustathius, all but forces the impression of English provocation:

> This Passage is translated with Liberty, for the Original comprizes a great deal in a very few Words . . . ; it will be proper to give a particular Explication of each . . . ἀφρήτωρ, says *Eustathius,* signifies one who is a Vagabond or Foreigner . . . . ᾿Αθέμιστος is one who had forfeited all Title to be protected by the Laws of his Country. ᾿Ανέστιος, one that has no Habitation, or rather one that was not permitted to partake of any Family Sacrifice.
>
> (TE, VII, 436n)

"Foreigner" is the most palpable of the clues to English glance, though it is not necessary to limit its application to George I, whom it fits less in the warmongering aspect than William. Otherwise—as sponsor of civil discord—George fits as well or better. There is no reason of course why the allusion cannot be thought to extend as well to those in ministerial place who would, and did, encourage strife among their own countrymen.[38]

The kingly reference continues under the rubric familiar from Books I and VIII. The epithet *tyrant*, again applied to Agamemnon, reappears in three places, all without precedent.[39] Even bolder is Pope's "stupid Prince" (v. 492), which in the Greek and the translations is either "him" or "he." Such kings, says Pope's Achilles, "Stand but as Slaves before a noble Mind" (v. 495). The idea of "slave" may have been appropriated (by way of alibi) from OBO, but the "noble Mind" is Pope's alone.[40] Again, the note is significant:

> The Words in the *Greek* are, *I despise him as a Carian*. The *Carians* were People of *Bœotia*, the first that sold their Valour, and were ready to fight for any that gave them their Pay. This was look'd upon as the vilest of Actions in those heroical Ages. I think there is at present but one Nation in the World distinguish'd for this Practice, who are ready to prostitute their Hands to kill for the highest Bidder.   (TE, VII, 456n)

Pope's modern mercenaries have to be German and his note therefore nothing short of an open sneer at the royal family. This is one of the most remarkable of all instances of Pope's boldness in political statement, Homeric or otherwise.

But he has not done yet. "Deceiv'd for once," says his Achilles, sounding the once-and-future motif, "I trust not Kings again" (v. 455). Inferential at best in the Greek, this statement (except for its "Kings") is a patchwork from Ogilby, Hobbes, and OBO.[41] Wakefield spotted it and made a perceptive observation: "Homer . . . says nothing about *kings* here: and it is observable with what eagerness our translator on every occasion, both in this version and in his original poetry, went out of his way to fall on *kings* . . . . This was the devotion of *popery* to the *Stuart* line."[42] But Wakefield missed another, and even bolder, Stuart glance: Achilles's statement to the Greek emissaries that, before an alliance "with a Tyrant's Race," he would prefer to rest

Content with just hereditary Sway (v. 521)

—what Homer and the earlier translators had called simply his patrimony.[43] Here, if ever, Pope proclaims his disdain of foreign tyrants and his allegiance to hereditary monarchy.

iv. *Iliad* XVI (1718)

Though the least allusive of the books we have made trial of, Book XVI is not devoid of political aside. It begins early on, in fact, with Patroclus's first speech to Achilles, appealing for succor of the stricken Greeks:

> Lo! ev'ry Chief that might her Fate prevent,
> Lies pierc'd with Wounds, and bleeding in his Tent.
> (vv. 33–34)

Pope's use of *chief* for warrior or hero, along with the reference to *fate*—both of which, wanting precedent here as elsewhere, we have already found tendentious—suggests a continuation of the English glance.[44] That this is likely is given added color by Patroclus's reference to the suffering of the Greeks as "More for their Country's Wounds, than for their own" (v. 37), a patriotic wording wholly without authority in any source.[45]

Still another allusion shifts the burden of reference to Hanover and the Whigs. Patroclus speaks now not in patriotism but in prophecy:

> ... Men unborn, and Ages yet behind,
> Shall curse that fierce, that unforgiving Mind.
> (vv. 44–45)

Wakefield (IV, 95n) styles the first verse an "explanatory amplification ... extremely happy and well timed," but does not say why he thinks it so. I suspect it, along with the verse following, a *political* amplification, intended as an admonishment to Hanover and the Whig avengers of the consequences of their punitive policies. It is true of course that Oxford was acquitted and released from the Tower in August of 1717, but

Bolingbroke was still in exile and the spirit of Whiggish rancor still very much alive.[46]

Pope resumes too the epithet *tyrant.* Achilles, speaking to Patroclus, complains of "The Tyrant's Pride" (v. 71), adding, significantly, "I made him Tyrant; gave him Pow'r to wrong / Ev'n me . . ." (vv. 74–75). Homer's Achilles speaks, in the first instance, only of "a man" (ἀνήρ, v. 53) who has wronged him; the second instance has no counterpart at all in Homer and only oblique precedent in translation.[47] We are accustomed to Pope's calling his kings tyrants, but Achilles's complaint that he *made* Agamemnon tyrant is reminiscent of Pope's following Dryden in turning the blame in the Statius on the people. Here the blame is placed in the aristocratic lap and may be intended to recall not only the invitation to William but the Act of Settlement as well, which created the "tyranny" of Hanover.

Another verse suspect for want of precedent occurs in Achilles's exhortation to Patroclus to "Arm, e'er the *Grecians* be no more a Name" (v. 159). Lacking authority, Greek or English, the exhortation suggests an opposition call to arms, lest the cause be lost forever.[48]

Finally, the note to v. 466 ff., describing the Jovian torrent sent to rescue Hector, reads like still another hint of Pope's allusive design:

> This is one, among a thousand Instances, of *Homer's* indirect and oblique manner of introducing moral Sentences and Instructions. . . . I must do a noble *English* Poet [Denham] the justice to observe, that it is this particular Art that is the very distinguishing Excellence of *Cooper's-Hill,* throughout which, the Descriptions of Places, and Images rais'd by the Poet, are still tending to some Hint, or leading into some Reflection, upon moral Life or political Institution . . . . (TE, VIII, 261n)

v. *Iliad* xxiv (1720)

Book XXIV again illustrates the impossibility, for Pope as well as for his tracker, of forcing Homer into straitjacket allegory or allusive docility. The shift of sympathy to the Trojans in this book puts Pope, at least for a time, in the position of investing Achilles (and the Greeks) with the allusive reproach he had hitherto located elsewhere. Apollo, for example, complains to his fellow Olympians that Achilles, like a lion,

> . . . hastes to murder with a savage Joy,
> Invades around, and breaths but to destroy.
>
> (vv. 54–55)

Pope, as we have said, must take his opportunities where he finds them, and he may have done so in this instance. It is not the substance but the wording and the vehemence of Pope's rendition that make Apollo's description of Achilles suspect. William is the obvious candidate, though Pope would doubtless have no objection if Hanover came to mind as well. Pope alone, at any rate, invokes such expressions as "murder," "Invades," and "destroy." Homer compares Achilles to a lion bent upon a human "feast." Chapman softens the reference to "silly sheepe," Ogilby omits it altogether, and Hobbes changes it to "cattle." OBO alone turns to a bitterness of moral reproach resembling Pope's, and it is possible that Pope—if he was indeed up to something—counted on that to justify (or even pale by comparison) his own wording.[49]

The Hanoverian implication is perhaps more nearly conjured in the lamentation of Hecuba (v. 253) for the loss of Hector and her other sons to the wrath of Achilles:

> So brave! so many fall'n! To calm his Rage.

Neither Homer nor any of the translators speaks of rage, but only of lost sons or children. But Achilles relents, as we know, and Pope may have taken advantage of that to bid for generosity in English Court and ministry. Jove himself says of Achilles:

> Some Thought there must be, in a Soul so brave,
> Some Sense of Duty, some Desire to save.
>
> (vv. 193–94)

By comparison with his sources, Pope's version has a noticeably petitionary tone and suggests appeal for clemency, perhaps with Bolingbroke especially in mind.[50] An even more striking example of this sort of thing occurs in Priam's invitation to Achilles to imagine *his* father beset with ills and without the protection of a son. Pope makes of the father's plight one of *exile*, a harsh turn of fate, of helplessness amidst strangers—a turnabout accountable only by supposing that he wants the passage to point to an English exile, Bolingbroke.[51]

The "better Day" that Pope as well as Priam hopes for is expressed in the same speech.[52] We may suppose that it was Pope's hope that the lesson of Achilles's compassion would carry itself to the tribunals of Georgian England, and that Bolingbroke, in the words of Hecuba, would come "Free, and a Hero, to the [English] Coast" (v. 949). Certainly the laments of Priam and Hecuba for their fallen son include expressions amenable to such an appeal. In Priam's petition to Achilles, the old King concludes by declaring that Hector had fallen "in his Country's Cause" (v. 621). For this Pope may have drawn somewhat on OBO, but he alone has distilled the heroism of Hector to something so patriotic as "his Country's Cause."[53] Hecuba had earlier gone even further and with even less dependence on precedent: Hector had fallen, Pope has her say, "a Hero in his Country's *Right*." This has no authority at all, Greek or otherwise.[54]

vi. *Odyssey* XXIV (1726)

We have already remarked Professor Fagles' comments on the larger political significance of Pope's *Odyssey* and Pope's own observation that the poem is "a moral and political work." It will not be amiss, before looking into the particulars of its political significance in Book XXIV, to cite Pope's note to Jove's disclosure of his will in vv. 552–53: "Since *Ulysses'* hand / Has slain the Suitors, heav'n shall bless the land." The design of the *Odyssey*, says Pope,

> is to shew virtue rewarded, and vice punish'd; here, to introduce this act of justice with greater solemnity, *Jupiter* is represented

giving his assent to it: "Let there be peace (says that Deity) but let justice be done, and the guilty punish'd;" the Reader must necessarily be satisfy'd with the equity of the cause of *Ulysses*, when he hears *Jupiter* himself directing in it. Besides, this conduct of *Homer* presents us with an excellent moral; it shews us that the Deity is the governour of human affairs, and arbiter of peace and war; as he directs, the scenes of blood are open'd or clos'd, and the words of *Homer* Διὸς δ' ἐτελείετο βουλή [*Illiad*, I, 5] may be apply'd to the *Odyssey* as well as the *Iliad*.   (TE, X, 374n)

The note is pregnant of point: reconciliation, or peace, but also justice ("virtue rewarded, and vice punished"), and the ultimate rulership of Heaven in the affairs of earth. Its principles are, I believe, meant to be understood as applicable to the world of Pope's England as much as to the world without end. Professor Mack has remarked the affinity of Bolingbroke with Ulysses (TE, VII, ccxxxiii–ccxxxiv). I believe Book XXIV of the *Oydssey* to be almost wholly an allusion to the return and pardon of Bolingbroke (1723): to the injustices done him (and Harley too, it may be), to his efforts to mount an opposition, to the kind of life befitting true nobility (the rural), and to the ratification of higher law and the prospect of peace in the restoration.

The explicit allusion may begin as early as Amphimedon's account of the story of Odysseus's return to Ithaca. Agamemnon, encountering Amphimedon in Hades, asks, "Say, for the publick did ye greatly fall?" (v. 139). The answer of course, to make Amphimedon's long story short, is *No*, that he died rather in the pursuit, along with other covetous suitors, of Odysseus's wife and kingdom.[55] Amphimedon's story opens a loose allegory of the Whigs (the suitors of power), their rivalry for position, failures already (compare the fall of Townshend), their confrontation by the returned Bolingbroke, and their baseness of motive in comparison with his. Amphimedon and the suitors did not fall in public service, but for private gain, unlike (Pope would seem to say) Bolingbroke, who fell "a Hero in his Country's Right."

Then came, in the fullness of their suit, Ulysses:

> Scorn'd by the young, forgotten by the old,
> Ill-us'd by all! to ev'ry wrong resign'd,
> Patient he suffer'd with a constant mind.
>
> (vv. 188–90)

This Odysseus may be something of a composite of Bolingbroke and Harley (the latter now dead, of course); but in the
story line it remains essentially the former, restored, it is true,
but still deprived and ill-used by the ministry.

Pope seems to introduce himself in the response of Achilles
to the narrative of Amphimedon. Enthralled with the story of
Penelope's faithfulness, he says,

> The Gods, to honour her fair fame, shall raise
> (Their great reward) a Poet in her praise.
>
> (vv. 224–25)

Only Ogilby specifies a poet, and he does so periphrastically
("Songs ... they shall write, / Shall Mortals ... ," p. 357).
Homer and the rest speak only of *song,* and that as if the affla-
tus of the gods. None speaks of the poet as the *reward* of the
gods. Pope's version could of course be a tribute to Homer, as
doubtless it is, but it might also be a tribute to himself.[56]

Homer made the transition from this to the Pope of Twickenham, but, more importantly, to the Bolingbroke of Dawley,
an easy one, moving as he does Odysseus to the farm of Laertes.
Here (vv. 234–68) is the example of agrarian nobility, of the
simple, hard-working life of the soil, a life—as opposed to that
of courts and courtiers—which Pope is at pains to see is not
overlooked by styling its noble farmer (Laertes) *king* and
kingly, designations appearing neither in Homer nor in the
translators.[57] Here, Pope seems to say, is the true kingly life
and work—such a life as he and Bolingbroke themselves led;
the life, in its way, of the Country Party.[58]

When Laertes, in response (vv. 326–28) to Odysseus's first
approaches, says,

> This is the land; but ah! thy gifts are lost,
> For godless men, and rude, possess the coast:
> Sunk is the glory of this once-fam'd shore!

the impression of English scene is further confirmed. Ithaca, we must remember, was also an island kingdom. Like it, moreover, England had fallen on evil days, its leader gone, and with him its former glory. In Georgian terms the account of Laertes points to a Whig regime of "godless," venal men and a loss of the old English virtues and repute. Pope alone styles the possessors of the island as "godless," and the island itself as "once-fam'd." Except for Ogilby, moreover, he is the only one to use language in any way calling attention to the country as an island.[59]

Pope's version of Odysseus's revelation of his identity to Laertes lends further credence to the suspicion that he is glancing at Bolingbroke's return. In Homer, Odysseus says,

> "Lo, father, I am here before thee, my very self, am that man of whom thou dost ask; I am come in the twentieth year to my native land."

> κεῖνος μέν τοι ὅδ' αὐτὸς ἐγώ, πάτερ. ὃν σὺ μεταλλᾷς, ἤλυθον εἰκοστῷ ἔτει ἐς πατρίδα γαῖαν.

> (vv. 321–22)

Pope retains the πατρίδα of Homer, omitted by the other translators, and draws into the announcement the surrounding Homeric context of grief and mourning expressed elsewhere in the Greek and not always included in the translations. But the principal clue lies in his use of the word *restored*:

> I, I am he; oh father rise! behold
> Thy son, with twenty winters now grown old;
> Thy son, so long desir'd, so long detain'd,
> Restor'd, and breathing in his native land.[60]

Pope is solely responsible, too, for the description "so long desir'd, so long detain'd," an account eminently suggestive of Bolingbroke's restoration.

When the story turns back to the Olympians for its close, Pope takes advantage of the opportunity to invoke Divine judgment and ratification of the English Odysseus and the English scene. Minerva opens this aspect with her question to Jove:

Oh Pow'r supreme, oh ruler of the whole!
Say, hast thou doom'd to this divided state
Or peaceful amity, or stern debate?
Declare thy purpose; for thy will is Fate.

(vv. 543–46)

The sentiment would lend itself to Georgian reading without particular clue, but Pope's "divided state" is a palpable giveaway. It is reminiscent of like expressions of English purport in the Statius: "divided Pow'r," "divide, and . . . reverse the State," and "our unhappy State."[61] Homer's Minerva speaks only of war (πόλεμόν), Chapman's Pallas of "grave encounter," Ogilby's of "ling'ring War," and Hobbes's of "war."[62] There is nothing in the Greek or elsewhere about "stern debate," a circumstance which suggests allusion to Opposition politics and pamphlet warfare at home both before and in the prospect. We may suppose Pope would like nothing better than "peaceful amity," but he is acknowledging the realities of division and debate.[63]

Jove ratifies the conduct of Ulysses and decrees peace in the land:

. . . Since *Ulysses'* hand
Has slain the Suitors, heav'n shall bless the land.
None now the kindred of th'unjust shall own;
Forgot the slaughter'd brother, and the son:
Each future day increase of wealth shall bring,
And o'er the past, *Oblivion* stretch her wing.
Long shall *Ulysses* in his empire rest,
His people blessing, by his people blest.
Let all be peace. . . .

(vv. 552–60)

With the exception of the penultimate line, and the fiat-like quality of the last half line, Pope follows Homer and the translators closely enough.[64] While the passage still carries a Bolingbrokian significance, it is likely that Pope is now also appealing to the royal ear to let bygones be bygones, bless his people with peace, and so be blessed by them.

In fulfillment Minerva descends to Ithaca (where Odysseus, his father, and son are facing the foe in final combat) and delivers Jove's orders, whereupon the warriors cease their strife, and, in Dryden's significant verse, the "Willing nations knew their lawful Lord." That Pope chose to end his translation quoting Dryden's great political poem celebrating justness in the King, peace and tranquility in the land, may be his way of bespeaking amity on all sides, could be an appeal to present royalty to assume patriotic leadership (while at the same time stirring the ashes of hereditary rule), but it is certainly a sign of his political tenacity to the very end.

POSTSCRIPT

·

IF POPE LISPED in numbers, as he claimed, they were likely as not satiric. So at least the record from his boyhood suggests. Satire, it would not be too much to say, was his ruling passion from the start. That it took a literary and social turn in the early years comes perhaps as no surprise, even for those unaccustomed to thinking of that part of his career as especially satiric. That it also took a political turn is another matter, something hitherto little remarked, perhaps because it came so often disguised as something else.

The truth is, nonetheless, that the political impulse in Pope was deep set and tenacious, living along the line of almost everything he put to paper. Whether he liked it or not, it was something apparently that he could not deny. Its voicing was dangerous, especially for one of his persuasion, but he never shirked it, though he did, as we have seen, grow proficient in devising ways of undertaking it with impunity. Not that he always resorted to subterfuge: even in the early career he could speak out with a daring that staggers belief.

As a Catholic in a militantly Protestant society, Pope was more than commonly sensitive to the "Change of Scepters" impelled by that militancy and visited upon the whole of his early life. He was born in the year of a determined Protestant takeover, one which, though it fanned partisan and popular fear more than it engaged in outright persecution, was still profoundly traumatic for the beleaguered Catholic. The reign of

Anne proved at best an uneasy interlude, marred as it was by the death of the heir apparent and the Act of Settlement, raising again the spectre of alien rule and Catholic reprisal, to say nothing of the threat to the Tory leadership Pope had come to find politically and personally reassuring. His anxieties were realized on the death of Anne, the succession of Hanover, and the resurgence of a willful Whiggery. The years immediately following were exacerbated by the Fifteen and other Jacobitical disquiet, by the dispersal of his friends in the wake of the changeover, and by the punitive measures invoked against the Catholics. It was an awkward time at best, as Pope stood by to probe the ills and seek for signs of remission.

At no point in this drama was Pope idle in the appraisal of its politics, from the *Ode on Solitude,* written when "not twelve," to the last book of the *Odyssey,* published in 1726. The appraisal was not that of a political theorist—for he was none—but of a concerned and vulnerable observer, not unenlightened and not indifferent to issues transcending his own interests. By birth and breeding, to be sure, Pope was, if not at least a nominal Jacobite, certainly a Stuart loyalist. Whatever the shortcomings of that House (and he was not unaware of them) it was the most congenial to his needs and instincts. Though Anne was clearly his ideal, better a Stuart in any case than an unknown factor, especially an alien, more especially if a Protestant champion, and more especially still if a Whig appointment.

But Pope's loyalty to the House of Stuart was based on more than personal grounds; it was based on dynastic convictions and a deep distrust of interruption, violent or otherwise. Like Dryden, Pope had a strong sense of social and political continuity, as a principle as well as a preference. He was not a Hobbist in politics, but neither was he a Lockean, at least in respect to revolution and social contract. He would have thought of himself as a constitutional monarchist, entertaining the highest expectations of that office, freedom of conscience under it, national rather than partisan government, and as much liberty as is consonant with order; but he would never, I believe, have regarded default in any of these particulars as grounds for dissolution.

It is the latter no doubt which accounts for his acceptance of the Revolution as fact, however much he disapproved of it in principle, and for his rejection, on the other side, of militant Jacobitism. As much as he disliked the Williamite "usurpation" and the Hanoverian reversion, his political conviction, as well as instinct, was for peace and simple freedom. "In my politicks," as he said in a letter quoted earlier,

> I think no further than how to preserve the peace of life, in any government under which I live .... I hope ... all governments are so far of God, as they are rightly understood, and rightly administred: and where they are, or may be wrong, I leave it to God alone to mend or reform them .... In a word, the [thing] I have always wished to see [is] not a King of Whigs, or a King of Tories, but a King of England. Which God in his mercy grant his present Majesty [George I] may be, and all future Majesties!

If, as he said to Harcourt on the eve of his testimony in the Atterbury trial, "to be a Papist, be to hold any [tenets] that are averse to, or destructive of, the present Government, King, or Constitution; I am no Papist." For all the obvious prudence in these declarations, there is no reason to believe them basically insincere.

But of all the grievances Pope entertained against the politics of his day, none was more offensive to him than the development of parties. This as much as rape upon the Crown and foreign rule he deemed an affront to the political sensibility. That he tended to associate it more with the Whigs than the Tories is not necessarily an inconsistency, since it was the Whig, or republican, impulse that gave rise to the system in the first place. Whether rightly or not, Pope tended to see the Tories as representing not only the monarchical continuity but the older, national principle of government. There were, to be sure, times when he perceived them more realistically, but not until 1740 did he abandon the hope that Toryism would eventually rise above its own partisanship, achieve a truly "broad bottom," and restore patriotism to government.

As a thinker about politics Pope held these essential views, but as a satirist he had neither the opportunity nor the inclination to argue them systematically. In that role he simply adopted the adversarial posture and let passion as much as doctrine define his case, except of course when he chose to broach the quarrel by way of allusion. Even then, for that matter, he let the pathetic rather than the rational govern his address.

Pope had not the advantages of Dryden, who wrote under the patronage of monarchs he sought no more than to serve; he had not therefore at his disposal the luxury to reason and argue his political views. Pope grew up and spent his life under a disability that Dryden knew only in retirement from the political scene. Pope's once and future kings were adversaries and aliens, and his Whigs, unlike those of Dryden's political period, were triumphant. It is doubtful therefore that Pope was ever even disposed to debate his politics, as Dryden did; his circumstances required and invited something less academic than that. There was in his case no standoff to admit of parley; the offense had been consummated and reconsummated, and there was no hope of reversing it by theoretical argument.

Partly on that account, partly no doubt because it was his nature, Pope fought his politics rather than talking it, and like a fighter he carried mainly belligerence and cunning into the fray. One way or another, at any rate, as the principal of the convent school now occupying the site of Twitnam once said, Pope gave them "what for." And he did so from the beginning.

NOTES

•

CHAPTER I

1. "Notes on the Canon of Pope's Works, 1714–20," *The Manly Anniversary Studies in Language and Literature* (Chicago, 1923), p. 170, as quoted in Guerinot, p. xxx.

2. *Epistle* II. ii. 58–67. I quote Pope from *The Twickenham Edition of the Poems of Alexander Pope*. Pope was "Convict a Papist" too, of course. His very name, as Guerinot remarks (p. xxxi), "lent itself to an inevitable pun that never seemed to grow stale, a useful shorthand for reminding the reader that the monkey satirist was no true Englishman, no friend to the Glorious Revolution."

3. The story of the Catholic penal laws, though still imperfect of record, is a dense and tedious one. This necessarily abbreviated account, though drawing on many sources, is principally indebted to the following: Maude Dominica Petre, *The Ninth Lord Petre* (London: SPCK, 1928); David Mathew, *Catholicism in England*, 3rd ed. (London: 1936; rpt. Eyre & Spottiswoode, 1955); Anthony H. Forbes, "Faith and True Allegiance: The Law and the Internal Security of England, 1559–1714" (unpublished diss., Univ. of California at Los Angeles, 1960); M.D.R. Leys, *Catholics in England, 1559–1829: A Social History* (London: Longmans, 1961); Martin J. Havron, *The Catholics in Caroline England* (Stanford: Stanford Univ. Press, 1962); and John Miller, *Popery and Politics in England, 1660–1688* (Cambridge: Cambridge Univ. Press, 1973). For a rather lurid pro-Catholic account, with some undeniably shocking documents, see St. George Kieran Hyland, *A Century of Persecution* (New York: Dutton, 1920).

4. Penalties to like effect had been part of the legislation of 1571. The *missionaries* were the so-called "seminary priests," trained in the new English colleges in Douai (1568) and later in Rome, Rheins,

Valladolid, and Seville. The first seminary priests began returning for missionary work c. 1574.

5. This act, as Havron remarks (p. 6), began the "policy of treating recusancy as a fruitful source of revenue."

6. See Havron, p. 111; Mathew, p. 50, n. 1.

7. The Bye Plot, sometimes called the Surprise Plot, was a conspiracy (1603) to seize the person of James I and extort certain religious concessions.

8. The penalty for violation of this provision was £100. Detection of Catholics was encouraged by rewards of up to £50, and by forfeiture, to be given over to informants. See Leys, p. 60. By this law, too, the Five-Mile Act was revised to require the signature of four justices of the peace to validate travel beyond that limit. See Havron, p. 15.

9. Leys, p. 55.

10. See Miller, p. 55.

11. Miller, p. 8. Pope's father, it might be noted, was born the year after the storming of Basing House.

12. Miller, p. 9. Another act of sequestration was passed in 1648. It should also be noted that acts and ordinances of February and March 1643 and October 1644 provided for double taxation of papists and other (Anglican) "delinquents."

13. Forbes, p. 138.

14. The obduracy of irrational and vindictive anti-Catholicism is nowhere better illustrated than in the attribution of the Great Fire of London in 1666 to Catholic conspiracy. The monument erected in memorial of the event carried two inscriptions in Latin commemorating the rebuilding; a third, in English, was added in 1681: "This pillar was set up in perpetual remembrance of the most dreadful burning of this ancient city, begun and carried on by the treachery and malice of the Popish faction . . . in order to the carrying on their horrid plot for extirpating the Protestant religion and old English liberty, and introducing Popery and slavery." The inscription was removed in the reign of James II but was restored at the Revolution, where it remained until 1831. (See W.E.H. Lecky, *A History of England in the Eighteenth Century* [New York: D. Appleton, 1883], I, 296.) Some even blamed the Catholics for the Medway disaster of 1667. See Miller, p. 105.

15. See Sir George Clark, *The Later Stuarts, 1660–1714*, 2nd ed. (Oxford: Clarendon Press, 1965), p. 96. This act revealed that there were twenty-one Catholic peers of age prepared to be so deprived as recusants. Some of course temporized, i.e., converted. See Mathew, p. 102.

16. Baxter, p. 170. I am much indebted to Baxter for my account

of William. Perhaps it should be added that the Prince more than once received and entertained Monmouth during this critical period, though obviously not in Monmouth's interests.

17. Baxter, p. 220.

18. Lecky, I, 297.

19. Both acts provided for a declaration against transubstantiation as a means of detecting Roman Catholics. Informers, if accompanied by a constable, were authorized to search the premises of papists at any hour, day or night, for the possession of arms.

20. In 1696 a royal proclamation called for enforcement of the Ten-Mile Act. It might have been this proclamation and a call the next year for stricter enforcement of the penal statutes that led the Popes to move to Hammersmith and subsequently to Binfield. See Ch. II.

21. A similar act had been passed in 1705, but was reenacted now after the union with Scotland.

22. For this and the following instances of Catholic reprisal, see John Ashton, *Social Life in the Reign of Queen Anne* (London: Chatto & Windus, 1883), pp. 347–49.

23. An earlier churchwardens' presentment for Binfield, May 1701, reported as follows: "We present as Reputed Papists in our parish Allixander Poope gent. and his wife." *Early Career*, p. 36.

24. *Corr.*, I, 240. Pope had taken a like pose earlier, in a letter to Caryll 31 August 1713: "The welfare of 'em all [Caryll's family] is to me of much more importance, than to the Government that of all or any Branch of the most illustrious House of Hanover." (*Corr.*, I, 188–89) Swift and Pulteney struck similar poses after the fact: see *Corr.*, II, 65, 419, 444.

25. 16 August 1714: *Corr.*, I, 241–42. Pope later mentions the prospect of losing his horse to Edward Blount, another Catholic friend; speaks of standing "in some fear of a country justice"; and makes light of the prospect of being disarmed. See *Corr.*, I, 246.

26. Pope had already indicated his awareness of the risks in the mails. In a letter to Caryll 21 December 1712, he quotes Homer in English, "for Greek characters might possibly be taken for cyphers should this letter be intercepted by any zealously affected to the government." *Corr.*, I, 166.

27. Basil Williams, *The Whig Supremacy, 1714–1760*, 2nd ed. (Oxford: Clarendon Press, 1965), p. 185.

28. Lecky, I, 298–99. Lecky has conflated several laws, principally 11 and 12 Will. III, c. 4, and 1 Geo., I, Stat. 2, c. 13; 1 Geo. I. Stat. 2, c. 55, and 3 Geo. I, c. 18. The law requiring papists to register their lands was passed in June 1716, following the first uprising. Its title was "An Act for appointing Commissioners to inquire of the

estates of certain traitors, and of Popish recusants, and of estates given to superstitious uses, in order to raise money out of them severally for the use of the public!" The tax upon property in 1722/23 was assessed at one quarter of the capital value of the land (see Leys, p. 119). At the same time Catholics and nonjurors were subjected to what amounted to an indemnity tax of 5s. on the pound. (See Williams, p. 183.) In practice, the tax was applied only to Catholics and was justified on the grounds of the expense to the nation of the Jacobite uprising.

CHAPTER II

1. See Pope's letter to Wycherley 26 December 1704. *Corr.*, I, 2.
2. For details see *Early Career*, pp. 29–37.
3. Cf. *Early Career*, p. 302.
4. Francis Beauchesne Thornton, *Alexander Pope: Catholic Poet* (New York: Pellegrini & Cudahy, 1952), pp. 39–40. Pope's enlightened attitude toward his religion owes much, obviously, to examples like Erasmus, Pascal, and Montaigne, among others. As for Pope's early reading in Catholic literature, see his letter to Atterbury 20 November 1711, *Corr.* I, 453.
5. Thornton (p. 29) thinks it more than possible that penal surveillance might have played a part in Pope's removal from Twyford.
6. For the Mannock story, see Spence, 26.
7. *Corr.*, I, 198–201.
8. 8 November 1717. *Corr.*, I, 451.
9. 20 November 1717. *Corr.*, I, 453–54.
10. 1 December 1739. *Corr.*, IV, 207. For Brooke's letter see *ibid*, 198.
11. 1 September 1742. *Corr.*, IV, 416. Racine replied most apologetically. See *Corr.*, IV, 422–23.
12. *Corr.*, I, 238–39.
13. *Corr.*, I, 246–47.
14. *Corr.*, I, 300. For Pope's reply, see *ibid.*, 303–4.
15. *Corr.*, I, 308–9.
16. *Corr.*, I, 384–85.
17. See *Early Career*, pp. 228–29.
18. See Pope's letter, 20 February 1723. *Corr.*, II, 161 and n. 2.
19. *Corr.*, II, 171–72.
20. *Corr.*, II, 172–73. In June Pope wrote to Judith Cowper of "the Loss of part of my Fortune by a late Act of Parliament." *Corr.*, II, 174.
21. See *Corr.*, I, 340 and n. 2.
22. Thornton, p. 97.

23. Hooker, I, 415.
24. Guerinot, p. 40. With few exceptions all the listings here are based upon this valuable bibliography.
25. Guerinot, pp. 43, 45.
26. Guerinot, p. 53.
27. See *Corr.*, II, 157–58 and n.

CHAPTER III

1. For a rhetorical analysis of Pope's use of the *Poems on Affairs of State*, see the unpublished dissertation of Stephen A. Miller, "The Satiric Rhetoric of *Poems on Affairs of State, 1660–1704*" (Vanderbilt Univ., 1976).

2. Published under various titles from 1689 to 1716, the *Poems on Affairs of State* has been newly edited and published under that title in seven volumes by Yale Univ. Press from 1963 ff. It is this edition that I follow, using the abbreviation POAS. As for Pope's acquaintance with this material, it must be remembered that manuscripts were in extensive circulation during this period, and that many of these came to press as well. Pope owned at least one of the printed collections, *A New Collection of Poems Relating to State Affairs*, 1705. Just when he acquired it or at what time he annotated it cannot be said for certain, but, as W. J. Cameron notes, Pope "must have been familiar with the original series," i.e., dating from 1689. See "Pope's Annotations on "State Affairs' Poems," *N&Q*, 203 (1958), 291. See also Benjamin Boyce, "An Annotated Volume from Pope's Library," *idem*, pp. 55–57.

Though Pope would have had little opportunity of access to the Restoration court libels and lampoons not appearing in POAS, there is little in them he would have found amenable to his taste or use anyway. Of the thirty-three "most interesting and most representative" pieces printed by J. H. Wilson from the hundreds that have survived, only four are of a quality or subject that Pope, if he saw them, would have found impressive: *Utile Dulci* (1681; 6 MSS.), *Satire on Both Whigs and Tories* (1683; 4 MSS.), *Madam Le Croix* (1686; POAS 1705), and the *Satire on Bent[in]g* (1689; 2 MSS.). See John Harold Wilson, *Court Satires of the Restoration* (Ohio State Univ. Press, 1976).

3. POAS, V, 40–45. The ballad survives in two MSS. and in Maidment's *Pasquils*. See *idem*, p. 549.

4. Vv. 1–8, 51–52, 79–82, 97–98, 123–26, 131–33, 138–45. POAS, V, 47–54. Sixteen MSS. of the poem survive. For satires on Mary alone, again as Tullia, cf. *The Female Parricide* (1689) and *The Duchess of York's Ghost* (1691), POAS, V, 156–57, 298–302. For per-

sistence of the charge (against William) of betrayal and usurpation, see *A Conference Between King William and the Earl of Sunderland* (1700), POAS, VI, 215.

5. See POAS, V, 117 ff. The poem survives in seven MSS. See *idem*, p. 557.

6. See vv. 72–82. For the opposite view, with James as the butt, cf. *Lilli burlero* (1688), which its author, Thomas Wharton, boasted "sung a deluded prince out of three kingdoms." See POAS, IV, 309 ff.

7. Spence, 120, 475. For later pieces by Mainwaring, see POAS, VII.

8. POAS, V, 151. Though not hitherto published, the *Metamorphosis* survives in seventeen MSS. The engraving is reproduced in POAS.

9. POAS, V, 219. The poem survives in but three MSS.

10. Cf. e.g., his own complaint of Dutch-fostered atheism in the *Essay on Criticism*, vv. 543 ff.

11. POAS, V, 456–57.

12. POAS, V, 483–84. In the same edition of POAS (1703) Pope would have found Tom Brown's *A Prophecy Found in a Football* on the same subject and concluding, "Then England, I tell thee, thou art cursedly shamed; / 'Tis too late to repent—sin on and be damned." See *idem*, p. 487.

13. Vv. 15–18, 139 ad fin. POAS, VI, 12 ff. Cf. the portrait of William presiding over the ruins of English liberty with the triumph of Vice in the *Epilogue to the Satires*. Cf. vv. 137–38 ("Opprest with clamour, Truth and Justice flies, / And thus pursued, down-hunted Reason lies") with the conclusion of the *Dunciad*.

14. *The Mourners*, POAS, VI, 362–63. Pope might also have read Thomas Smith's *Upon Sorrel*, published in *The Observator* on 22 April 1702, and Defoe's *The Mock Mourners*, a defense of William published in the same year. See POAS, VI, 364–66, 372–97.

15. Vv. 7–8. POAS, VI, 453.

16. Vv. 95 ad fin. Cf. *Windsor Forest*, vv. 407–22. The Virgilian analogy, *Eclogue* IV, is not nearly so close to Pope's lines as those in *The Golden Age*.

17. Vv. 9–12, 19–23, 458–59, 486–89. See POAS, VI, 648 ff. The poem was reprinted in 1707 (POAS) and in 1709.

18. For Pope's early expression of the principle, see his letter to Atterbury quoted above, p. 25. Pope may have owed something of this view to Defoe as well. See below, p. 51.

19. See Pope's *Statius*, vv. 234 ff. Dryden of course had a hand in Pope's view of English political inconstancy and instability. See below, Ch. V.

20. Cf. "Th'according music of a well-mix'd state," v. 294. Dryden contributed to this concept too. See *Absalom and Achitophel*, vv. 753–810, 939–1025. Pope also knew and doubtless absorbed much from Shippen's *Moderation Display'd* (1704), which may have furnished him, in addition to political philosophy, with hints toward the *Duniciad*. See POAS, VII, 19–42.

21. Spence, 583. Pope's indictment of both Jameses must be understood as a judgment upon their ineptness, not upon their intentions or any disposition on their part to persecute for conscience. Their fault lay in playing into the hands of parliaments determined to root out popery and dissent.

22. *A Very Heroical Epistle in Answer to Ephelia* (1679), vv. 30–31. See POAS, I, 346; see also *The Complete Poems of John Wilmot*, ed. David M. Vieth, pp. 114, 204–5. Cf. Pope's *Epistle to a Lady*, vv. 241–42, dating from at least 1730.

23. *An Epistolary Essay from M. G. to O. B. upon their Mutual Poems* (1680), vv. 40–41, 69–70, 87–88. POAS, I, 350–51; Vieth, pp. 145–47, 214. Vieth uses a different copy text. Cf. Pope's *Essay on Criticism*, vv. 606–7, 1–18, and the 1713 version of *The Second Satire of Dr. Donne*, vv. 39–40 (TE, IV, 136).

24. *An Allusion to Horace* (1680), vv. 43, 90, 120–24. POAS, I, 360–63; Vieth, pp. 123–26, 207. Cf. Pope's *Ep*. II. i (Augustus), v. 85; *Essay on Criticism*, vv. 1–2, 657; and *Epistle to Arbuthnot*, vv. 135–46.

25. *My Lord All-Pride* (1697), vv. 6–12, 23. POAS, I, 414–15; Vieth, pp. 142–43, 213. Cf. Pope's *Essay on Criticism*, v. 601; the 1713 version of Donne's *Second Satire* (*loc. cit.*); *Epilogue to the Satires*, Dialogue ii, 171–80; and the *Dunciad*, v. 2. The "filthy Simile" of the Westphaly hogs in the *Epilogue* was earlier (Sherburn says 1715) given a more Rochesterian turn in a protodraft of the Atticus portrait. See *Early Career*, p. 146 and plate 3; also TE, IV, p. 323n.

26. Vv. 40–45, 72–81 (note also the "Cornus" of v. 92). The poem first appeared in print in *The Miscellaneous Works of His Grace, George, Late Duke of Buckingham* (1707). Seven MSS. survive. For the text see POAS, I, 364 ff. Cf. Pope's *Sat*. II. i. 41, 76; *Epilogue to the Satires*, ii, 1 ff., but esp. vv. 59–60, 157–67; *Epistle to Arbuthnot*, vv. 283–86, the "Cornus" of v. 25 and the *why write, why publish* of vv. 125, 135; and *Sat*. II. i. 42–44, 69. Where this particular Horatian satire is concerned, Scroope is decidedly closer to Pope than Horace is.

27. Vv. 7–8, 20, 71, 185, 266–67. POAS, I, 401 ff. Cf. Pope's *Ep*. II. i (*Augustus*), 241–62; *Essay on Criticism*, vv. 362–63, 599; *Epistle to a Lady*, v. 72; *Dunciad*, I, 63–64. Again, Dryden is involved, not

only as collaborator in Buckingham's poem but as critic in his own right. Pope would have read his *Discourse of Satire*.

28. V. 607. Cf. "the dregs and squeezings of his rage" in *Satires upon the Jesuits* (1679, 1681), II, 25. POAS, II, 34. For other possible commerce with Oldham, see below, Ch. VI.

29. Still, Pope apparently studied him early and closely. See Spence, 473n.

30. Vv. 60, 177. POAS, II, 82 ff. Cf. Pope's "Paternal Cell," *Ep.* II. ii. 59, and *Epistle to Arbuthnot*, v. 319. See also Caryll's*The Hypocrite*, POAS, II, 103–6.

31. POAS, VI, 158.

32. The *Pacificator*, except for being in verse, is much nearer the mood and manner of Swift's *The Battle of the Books*, though there can be no question of causal relationship either way. Defoe's account of wit and judgment ("sense") in vv. 355 ff. may well have said something to Pope's *Essay on Criticism*, vv. 82–83, and its psychological counterpart in the self-love and reason of the *Essay on Man*, II, 53 ff.

33. Ellis also associates the *Lent-Entertainment* with the *Dunciad*. See POAS, VI, 189.

34. Vv. 23, 52–53. POAS, VI, 202–5. Cf. Pope's *Epilogue to the Satires*, ii. 226 and *Ep.* II. i (*Augustus*), 385–87.

35. *The Art of Sinking in Poe*try, ed. Edna Leake Steeves (New York: King's Crown Press, 1952), pp. 38, 27, respectively.

36. See *The Dunciad Variorum*, ed. R. K. Root (Princeton: Princeton Univ. Press, 1929), I, 101 and n. Pope later (II, 139) includes Defoe in the tapestry depicting the martyrs of dullness: "Earless on high, stood un-abash'd Defoe."

37. Spence, 498.

38. Vv. 216–33. POAS, VI, 408–9. Pope would not have cared for the alexandrine. The *Reformation of Manners* abounds in portraits. To see how closely Defoe approaches the Popeian character, cf. the portraits in Shippen's *Moderation Display'd* (POAS, VII, 23 ff.).

39. Vv. 409–14. POAS, VI, 416. Cf. also "No Civil Government resents the Wrong; / But all are touch'd and angry at thy Song" (vv. 417–18) with Pope's "Safe from the Bar, the Pulpit, and the Throne, / Yet touch'd and sham'd by *Ridicule* alone" (*Epilogue to the Satires*, ii, 210–11).

40. Vv. 467–68, 479–80. Cf. Pope's *Cobham*, vv. 228–31; *To a Lady*, vv. 71 ff.

41. Vv. 865–72. POAS, VI, 434. Cf. *Essay on Criticism*, 440–45, 687–96; *Essay on Man*, III, 305–10 and passim. Cf. to Pope's Triumph of Vice (*Epilogue to the Satires*, I, 145 ff.) the following: "*Vice*

binds the Captive World in hostile Chains" (v. 908) and "While *Harlot Morgan* rides in Coach of State" (v. 1215).

42. See vv. 1044 ff. Defoe scores the *"vile Obscenity"* Pope singled out in the *Essay on Criticism* (v. 530); see vv. 1124 ff. and 1246–47.

43. Vv. 250–51, 305, 316, 439–40, 649, 911–12, 1060–61, 1298. For the poem, see POAS, VII, 72 ff.

44. Quoted in James Sutherland, *Defoe*, 2nd ed. (London: Methuen, 1950), p. 100.

45. Between their beginning, in 1689, and the *New Collection* (1705) owned by Pope, there were at least eighteen distinctive collections of state poems. Spence records this cryptic statement by Pope in 1733 or 1734: *"State Poems* proper, etc." To which Professor Osborn, in his edition of Spence, appends the following note: "Just what Pope may have considered the *Poems on Affairs of State* proper for is an enigma. Perhaps for the study of satire, in which their place in literary history has been much neglected before the Yale edition was undertaken." See Spence, 476 and n.

CHAPTER IV

1. Pope may have written "rhymes" before this, though no poems of which we have record. See Spence, 11, and Warburton's edition of *The Works of Alexander Pope* (London, 1751), IV, 18n. For the Twyford satire, see Spence, 15, 19, 20.

2. See the letter from "E. P." published by Curll in *Mr. Pope's Literary Correspondence* (1735), *Corr.*, III, 359–60. See also Spence, II, 609, appendix to entry No. 18.

3. TE, II, 233. Cf. Dryden's *To Sir Godfrey Kneller*, v. 94.

4. *The Garden and the City: Retirement and Politics in the Later Poetry of Pope* (Toronto: Univ. of Toronto Press, 1969).

5. *Epodon* II, v. 1.

6. For the variants, see *Minor Poems*, pp. 3–4 and notes. For the autograph date, cf. *Corr.*, I, 66 n. 2.

7. Sherburn, describing it as Pope's "first published satire," associates the poem with Pope's resentment of Settle's "anti-Catholic pamphleteering," his (i.e., Pope's) "hostility to the Hanoverian succession," and his "Jacobite tendencies." See *Early Career*, pp. 84, 99, 117. "Successio" is Pope's title for Settle's *Eusebia Triumphans, the Hanoverian Succession to the Imperial Crown of England*, 1702, reissued or re-edited five times between that date and 1711. See F. C. Brown, *Elkanah Settle* (Chicago: Univ. of Chicago Press, 1910), pp. 111–15.

8. See *Minor Poems*, p. 17n.

9. The autograph is reprinted in *Minor Poems*, pp. 463–64. A second MS., part of the Caryll papers in the British Museum, is reprinted and discussed briefly by Howard Erskine-Hill in "Alexander Pope at Fifteen: A New Manuscript," *RES*, n.s., 17 (1968), 268–77. The Caryll transcript differs from the autograph chiefly in accidentals, though there are a few minor substantive differences.

10. *Minor Poems*, p. 464. I should repeat that in quoting poetry I alter terminal punctuation at convenience.

11. Some of the refinement, it should be noted, took place as early as the Caryll transcript, which includes, e.g., "The Country Wit" and "The Courtier's Learning."

12. *Minor Poems*, p. 18. Originally the first line read, "Thou Cloak of Vice that hid'st the Rascals name." *Idem*, p. 464.

13. Stanza 13 of the autograph: *Minor Poems*, p. 464.

14. The peculation ("What Fav'rites gain," v. 35) is probably an allusion to Marlborough.

15. Revision seems to have gone forward to the end of 1707. See TE, I, 14, 37 ff. The *Pastorals* were published in 1709.

16. TE, I, 59n. In the MS. of the *Discourse on Pastoral Poetry* Pope added the names of Congreve, Southern, Sir H. Sheers, Wharton, Dorchester (Lady Mary's father), and Buckingham. See also "Who read Pope's *Pastorals?*" in Spence, II, 616–18.

17. See TE, I, 39–41, 69n. Pope himself declared the lines allusive to "ye Arms of Scotland & France." See "Alterations to the Pastorals," TE, I, 479.

18. J. R. Moore, "*Windsor Forest* and William III," *MLN*, 66 (1951), 451–54; rpt. in *Essential Articles for the Study of Alexander Pope*, ed. Maynard Mack, rev. ed. (Hamden, Conn.: Archon Books, 1968), pp. 242–46. For the Stuart-Tory "propaganda" in the poem, see TE, I, 137.

19. TE, I, 159n. Moore says the lines could be read "in a sense . . . hardly short of treasonable." *Essential Articles*, p. 245.

20. Moore, in *Essential Articles*, p. 245. Moore's statement of the political implications of *Windsor Forest* can hardly be improved upon. One might add to it however the resumption of the retirement-politics theme in vv. 235 ff., concluding "Such was the Life great *Scipio* once admir'd, / Thus *Atticus*, and *Trumbal* thus retir'd."

21. On Williamite heresies and impieties, cf. *Essay on Criticism*, vv. 544 ff., TE, I, 300 ff. and notes.

22. *January and May*, published 1709; *The Wife of Bath her Prologue*, published 1713 (dated 1714).

23. See vv. 80, 144, 310, 424–25, 816.

24. I quote Chaucer, here and elsewhere, from *The Complete*

Works of Geoffrey Chaucer, ed. F. N. Robinson (Boston: Houghton Mifflin, 1933), p. 142, vv. 1491 ff. The passage in Pope is vv. 156 ff.

25. The poem is not canonically certain, but I am inclined to follow Sherburn and Ault in supposing it Pope's. Pope himself apparently alludes to it as his in another verse *Letter to Cromwell,* 1708. See *Minor Poems,* pp. 24–29, 39–40.

26. Pope acknowledges this borrowing from Donne.

27. *Minor Poems,* pp. 39–40.

28. *Corr.,* I, 11.

29. *Ibid.,* p. 12.

30. *Ibid.,* pp. 31–32, 34.

31. *Ibid.,* p. 59.

32. *Ibid.,* p. 62.

33. Vv. 3–6. Cf. *The Rape of the Lock,* III, 5–6. The resemblance has not, I believe, been hitherto remarked.

34. Vv. 22–30. Cf. the arguments in *The Dunciad, Epistle to Burlington,* and *Sat.* II. ii ("Bethel's Sermon").

35. Presumably out of deference to Rowe this epigram was not printed until 1727 and was never expressly acknowledged by Pope. Pope delivered himself of at least four other epigrams on literary topics in his correspondence with Wycherley and Cromwell between 1708 and 1710. See *Minor Poems,* pp. 74–76.

36. "Memorial List of Departed Relations and Friends." See Spence, 75n.

37. *The Odyssey of Homer,* tr. Alexander Pope, ed. Gilbert Wakefield (London, 1806), IV, 339.

38. *Minor Poems,* p. 31n.

39. Cf. especially v. 27: "And Curs, Girls, Boys, and Scolds, in the deep Base are drown'd." *Minor Poems,* p. 44.

40. Warton first made the association; see TE, III–II, 49n. For the imitation, see *Minor Poems,* pp. 48–49.

41. *Minor Poems,* pp. 49–51. One is tempted to read into this life cycle the careeers of George I's mistresses, the Duchess of Kendal, the Countess of Darlington, and (perhaps) the Countess von Platen.

42. *Minor Poems,* p. 61.

43. *Minor Poems,* p. 68. For the group, see pp. 66–74.

44. *Minor Poems,* p. 74n.

45. See *Epistle to Dr. Arbuthnot,* vv. 340–41.

46. See *An Essay on Man,* IV, 391–92.

CHAPTER V

1. These correspond to vv. 178–99 and 224–442 of Pope's translation: the discord sown in the breasts of Eteocles and Polynices by

Tisiphone, the popular murmur over the plight of the Thebans, and the council of the gods. See *Corr.*, I, 36–38.

2. *Corr.*, I, 56.

3. *Spence*, p. 103.

4. *Ibid.*, n.

5. *Early Career*, p. 60.

6. Only the Elwin-Courthope editors appear to have suspected anything allusive in the Statius, and they only to the extent of the couplet beginning "New Lords they madly make" (vv. 228–29), which, they remark, "was interpolated by Pope, and seems to have been suggested by his hostility to the revolution of 1688." See *The Works of Alexander Pope*, ed. the Rev. Whitwell Elwin and W. J. Courthope (London, 1871), I, 61n.

7. I quote Statius from the Loeb edition with the translation by J. H. Mozley (London and New York, 1928). In translating I sometimes follow Mozley, sometimes not. For William's long-standing desire and scheming to rule England, see Baxter, Ch. XVII.

8. Stephens's translation was titled *The Five First Books of Publ. Papinius Statius his Thebais, Done into English Verse* (London, 1648). The corresponding passage in Stephens is I, 210–44; in Statius, I, 168–96. I quote Pope from the text in TE, I.

9. *Absalom and Achitophel*, vv. 45, 216–19. Cf. "Rascall Rabble" (579) and "fickle rout" (785); also vv. 61–66. I quote Dryden from *The Poems of John Dryden*, ed. James Kinsley (Oxford: Clarendon Press, 1958). Editors are fond of pointing out the parallels between Pope's Statius and Dryden's *Aeneid*, but no one so far as I know has remarked the influence of *Absalom and Achitophel* or *The Medal*. For the latter, cf. vv. 89–94 and 127–30.

10. The Drydenian turn is one of the clues to Pope's motive here and elsewhere in the translation, which was to draw Statius into the orbit of Stuart apologetics and anti-revolutionary polemic. Busy about the accuracy of the translation, Elwin and Courthope miss this point altogether. Statius, they tell us, does not "call the populace 'vile,' or say that they are always 'discontented,' or that they are 'still prone to change, though still the slaves of state.' Neither does he say that they 'are sure to hate the monarch they have,' but he says that their custom is to love his successor, which is a sentiment more in accordance with experience" (*Works*, ed. Elwin and Courthope, I, 61n.). Such a sentiment may be more in accord with the experience of Elwin and Courthope, but clearly not with that of Catholic Pope, or ruefully Jacobitical Pope, or anti-Williamite Pope.

11. For other differences between Pope and Dryden on the subject of monarch and mob, see my article, " 'The Change of Scepters, and impending Woe': Political Allusion in Pope's Statius," *PQ*,

52 (1973), 733–34. On the whole question of Restoration usage in respect to mob (*mobile vulgus*), see the excellent study by Michael Seidel, "The Restoration Mob: Drones and Dregs," *SEL,* 12 (1972), 429–43.

12. The term *exil'd* is, as Pope would have known, no barrier to the English application. *Exile* is related etymologically to the noun *exsul* (*exul*), signifying, by extension, *estranged;* and to the verb *exsulo* (*exulo*), signifying, metonymically, *to be a stranger.* Cf. Stephens's use of *stranger* in the following: "Must we exchange our fears still? and indanger / Our subdu'd heads by course to serve a stranger?" (vv. 217–18). Pope would have been aware too that in English the noun *exile* includes the meaning of "waste or devastation of property; ruin . . . impoverishment." See Charlton T. Lewis, *A Latin Dictionary for Schools* (Oxford: Clarendon Press, 1962); *Thesaurus Linguae Latinae* (Leipzig, 1953); and the *NED.*

13. It will be recalled that as recently as the spring of 1708 the French had again attempted, without success, to land "James III" in Scotland.

14. Stephens says, "Think you, that this man will be e're brought down / To his own private fortunes? Yet we find / That none was once more gentle, just, and kind" (vv. 234–36).

15. *nos villis in omnis / prompta manus casus, domino quicumque parati* (vv. 191–92).

16. Freely from *heu dubio suspensa metu tolerandaque nullis / aspera sors populis!—hic imperat, ille minatur* (vv. 195–96).

17. Pope's description of Stephens: Spence, 30.

18. TE, I, 352.

19. See the title page to the poem in *The Works of Mr. Alexander Pope* (1717) and *Corr.,* I, 154n.

20. TE, II, 382.

21. TE, II, 223–24. Elwin's complaint is not so much "irrelevant" as inobservant.

22. TE, II, 233, 235.

23. See vv. 151–55. Cf. Swift on Marlborough in *The Conduct of the Allies* (*Political Tracts,* 1711–1713, ed. Herbert Davis [Oxford: Blackwell, 1951], pp. 44–45). Cf. also the account of the Duke's return to England in November of 1711, in *The History of the Four Last Years of the Queen,* ed. Davis (Oxford: Blackwell, 1964), p. 28, and the remarks in *The Examiner,* passim. For Pope on the subject, see Spence, Nos. 366–72, and the cancelled "Character" of Marlborough in *Minor Poems,* pp. 358–59.

For all its awkwardness, I am also inclined to read more than meets the eye in the lines on Caesar (155–58), especially those that read, "Unmov'd, superior still in every State; / And scarce detested in his

Country's Fate," which look rather like an oblique reference to the late debacle and its victim, Harley.

24. Plutarch, *The Lives of the Noble Grecians and Romans*, tr. John Dryden, rev. Arthur Hugh Clough (New York: Modern Library, n.d.), p. 961. Though Plutarch might well spring to mind, Pope is at pains in his notes to refer the reader to him. Dryden's only part in the Plutarch of course was the Preface and the Epistle Dedicatory.

25. See *The Examiner* (passim); *The History of the Four Last Years*, pp. 67, 70; and *The Conduct of the Allies*, pp. 10, 53. But the point is nowhere better made than in Bolingbroke's "Letter to the Examiner" (August 1710). See *The Examiner*, p. 224.

26. Pope may have hoped it would be recalled or pointed out that in Chaucer the goddess grants the petition of his suppliants.

27. From Dilke's MS. note in the British Museum, as quoted in TE, II, 382.

28. Swift constantly complains in *The Examiner* of the indignities and insolence offered the Queen by the Whigs. See pp. 38, 89, 117, 121, 139. Cf. *The Conduct of the Allies*, pp. 43, 44, and *A Letter to a Whig-Lord* (*Political Tracts*, 1711–1713, p. 128), Bolingbroke's "Letter to the Examiner," and *The Examiner*, p. 226.

29. It is not easy to pinpoint the allusion, if any, in "Friends betray'd"; but, if it is not a reference to William's supporters given the cold shoulder by their new king, it may be a reference to Marlborough's desertion of James for William at the time of the invasion.

30. Vv. 454–57. Chaucer speaks of "dyvers transmutacions / Of estats, and eke of regions; / Of trust, of drede, of jelousye, / Of wit, of wynnynge, of folye; / Of plente, and of gret famyne, / Of chepe, of derthe, and of ruyne; / Of good or mys governement, / Of fyr, and of dyvers accident" (vv. 1969–76). The changes are indicative of Pope's finesse as well as of his intent. *Estats* becomes "the State" (*regions* is omitted as beyond target); the rest is whole Pope, though he could always appeal fallen favorites to *trust* and *jelousye*, "old Mismanagements" to *mys governement* (omitting the *good*), which would also accommodate "Taxations new," not mentioned by Chaucer.

31. TE, II, 268n. In the note following, Tillotson rightly calls attention to Pope's special interest as a Catholic in the "Taxations new," though again he limits the allusion to pre-1714.

32. Tillotson is surely mistaken in suggesting that the lines allude to Bolingbroke's impeachment, which did not take place until after Pope's poem was published. Even then the impeachment proceedings were suspended after Bolingbroke fled to France, and he was attainted instead, in September 1715.

33. *New Light on Pope* (1949; rpt. 1967), pp. 109–10. For Addison, see *Spectator* 253, in *The Spectator*, ed. Donald F. Bond (Oxford: Clarendon, 1965), II, 481–86.

CHAPTER VI

1. Dennis was in no doubt about the satirical character of the poem, styling it libelous, insolent, censorious, impudent, impertinent, arrogant, bullying, venomous, and the like. Nor was Addison, who deplored the strokes of "Detraction" in the *Essay* which he otherwise praised. See *Spectator* 253.
   2. See *The Art of Poetry, The Poetical Treatises of Horace, Vida, and Boileau*, ed. A. S. Cook (Boston, 1892).
   3. *L'Art poétique*, IV, 85, italics mine. I quote here and elsewhere from *Oeuvres Complètes de N. Boileau*, ed. M. Paul Cheron (Paris: Librairie Garnier Frères, n.d.).
   4. To say nothing of "Flecknoe" for *Typhon*. For the French, see *L'Art poétique*, I, 81–97. The translation is quoted from *The Poems of John Dryden*, ed. James Kinsley. The English Boileau is laced with this racier style. Cf. (English > French) I, 225–30 > 225–32; II, 326 > 100, 424 > 200; III, 541–42 > 115–16, 576 > 149, 853–54 > 424–25; IV, 909 > 54.
   5. Quoted from *The Works of Mr. John Oldham, Together with his Remains* (London: H. Hindmarsh, 1698). The translation may also be consulted in *Poems of John Oldham*, ed. Bonamy Dobrée (Southern Illinois Univ. Press, 1960), pp. 144 ff. Neither text numbers the lines.
   6. Cf. "The things, we know, are neither rich nor rare, / But wonder how the Devil they got there?" (*Epistle to Arbuthnot*, vv. 171–72).
   7. Spence, 473.
   8. Vv. 1–4. See POAS, I, 358 ff.
   9. Vv. 11–20. See POAS, I, 396 ff., and supra, Ch. III. Cf. *Essay on Criticism*, v. 3; *Essay on Man*, I, 13.
   10. Vv. 53–62. Quoted from the text in *Critical Essays of the Seventeenth Century*, ed. J. E. Spingarn, II, 286 ff. With the last line cf. "Fear not the Anger of the Wise to raise; / Those best can bear Reproof, who merit Praise" (*Essay on Criticism*, vv. 582–83).
   11. Spingarn, II, 288, 289, 290, 294.
   12. *Ibid.*, p. 290. Cf. Pope's *Ep.* II. i (*Augustus*), vv. 261–62.
   13. Quoted from the text in Spingarn, II, 306, and ante.
   14. For Granville's poem, see Spingarn, III, 292–95. Cf. "From Pulpits banisht" (p. 295) with Pope's "*Pulpits* their *Sacred Satire* learn'd to spare" (*Essay on Criticism*, v. 550).

15. Cf. (Blackmore > Pope) "Insect-Wits" (Spingarn, III, 325), "half-form'd Insects" (*EC*, 41); "They justly Wits and Fools believ'd the same" (p. 325), "Some have at first for *Wits*, then *Poets* past . . . prov'd plain *Fools* at last" (*EC*, 36–37); "The Mob of Wits" (p. 326), "The Mob of Gentlemen who wrote with Ease" (*Epistle to Augustus*, v. 108); "Declare that what's Obscene shall give Offence" (p. 331), "vile *Obcenity*" (*EC*, v. 530); "none praise a Wealthy Fool" (p. 332), "Fear most to tax an *Honourable* Fool" (*EC*, v. 588), et al.

16. Vv. 396–97, omitting the parentheses.

17. See TE, I, n. to vv. 396 ff.

18. Pope is surely alluding in this to the Catholic as well as the sectarian plight.

19. Cf. Dryden, Dedication to *Examen Poeticum* (*Poems*, ed. Kinsley, II, 793).

20. See TE, I, n. to v. 509 and E. N. Hooker, "Pope on Wit: *The Essay on Criticism,*" *Hudson Review*, 2 (1950), 84–100 (rpt. in *Essential Articles*).

21. The couplet originally followed v. 545.

22. Cf. Ch. III and the annotation in TE, I.

CHAPTER VII

1. *Early Career*, p. 82. Professor Sherburn did not of course intend to include under this rubric all that I do.

2. *The Critical Specimen* was published pseudonymously and never owned by Pope, but I accept Norman Ault's arguments for his authorship. See *Prose Works*, I, xi–xviii and xxviii–xxxiii. Ault speculates that the *Specimen* followed hard on Dennis's *Reflections*, published 20 June 1711.

I quote Pope's prose throughout from the edition by Ault, normalizing italic usage where convenient. Since most of the pieces are brief, I make no effort to cite page references in every instance.

3. Sherburn doubts Pope's authorship of the *Specimen*, but says that Dennis must have thought, upon seeing it, "*Aut Pope aut diabolus*" (*Early Career*, pp. 93–94).

4. *PW*, p. 7. Dennis's *Grounds of Criticism*, also in folio, was offered on the same terms. See Hooker, I, 333.

5. Pope, perhaps in mockery, calls Bellerophon the horse.

6. For the arguments for and against Pope's authorship, as well as the question of motive, see Ault's *PW*, pp. xviii–xxviii, and Sherburn's *Early Career*, pp. 104–13. Sherburn, though hesitant to give the piece solely to Pope, concedes that "We must believe that Pope

had at least a hand in this whim." "If Pope is the sole author," he says, "it is one of the liveliest pieces of prose he ever wrote." I take Ault's arguments to put the matter beyond dispute.

7. Quoted in *PW*, p. xxi. Norris had advertised in other periodicals from at least late 1711. See *Early Career*, p. 106.

8. The "Grammarian" was taken to be Pope's crony, but also Dennis's friend, Henry Cromwell. It may be on this account, as well as Pope's promise to Caryll that he would "never make the least reply" to Dennis, that he disavowed at the time any connection with the piece.

9. Dennis's adaptation of Shakespeare's play, titled *The Invader of His Country: or The Fatal Resentment*, published in 1720. It had been performed, unsuccessfully, at Drury Lane in 1705. See H. G. Paul, *John Dennis, His Life and Criticism* (New York: Columbia Univ. Press, 1911), pp. 43–44.

10. Sherburn (*Early Career*, pp. 74–75, 100, n. 1) attributes these to Pope. For Ault's argument for the attribution, see *PW*, pp. xxxv–xxxviii.

11. The *Memoirs* were not published until 1741, under Pope's initiative and editorship. For details of authorship, composition, and publication, see Charles Kerby-Miller, ed., *Memoirs of the Extraordinary Life, Works, and Discoveries of Martinus Scriblerus* (New Haven: Yale Univ. Press, 1950; rpt. New York: Russell and Russell, 1960), pp. 57–67. Because of the uncertainties surrounding most or all of these factors, and the careful work of Professor Kerby-Miller himself, I have not included the *Memoirs* in this discussion.

12. Cf. "dull Receits how Poems may be made," *Essay on Criticism*, v. 115. Lloyd Douglas, in "A severe animadversion on Bossu," *PMLA*, 62 (1947), 690–706, is at pains to point out that Pope was not here ridiculing Le Bossu, whom he admired, but Le Bossu's English disciples, especially Blackmore.

13. The quotation is rendered in some editions, "A larger portion of heroic fire / Did his small limbs and little breast inspire." Pope had published his translation of the first book of Statius just the year before.

14. Ault is inclined to assign *Guardian* 106 ("On a Dream of a Window in his Mistress's Breast") to Pope, on the grounds of its resemblance to passages in *The Rape of the Lock*. He says nothing of its resemblances to Addison's "Dissection of a Beau's Head" or of "a Coquette's Heart" (*Spectator* 275, 281). The attribution seems to me unconvincing.

15. The lines have no counterpart in the two-canto (1712) version of the poem.

16. The subtitle reads, "A Treatise proving, beyond all contradiction, the dangerous Tendency of a late poem, entituled, *The Rape of the Lock*."

17. The first of these lines would seem (appropriately enough) to be drawn from the Prologue to Oldham's *Satires upon the Jesuits*. Oldham invokes the various passions to prompt his pen, "That its each home-set Thrust their *blood* may draw, / *Each drop of Ink* like Aqua-fortis gnaw." (*Works*, ed. cit., p. 4. I have dropped Oldham's italics and added my own.) Cf. also Garnet's ghost on the theme of blood revenge.

18. See *Minor Poems*, p. 136n. It is not impossible that the lines in which this wish is conveyed bear a sidling glance at kings as well as commoners: "Knighthoods on those have been conferr'd of late, / Who save our Eyesight, or wou'd save our State, / Unenvy'd Titles grace our mighty Names, / The learn'd Sir *William*, or the deep Sir *James*."

19. A Dutch barrier had been part of the negotiations for the Grand Alliance in 1701. The first treaty (1709) had given the United Provinces possession and/or promise of nineteen fortified garrisons for the protection of the Dutch frontiers. It was the reduction of this protective allotment in one of the treaties associated with Utrecht that constitutes the grounds of Barnivelt's complaint and allegation. One should bear in mind, too, Swift's *Remarks on the Barrier Treaty*, 1712.

20. The allusion is probably to the Earl of Nottingham, the Tory defector nicknamed "Dismal" and already scored by Swift in two verse lampoons and a prose broadside.

21. Curll had begun his baiting of Pope before of course, especially in publishing (1714) Charles Gildon's *A New Rehearsal, or Bays the Younger*, an attack on Pope and Rowe, but also in several petty larcenies of Popeian bawdy and the like. See *Early Career*, pp. 164–66, and Ralph Straus, *The Unspeakable Curll* (London: Chapman and Hall, 1927), pp. 49–64.

22. Oldmixon, it is amusing to note, published a disclaimer of this transaction in the *Flying Post*. See Straus, p. 57.

23. I accept Ault's arguments for putting the publication of *A Further Account* late in the year rather than hard on the heels of the *Full and True Account*. See *PW*, pp. xcviii–cvi. There is reason, however, to place its publication *after* rather than *before* Curll's advertisement in *The St. James's Post* (7–12 December), as Ault argues. Ault seems to have overlooked the allusion of the title page of *A Further Account* to that advertisement, which in announcing "A Satyr, entitled, Pope on the Stool of Repentance" says it "will be compleated in a Book of 1s. price, or else will be inserted in [Dun-

ton's] Weekly . . . till the whole is compleated." Pope's title page
bears the announcement, "To be publish'd Weekly." See *PW*, p. 273.
24. See *PW*, pp. cvii–cix.
25. I am unconvinced by Ault's attribution to Pope of *A Sermon
on Glass Bottles* (1715).
26. See *PW*, pp. civ–cv.
27. The Bodleian copy of *God's Revenge* identifies these nobles
as Hervey, Stanhope, and Warwick. See Swift, *A Proposal for Correcting the English Tongue, Polite Conversation, Etc.*, ed. Herbert
Davis (Oxford: Blackwell, 1964), p. 299n. This volume contains
A Modest Defence of Punning, a Swiftian take-off on *God's Revenge*.
28. It is hard to say which Lord Hervey the Bodleian MS. refers
to. The titular Lord Hervey since 1714 and until 1723 was Carr
Hervey, half-brother of the Lord Hervey of later Popeian notice. See
Robert Halsband, *Lord Hervey: Eighteenth Century Courtier* (Oxford: Clarendon Press, 1973).
29. See *PW*, p. cxviii.

CHAPTER VIII

1. Vv. 15–24. Except as indicated I quote Pope throughout from
Minor Poems, ed. cit.
2. For attribution, composition, and text, *Minor Poems*, pp. 183,
187. For the reception of the ballad by the ladies, see *Early Career*,
pp. 153, 198.
3. The *Epitaph on Sir William Trumbull*, published without assignment in the *Works* (1717), speaks of his "scorn of wrangling
. . . zeal for truth; / . . . gen'rous faith, from superstition free, / . . .
love to peace, and hate of tyranny." *Minor Poems*, p. 169.
4. Sherburn notes that the younger Caryll's visit to France in the
summer of 1712 to settle the estate was a matter of suspicion to Hanoverians, and that the *Flying Post* commented on Caryll in a way
that offended Pope almost to the point of reply. *Early Career*, p.
99. Pope may have thought of the lines as advertising himself as
well as Caryll—as constituting a kind of brief for Jacobitism as not
necessarily treasonable.
5. *The Second Satire* was not published until 1939, in the Twickenham edition. For date of composition see *TE*, IV, xlii. I quote from
this text. When Pope revised the poem for inclusion in his *Works*
(1735), he retained "only some 30 of the 120 and odd lines." *TE*,
IV, xlii. In this later version Pope gives the satire a contemporary
political turn, with allusions to the excise, the standing army, Germans, venality, Peter Walter, and court sycophants.

6. Vv. 11–12. Donne reads, "yet their State / Is poor, disarm'd, like Papists, not worth hate."

7. See Donne, vv. 25–30; Pope, vv. 33–40.

8. See *Minor Poems*, p. 112. Ault puts the *Gentle Shepherds* "not long after" Pope's *Guardian* 40, though it was not published until 1726. I am convinced of Pope's authorship. See Ault's note.

9. So described by Sutherland, TE, V (1953), p. 430.

10. Vv. 19–30. The poem was first published in *Minor Poems*, 1954. See note, p. 124. Though the timing makes it difficult to be sure, it is possible that the line, "You may, with *Addison*, do wonders," is not so simple as Ault's explanation (that Addison and Budgell were cousins). It is possible that by this time Pope knew, or suspected, that Addison was the prime mover behind Tickell's plans to translate the first book of the *Iliad*.

11. For composition and publication of these sketches, see *Minor Poems*, pp. 138–39, 140–41, 144–45.

12. See *Early Career*, pp. 147–48. Sherburn quotes Burnet's letter to Duckett (1 June 1716) to the effect "that Addison and the rest of the Rhiming Gang have dropt their Resentment against the Lordlike Man [Pope]." For Pope's version of the effect of the portrait, see Spence, 166: "Mr. Addison used me very civilly ever after."

13. Vv. 23–24; *Minor Poems*, p. 143.

14. I don't know that it has been noticed that *The Worms* bears a marked similarity to an anonymous satire, also in quatrains, called *The Tack*, published in 1705 and again in 1712. See POAS, VII, 71 and 637–38. For Pope's poem, see *Minor Poems*, pp. 161–64.

15. For attribution and date, see *Minor Poems*, p. 174n.

16. *Corr.*, I, 175.

17. See *Minor Poems*, p. 98, and Warburton (ed.), *The Works of Alexander Pope Esq.* (London, 1751), I, 271n.

18. See *Minor Poems*, p. 154n. The tragedy was Buckingham's, not produced in Pope's time and not published until Pope's edition of the Duke's *Works*, 1723.

19. The poem was not published until 1775, in *The St. James Chronicle*. Ault places the composition between 19 May (Halifax's death) and 12 June, when Jervas refers to it in a letter. *Minor Poems*, p. 130n. To say that it missed of its mark does not apply, obviously, to Pope's contemporaries, few of whom ever saw it.

20. See *Early Career*, p. 157. Sherburn speaks of "the lamentable implications of certain lines," but it would appear that he is referring to Pope's affectation of whoring.

21. For an account of the disarray and disappointment in the Tory camp from the standpoint of Swift, who was in close touch with Pope during this time, see Irvin Ehrenpreis, *Swift: The Man*,

His Works, and the Age (Cambridge, Mass.: Harvard Univ. Press, 1962, 1967), II, 728–63, and Swift's own *Political Tracts, 1713–1719*, ed. Herbert Davis and Irvin Ehrenpreis (Oxford: Blackwell, 1964). The "Whimsicals" were those Tories, led by Sir Thomas Hanmer, who opposed the commercial treaty with France in the settlement of Utrecht, and who on the issue of succession drifted to the Hanoverian side (hence Hanoverian Tories). Swift describes them as follows in *Some Free Thoughts*: "that Race of Politicians, who in the Cant Phrase are called the Whimsicalls, was never so numerous or at least so active, as it hath been since the great Change at Court; Many of those who pretended wholly to be *in* with the Principles upon which Her Majesty and her new servants proceeded, either absenting themselves with the utmost Indifference, in those Conjunctures upon which the whole Cause depended, or siding directly with the Enemy. All which indeed arose from a very unjust and perhaps an affected Diffidence towards those at the Helm." See *Political Tracts*, cited above, pp. 82–83.

22. Postdated 1722.

23. "Pope's 'Epistle to Harley': An Introduction and Analysis," in *Pope and His Contemporaries: Essays Presented to George Sherburn*, ed. James L. Clifford and Louis A. Landa (Oxford: Clarendon Press, 1949), p. 75 and n. Cf. Pope's letter to Harley, 21 October 1721 (*Corr.*, II, 90).

24. Vv. 8–10. See *Minor Poems*, pp. 238–40.

CHAPTER IX

1. For Pope's awareness of a tradition of satirical passages in Homer himself and of translational embellishments thereon, see his note to *Iliad*, I, 698 (TE, VII, 120–21).

2. In the second *Homerides* it is alleged that "This *Papish Dog has . . . translated Homer for the Use of the Pretend*er. . . ." See Guerinot, p. 40. Oldmixon's *Catholick Poet* is addressed on its title page "To all Gentlemen, Authors, Translators, or Translating Poets, who are Protestants, and well affected to the present Establishment in the most Illustrious House of Hanover." Dennis, as we have seen, complains of Protestant toleration of the papistical and Jacobitical drift of Pope's translation. The French text of Madame Dacier's *Remarks* appeared in 1719. The pertinent part of that is her observation that a man so clever as Pope would hardly confine himself to perfecting the art of epic poetry, but would be about the perfecting of politics as well. In a letter to the bookseller Buckley, Pope expresses both alarm and amusement at this. He has now, he says, given up any thoughts of translating the *Odyssey* and hopes Mr.

Tickell will take it on, "for the honour & safety of the Protestant Religion & Establishment, which otherwise (according to M. Dacier) a Papist may do much damage to. I did not think I had such Talents in Politicks, but I will now begin to look about me, since I am thought so capable of great affairs, by the consent of two nations."

3. Yale Univ. Press, 1951, p. 48.

4. *Alexander Pope: The Poetry of Allusion* (Oxford: Clarendon Press, 1959), Ch. IV, "True Heroic Poetry."

5. *To Homer Through Pope* (New York: Barnes & Noble, 1972), p. 51.

6. TE, VII, xlvi and passim ccxxvi–ccxlii.

7. *Ibid.*, passim lxxviii–ciii.

8. *Ibid.*, passim cxxxiv–clxxxiv.

9. *Ibid.*, ccxxi. The lines from the Postscript are worth repeating: "Tho' I am a Poet, I would not be an Enthusiast; and tho' I am an Englishman, I would not be furiously of a Party. I am far from thinking myself that Genius, upon whom at the end of these remarks Madam *Dacier* congratulates my country: One capable of 'correcting *Homer,* and consequently of reforming mankind, and amending this Constitution.' It was not to *Great Britain* this ought to have been apply'd, since our nation has one happiness for which she might have preferr'd it to her own, that as much as we abound in other miserable misguided Sects, we have at least none of the blasphemers of *Homer.* We stedfastly and unanimously believe, both his Poem, and our Constitution, to be the best that ever human wit invented: That the one is not more incapable of amendment than the other; and (old as they both are) we despise any *French* or *English* man whatever, who shall presume to retrench, to innovate, or to make the least alteration in either. Far therefore from the Genius for which Madam *Dacier* mistook me, my whole desire is but to preserve the humble character of a faithful Translator, and a quiet Subject" (TE, X, 397). This is a masterful piece of equivocation.

10. My choice of books was determined by the desire to test the allusiveness (where the *Iliad* is concerned) from year to year as the installments appeared, and by my feeling that the choice should include at least the first and last books, with such between as would (a) be likely, by subject matter, to prove allusive and (b) test the allusiveness under varying rubrical conditions, such as battle scenes, Olympian episodes, etc. The *Odyssey* appeared in two installments only, 1725 and 1726, by reason of which I felt justified in limiting the test in that case to one volume only, and of that to the last book.

11. TE, VII, ccxxxiv. Pope is not remiss in leaving clues of course. His Preface, which throws off various hints, concludes with acknowledgments to persons of political as well as literary reputation,

most suggestively perhaps, Bolingbroke, still in political exile, one "not," as Pope says, "more distinguished in the great Scenes of Business than in all the useful and entertaining Parts of Learning" (TE, VII, 24). Parnell's "Essay on Homer," prefixed to the first volume, includes a section of Homer's own "Politicks," and the "Poetical Index" opens, under FABLE, with the observation that the "great *Moral* of the Iliad [is] that *Concord, among Governours, is the preservation of States, and Discord the ruin of them*" (TE, VIII, 591). The notes themselves afford abundant suggestion of contemporary appplication. Pope's comments in the first note, on *Amphibologies*, may indeed have been intended as a signal of such activity and at the same time an ostensible disclaimer of tolerance for such a practice.

12. For Pope I use the Twickenham text (TE), volumes VII, VIII, and X; for Homer and the English translations to the time of Pope the following: the Loeb Classical Library editions of the *Iliad* and *Odyssey; Chapman's Homer,* ed. Allardyce Nicoll, 2 vols., Bollingen Series XLI (New York: Pantheon Books, 1956); *Homer His Iliads Translated . . . By John Ogilby* (London: Thomas Roycroft, MDCLX) and *Homer His Odysses Translated . . . By John Ogilby, Esq.* (London: Roycroft, MDCLXV), both cited by page reference; *The English Works of Thomas Hobbes,* ed. Sir William Molesworth, Vol. X (London: Longman, Brown, Green and Longmans, 1844); Dryden, *The First Book of Homer's Ilias,* in *The Poems of John Dryden,* ed. James Kinsley, Vol. IV (Oxford: Clarendon Press, 1958); Congreve's *Priam's Lamentation and Petition to Achilles* and his *Lamentations of Hecuba, Andromache, and Helen* in TE, X, 542–49; Thomas Yalden's *Patroclus' Request to Achilles* in TE, X, 554–56; Arthur Mainwaring, *The First Book of Homer's Iliads* in TE, X, 560–72; and *The Iliad of Homer . . . By Madam Dacier, Done from the French by Mr. OZELL,* cited herein as OBO, by volume and page.

13. ἀλλ' οὐκ Ἀτρείδῃ Ἀγαμέμνονι ἥνδανε θυμῷ, / ἀλλὰ κακῶς ἀφίει, κρατερὸν δ'ἐπὶ μῦθον ἔτελλε (I, 24–25). Chapman calls Agamemnon "General" (I, 24), Ogilby calls him "Atrides" (p. 2), Hobbes "King Agamemnon" (I, 26), Dryden "The King of Men" (I, 37), and Mainwaring "King Atrides" (I, 31). OBO does not specify a title (see vol. I, p. 5). Hereafter OBO references will be given without the abbreviations for volume ·and page but should be understood to signify those, not book and verse.

14. Ἀτρείδη κύδιστε, φιλοκτεανώτατε πάντων (I, 122). OBO furnishes Pope with *insatiate* (I, 15), but Pope alone is responsible for the coupling with *King*.

15. Wakefield, I, 161n.

16. See Pope, I, 194, 215, 388, 443; Homer, I, 149, 163–64, 293 ff.,

340. Dryden speaks of "A Tyrant's Curb" (I, 416) and Mainwaring twice uses the epithet "Tyrant" (I, 175, 367).

17. See Pope, I, 175, 189, 196, 221, 228, 283, 466, 660. Only twice in these places does Homer describe Agamemnon, and then in the honorific style: "son of Atreus, wide-ruling Agamemnon" (I, 355) and "Agamemnon, king of men" (I, 506). Cf. Dryden I, 206–7, 227, 320, 683; and Mainwaring ("That haughty King"), I, 226.

18. See Pope, I, 236, 247–48. Homer says only "rule thy Myrmidons" (Μυρμιδόνεσσιν ἄνασσε, I, 180) and nothing to Pope's wording in the second instance (see I, 185–86). The other translators follow Homer closely.

19. Pope, I, 250. See Guerinot, p. 55.

20. Pope, I, 383. Homer and all but one of the English translators speak only of Agamemnon's interest in sway. Mainwaring may have encouraged Pope to generalize: "Affecting Empire, which no Prince will yield" (I, 314).

Cf. too the tendentiousness of Pope's rendering of Homer's δημοβόρος βασιλεύς, ἐπεὶ οὐτιδανοῖσιν ἀνάσσεις (I, 231) and ἵνα πάντες ἐπαύρωνται βασιλῆος (I, 410): "Scourge of thy People, violent and base! / Sent in Jove's Anger on a Slavish Race" (I, 305–6) and "bring / The Greeks to know the Curse of such a King" (I, 534–35). The earlier translators contented themselves in the main with the idea of *devouring* in the first instance and, with the exception of Chapman, with that of *sharing* or *enjoying* in the second. Chapman says, "their pains paying the wreake of their proud Soveraign's heart" (I, 404).

21. See Dryden, I, 398–99; Pope, I, 365; Homer, I, 278–79, 282.

22. Pope, I, 345–46; Homer, I, 260–63.

23. Wakefield was right in declaring Pope's "foreign Contests" a gratuitous addition, but he apparently missed the point in adding that it weakens "the purport of the passage." It is, with "domestic Rage," part of Pope's equation for the call of foreign monarchs to England's throne. The "foreign Contests" may also, in the way of Professor Callan's "two or more meanings" in Popeian translation, glance at the *foreign* policy of recent and present *foreign* rulers of England.

24. Only Pope speaks of "wretched Quarrels" and of "senseless Strife." Cf. Homer, I, 573–74; Chapman, I, 556 ff.; Ogilby (who does speak of "factious parties," but amongst the gods, p. 29); Hobbes, I, 538 ff.; Dryden, I, 772–73; and OBO, I, 51.

25. See, respectively, I, 71–73, pp. 5–6; I, 80–84.

26. See Mainwaring, vv, 89–92 ff.; OBO, I, 11.

27. Perhaps further hint that Pope is identifying with Calchas is to be found in his note to I, 117, where he styles Calchas "blameless" (from Gr. ἀμύμων). The epithet, says Pope, "is not only apply'd [in Homer] to a Priest, but to one who being conscious of the Truth, prepares with an honest Boldness to discover it" (TE, VII, 92n).

28. Homer, I, 106–8; Chapman, I, 103–5 ff.; Ogilby, p. 17; Hobbes, I, 105–6 ff.; Dryden, I, 155–56 ff.; Mainwaring I, 119–20 ff.; OBO, I, 13. For another teasing Popeian note, see that appended to this passage: TE, VII, 93n.

29. καὶ νῦν ἐν Δαναοῖσι θεοπροτέων ἀγορεύεις (vv. 109 ff).

30. TE, VII, 403n.

31. Vv. 340–42. Pope's description of the Teucrian strategy— "With ev'ry Shaft some hostile Victim slew, / Then close beneath the sev'nfold Orb withdrew" (vv. 323–24)—should be compared with the Greek, which even more precisely expresses the Popeian satiric-allusive strategy: "Then would Aias move his shield aside from over him, and the warrior would spy his chance." See vv. 268–69 and ff.

32. Vv. 430–32. Pope is the only one to divide the rage into what has gone before and what shall yet befall. Cf. Homer, VIII, 354–56; Chapman, VIII, 306–9; Ogilby, p. 187; Hobbes, VIII, 322–23; and OBO, II, 205.

33. Pope's *tyrant* is Homer's "dread son of Cronos" (VIII, 462), Chapman's, Ogilby's, and Hobbes's *Jupiter* or *Jove*, and OBO's "cruel son of Saturn." Pope's "unmeasur'd Hate" (VIII, 579) is *wrath* or *anger* in all the rest. In VIII, 587, Pope speaks of "th'Almighty Thunderer in Arms." This is Homer's "mighty son of Cronos" (VIII, 470), Chapman's "great Saturnides" (VIII, 415), and OBO's "The Master of the Thunder" (II, 212).

34. Pope, VIII, 512. Homer speaks of *striving*, Chapman of *fighting* (VIII, 420; VIII, 365). Note that Pope's word is now *Rebellion*.

35. Only Chapman and OBO use *king,* the former in the singular and referring to Agamemnon (IX, 58–60), the latter in the generalized plural (II, 227). Homer's βασιλῆας is appropriately rendered "princes" in the Loeb translation by A. T. Murray. See IX, 59.

36. Homer speaks only of the need of the *Achaeans* (IX, 75), Chapman of the *Greeks* (IX, 81). The rest do not specify. Pope's Nestorian advice that it befits Agamemnon to hear all counsel "And ratify the best, for publick Good," even though offered by a lesser person (IX, 133–38) probably owes something to OBO's "Projects conducive to the Publick Good" (II, 230), though no one, even Homer, speaks of the advice coming from a "meaner" person. This too looks like interested translation.

37. For comparison, see Homer, IX, 110–11; Chapman, IX ,114–15; Ogilby, p. 119; Hobbes, vv. 101–3; and OBO, vol. II, 231.

38. Another ministerial glance may lurk in v. 305: "*Troy* and her Aids for ready Vengeance call," which in the Greek is simply, "the Trojans . . . and their far-famed allies . . . deem they shall no more be stayed." None of the English versions mentions *vengeance*, which is the allusive clue.

39. See vv. 481, 515, 759. For the first, the Greek has simply, "lord Agamemnon, son of Atreus" (κρείων Ἀγαμέμνων / Ἀτρεΐδης), IX, 368–69. He is called either *Agamemnon* or *Atrides* in the translations. Neither Homer nor the translators say anything to Pope's other uses of the epithet.

40. The Greek says simply, "Hateful in my eyes are his gifts" (ἐχθρὰ δέ μοι τοῦ δῶρα), IX, 378.

41. In Homer, Achilles says only "let him [Agamemnon] not tempt me that know him well; he shall not persuade me" (IX, 345). See Ogilby, p. 206; Hobbes, IX, 345; OBO, II, 248. None speaks of *Kings*, only of Agamemnon.

42. Wakefield's note to v. 455, ed. cit., III, 48.

43. See Homer, IX, 400; Chapman, IX, 388; Ogilby, p. 208; Hobbes, IX, 393; OBO, II, 252.

44. Chapman speaks of "Our greatest Greeks" (XVI, 21), Hobbes of those "that excel the rest" (XVI, 19–20), and OBO of "her bravest Heroes" (IV, 7). Homer speaks of the ἄριστοι (XVI, 23).

45. Wakefield calls the line "superfluous" (IV, 94n). That is true only if by *superfluous* he means that it is not in Homer.

46. The speech in Homer reads, "Wherein shall any other even yet to be born have profit of thee?" (τί σευ ἄλλος ὀνήσεται ὀψίγονός περ), XVI, 31. Cf. also ὅτι τοι νόος ἐστὶν ἀπηνής ("for that thy heart is unbending"), v. 35. Chapman says (vv. 26–27), "How shall our progenies . . . / . . . enjoy thine aide?" Yalden renders it, "What injur'd Friend from thee shall hope redress!" (v. 49, TE, X, 555). Ogilby, Hobbes, and OBO say nothing to this effect at all.

47. Neither Chapman nor Hobbes uses the expression, and Ogilby and OBO use only inflections: "tyranny of his Prerogative" (Ogilby, p. 349) and "this Tyrannizing Man" (OBO, IV, 8–9).

48. For a similar summons, cf. "And give the *Greeks* to visit *Greece* again" (XVI, 107). Homer says only, lest they fire the ships "and rob the Greeks of their desired return" (XVI, 82). Chapman speaks of "Our sweet home-turning" (XVI, 74–75); Ogilby of "the only Hope of our return" (p. 350); Hobbes of their retiring to their country (XVI, 80); and OBO of "the Hope of seeing *Greece* again" (IV, 10).

49. Cf. OBO's "a wasting Monster, who knows no Justice, Equity, or Mercy" (V, 92).

50. Pope alone speaks of "a Soul so brave" and of a "sense of Duty." See Homer, XXIV, 157–58; Chapman, XXIV, 160–62; Ogilby, p. 502; Hobbes, XXIV, 145–46; and OBO, X, 99.

51. See Pope, XXIV, 604–7. Pope alone speaks of Achilles's father as "perhaps, [by] some Turn of human Fate / [Expell'd] . . . helpless from his peaceful state," of his having to fly "from some pow'rful Foe." Chapman speaks of his "being outrunne" by such woes as beset Priam (XXIV, 433–36); however, *outrunne* in Chapman does not mean *expelled* or *exiled*, but "oppressed" or "worn out." See Nicoll's edition, I, 723. Others, including Homer (XXIV, 448–49) speak either of being *troubled* by neighboring people or of being *invaded* by them. Cf., among these, Congreve's *Priam's Lamentation*, vv. 40–45, in TE, X, 453.

52. Only Pope speaks of "a better Day." All others (including Congreve) speak only of the return of the son.

53. See Pope, XXIV, 621. Homer says only that Hector "guarded the city" (XXIV, 499). Congreve speaks of him as "his Country's prop" (*Priam's Lamentation*, vv. 61–65; TE, X, 543) and OBO as the "Prop of all my House" (V, 115).

54. V. 266. Italics mine. OBO perhaps comes closest: "Sav'd us from Bondage" (V, 102). Homer has Hector slain in defense of "the men and deep-bosomed women of Troy" (XXIV, 215–16).

55. Cf. Amphimedon's account of Odysseus's cutting them down with the bow, vv. 201–17.

56. See Homer, XXIV, 196–98; Chapman, XXIV, 260–63; Ogilby, p. 357; and Hobbes, XXIV, 185–86. On the poet as *reward*, cf. Pope's lines to Martha Blount in *To a Lady*, vv. 291–92. Pope may have recalled those lines from the *Odyssey*.

57. One is invited to think, as Pope did early and late, of the Sabine farm, the Ofellian Horace and Umbrician Juvenal, the Pope of Windsor, Twickenham and Bethel, the Pope of Donne's *Second Satire*, of Horace's *nil admirari* and *Hoc erat in votis* (trailing clouds of Swift), the Pope of *Ep*. I. vii and the Bolingbroke of *Ep*. I. i— in short, the Pope of the *secretum iter* so sensitively delineated by Maynard Mack. For an interesting account of Dawley and its "goodman," Bolingbroke, see Walter Sichel, *Bolingbroke and His Times* (rpt. New York: Haskell House, 1968), II, 215 ff.

58. Cf. Pope's note on the "kingly Gardner," TE, X, 361–62.

59. Pope, XXIV, 326–28. Ogilby speaks of "Coast" (p. 359); Chapman and Hobbes say only "Ithaca."

60. Vv. 375–78. Chapman speaks of being "returned" (XXIV,

435), Ogilby of being "here" (p. 360), and Hobbes of being "come" (XXIV, 299).

61. See above, Ch. V.

62. See, respectively, XXIV, 475; 637–44; p. 364; 429.

63. Though "stern debate" may be, as someone has suggested, a Miltonism for "war," there is no reason why it may not also accommodate the notion of partisan polemics.

64. Cf. Homer, XXIV, 482–86; Chapman, XXIV, 649–58; Ogilby, p. 364; Hobbes, XXIV, 431–36.

INDEX

.

Index